AF865655

Wood Industry - Past, Present and Future Outlook

Edited by Guanben Du and Xiaojian Zhou

Published in London, United Kingdom

Wood Industry - Past, Present and Future Outlook
http://dx.doi.org/10.5772/intechopen.100751
Edited by Guanben Du and Xiaojian Zhou

Contributors
Kaimeng Xu, Yu Chen, Guanben Du, Siqun Wang, Maryam Shirmohammadi, Hüseyin Emre Ilgın, Markku Karjalainen, Amjad Zaki Almusaed, Asaad Almssad, Abel O. Olorunnisola, Tomasz Krystofiak, Shamsul Haq, Amit Prem Khare, Nidhi Dwivedi

© The Editor(s) and the Author(s) 2023
The rights of the editor(s) and the author(s) have been asserted in accordance with the Copyright, Designs and Patents Act 1988. All rights to the book as a whole are reserved by INTECHOPEN LIMITED. The book as a whole (compilation) cannot be reproduced, distributed or used for commercial or non-commercial purposes without INTECHOPEN LIMITED's written permission. Enquiries concerning the use of the book should be directed to INTECHOPEN LIMITED rights and permissions department (permissions@intechopen.com).
Violations are liable to prosecution under the governing Copyright Law.

(cc) BY

Individual chapters of this publication are distributed under the terms of the Creative Commons Attribution 3.0 Unported License which permits commercial use, distribution and reproduction of the individual chapters, provided the original author(s) and source publication are appropriately acknowledged. If so indicated, certain images may not be included under the Creative Commons license. In such cases users will need to obtain permission from the license holder to reproduce the material. More details and guidelines concerning content reuse and adaptation can be found at http://www.intechopen.com/copyright-policy.html.

Notice
Statements and opinions expressed in the chapters are these of the individual contributors and not necessarily those of the editors or publisher. No responsibility is accepted for the accuracy of information contained in the published chapters. The publisher assumes no responsibility for any damage or injury to persons or property arising out of the use of any materials, instructions, methods or ideas contained in the book.

First published in London, United Kingdom, 2023 by IntechOpen
IntechOpen is the global imprint of INTECHOPEN LIMITED, registered in England and Wales, registration number: 11086078, 5 Princes Gate Court, London, SW7 2QJ, United Kingdom

British Library Cataloguing-in-Publication Data
A catalogue record for this book is available from the British Library

Additional hard and PDF copies can be obtained from orders@intechopen.com

Wood Industry - Past, Present and Future Outlook
Edited by Guanben Du and Xiaojian Zhou
p. cm.
Print ISBN 978-1-80356-449-4
Online ISBN 978-1-80356-450-0
eBook (PDF) ISBN 978-1-80356-451-7

We are IntechOpen, the world's leading publisher of Open Access books

Built by scientists, for scientists

6,200+
Open access books available

168,000+
International authors and editors

185M+
Downloads

156
Countries delivered to

Our authors are among the
Top 1%
most cited scientists

12.2%
Contributors from top 500 universities

CLARIVATE ANALYTICS BOOK CITATION INDEX INDEXED

WEB OF SCIENCE™

Selection of our books indexed in the Book Citation Index in Web of Science™ Core Collection (BKCI)

Interested in publishing with us?
Contact book.department@intechopen.com

Numbers displayed above are based on latest data collected.
For more information visit www.intechopen.com

Meet the editors

Guanben Du is a full professor of wood science and technology at Southwest Forestry University, China. He was elected a fellow of the International Academy of Wood Science (IAWS) in 2010 and is serving as a board member from 2018 to 2028. Prof. Du's research focuses on wood adhesives, wood composites and wood surface treatment, with the goal of upgrading the wood panel and wood adhesives industry. His research has been supported by the EU, the National Natural Science Foundation of China, and others. He has published more than 300 articles/books and 31 patents and is the recipient of many awards. As a director, he has successfully built multi-research platforms, such as the International Joint Research Center for Bio-materials.

Xiaojian Zhou received his Ph.D. in wood and fiber science from the University of Lorraine in France in 2013 and then joined the Luleå University of Technology in Sweden. He has been a professor at Southwest Forestry University in China since 2019. Dr. Zhou's research, which has been supported by the EU, NSFC, and others, focuses on the processing and evaluation of wood adhesives and composites. He has published over 80 articles, five books or book chapters, served as a reviewer, editor or editorial board member for many international journals, and obtained eight authorized patent rights He has twice received Youth Technology Awards, and has gained three provincial and one national Science and Technology Progress Awards.

Contents

Preface

Wood, a most important renewable and sustainable material resource, has been widely used in daily life for thousands of years and represents a bridge between tradition and modernity. In the course of manufacturing this bridge, new materials, new connections and new adhesives, as well as better logistics, have influenced the quality, manufacturing and efficient transport of wooden products – in short, the entire wood industry. Wood is used in every possible unit size, from macro- to micro- and even nanoscale. It also can be combined with various polymers to obtain composites that can achieve excellent performance.

The aim of this book is to present traditional, present and future advanced functional wooden composites, from traditional timber to currently popular wood-based panels, wooden buildings, wood bio-energy, wood carbon stock, and woodland biodiversity. Lightweight wooden materials, the use of alternative fast-growing species and recycled wood, and many new hardwood and softwood adaptation processes from different countries are discussed. The most recent research into "super wood" functionalities and products using novel advanced techniques in high value-added sectors will also be covered.

I believe that the excellent work of this volume's authors will have significant academic value and a far-reaching impact on the wood industry.

Guanben Du and Xiaojian Zhou
Professor,
International Joint Research Center for Bio-Materials,
Southwest Forestry University,
Kunming, China

Section 1

Wood Construction

Chapter 1

Massive Wood Construction in Finland: Past, Present, and Future

Hüseyin Emre Ilgın and Markku Karjalainen

Abstract

Finland has a long history of massive wood construction such that the log construction technique has been used as a traditional method of Finnish residential construction for thousands of years, and the entire history of Finnish architecture is based on this technique. Today, almost all leisure buildings, for example, cottages in Finland are made of wood and mostly log construction. Also, today 90% of Finland's detached houses have timber frames, and a quarter of them are made from industrial glue logs. Apartment buildings began to be made of wood, especially cross-laminated timber (CLT) and laminated veneer lumber (LVL). The most common way of constructing wooden apartments is to use volumetric elements as compared to load-bearing large elements and post-beam systems. The increase in environmental awareness in Finland, as in many European countries today, strengthens the popularity of wood construction, and this brings the search for innovative and environmentally friendly engineered wood product solutions (e.g., dovetail massive wood board elements) as a future vision. The chapter aims to identify, combine, and consolidate information about massive wood construction in Finland from past, present, and future perspectives. This study will assist and guide Finnish key professionals in the design and implementation of timber buildings.

Keywords: timber/wood, construction, log construction, engineered wood products, sustainability, dovetail massive wooden board elements, Finland

1. Introduction

Finland has a long history of using massive wood in construction, starting with thousands of years of log building techniques [1]. Log, which was traditionally carved by hand from single trees, has been the main material of all types of buildings, for example, residences and religious buildings. In the early phases of industrialization, the log was used merely for the construction of sauna huts and summer cottages (**Figure 1**) [2–4]. Today's logs are produced industrially in factories, using sophisticated woodworking machines from glued laminated wood (**Figure 2**) [5]. Moreover, in the last 10 years, log construction doubled the share of all new prefabricated detached houses sold in Finland [6]. Overall, there is a swift development going on right now, where the use of log construction is growing, and neither the usage context of the logs nor the log itself is the same as in the past [7].

Figure 1.
Log cottage example from Finland (photo courtesy of Lotta Häkkänen).

Figure 2.
A modern log cottage example from Finland (photo courtesy of Lotta Häkkänen).

Finland has been experimenting with wood-frame multi-story construction since the mid-1990s due to industrialized prefabrication of engineered wood products (EWPs) such as CLT, and LVL [8], which allowed the use of wood in large-scale construction, for example, multi-story apartment buildings [9]. Furthermore, as timber construction research has increased in Finland in recent years, the use of EWPs in the construction sector has become gradually more prevalent (e.g., [10–12]). The most popular way of constructing wooden apartments is to use volumetric elements as compared to load-bearing large elements and post-beam systems [13]. Here, wooden multi-story refers to buildings more than 2-story with a wooden structural frame and, in some cases, with timber facade cladding [14, 15]. Moreover, the Finnish fire code was revised so that residential and office buildings with timber structures and facades could rise to 4-story and then 8-story in 1997 and 2011, respectively [16]. With the revision in 2018, it has become possible to design and construct housing and office buildings with timber structures and facades up to 8-story and, due to functional fire planning, wooden buildings higher than 8-story (e.g., apartments, dormitories, hotels, and offices) are also possible [17]. Currently, there are two wooden tall residential buildings (≥9-story), 14-story Lighthouse Joensuu (2019) with LVL (**Figure 3**), and 13-story HOAS Tuuliniitty (2021) with CLT (**Figure 4**).

In line with "Finnish National Energy and Climate Strategy" [18] and "Guidelines on State Aid for Climate, Environmental Protection and Energy 2022" [19], as a reflection of environmentally friendly approaches to reduce greenhouse gas emissions and carbon footprint on the construction industry, the use of wood has become more prevalent, especially by being encouraged by many government-supported

Figure 3.
Lighthouse Joensuu (photo courtesy of Arcadia).

Figure 4.
HOAS Tuuliniitty (photo by Miika Ullakko, courtesy of Arkkitehti toimisto Jukka Turti ainen/Arkkitehti palvelu Oy).

institutions, organizations, and regulations in Finland [20–28]. As a result, the search and trend towards innovative and "green" wood products such as adhesive- and metal fastener-free dovetail wood board elements (**Figure 5**) seem to shape the future of the Finnish construction industry [29, 30].

Overall, this chapter examines massive wood construction in Finland from past, present, and future perspectives. It is thought that this study will assist and guide key professionals in the design and implementation of timber buildings in Finland.

Figure 5.
Test specimen of adhesive- and metal fastener-free dovetail wood board element (photo by Hüseyin Emre Ilgın).

The chapter is structured as follows. The next section presents Finnish massive wood construction by detailing the history of log-based wood construction, the current state of the art, and finally the future of the Finnish wood construction industry. The last section provides our concluding remarks.

2. Massive wood construction in Finland

2.1 Past

The entire Finnish wooden building tradition is based on the use of logs (**Figure 6a**). The art of building logs has been developing in the northern coniferous region for more than a thousand years. The log structure is a traditional wooden construction method in which load-bearing walls are made of logs. In Finland, logs are usually arranged horizontally and joined by special corner joints (**Figure 6**) [31]. The horizontal log technique, which resulted in simple rectangular building volumes with scale uniformity relative to the length of the log, has been used in Finland for over a thousand years. Due to the always availability of trees, logs have become a natural building material in Finland.

In the first decades of the twentieth century, a new American-style lightweight timber-frame construction system began to be used in Finland [32] and log construction was the most used practice for residential buildings until the 1930s before the dominance of the American light frame in Finnish wooden construction industry [33].

In the 1930s, the Finnish forest, used for the paper and timber market, contributed to the industrialization of the country. In this period, when the international

(a) (b)

Figure 6.
Log construction (a) earlier corner detail (photo courtesy of Lotta Häkkänen) and (b) modern corner detail (photo by Hüseyin Emre Ilgın).

style influenced Finnish architects, the Finnish wooden building tradition was heavily applied [34]. Rising labor costs spurred single-home builders to seek alternatives for industrial-scale housing solutions. The American-style urbanization and industrialization at the time gave architects like Alvar Aalto, designing numerous multi-dwelling accommodation facilities, enough inclination to explore possibilities including prefabricated solutions [35]. The focus of the construction was solely derived from natural resources, for example, the abundance of Finnish forests. Single houses were built utilizing massive wood logs harvested directly on the site [36].

In the 1940s, World War II led to a shortage of building materials and a demand for community and residential construction in a timely and cost-effective way. It's worth noting here that Alvar Aalto's approach relied on the use of prefabricated elements specifically to maximize Finland's use of forest resources, as a continuation of the framing system experiment Finland modeled on its previous American predecessor [34]. Nevertheless, despite heavy investments and the overall positive impact of the practice on Finland's architectural development, adverse weather conditions, and high labor costs resulted in low participation in this practice.

The arrival of wooden facades coincided with the end of World War II. The peculiarities of prefabrication during the war, especially due to the fast pace of construction, cemented the position of this private residential solution in Finnish construction history. Prefabrication provided an effective solution to the population boom, rapid urbanization, and migration from more rural areas to urban centers in Finland. Finnish log construction took on new vitality in the early 1950s, with the industrial production of log houses (**Figure 6b**). Due to their nail-free structure and good availability of timber, logs were again a beneficial building material, which was mostly used in single-family houses. On the other hand, with the emerging modernist movement internationally, concrete flourished on the construction scene in the late 1960s and became a generally common material for medium to large-scale building designs.

In the early 1990s, Finland started a piloting effort to explore the potential to return to wood construction, which was a background indicator of the relevance of Finnish buildings to traditional Finnish cultural values and the return to deindustrialization. However, although this effort was reflected in several pioneering projects that promoted the validity of wood as the next major building material, it later lost power due to the general economic fluctuation at the national level. Even though the economic boom of the late 1990s greatly boosted development in the construction industry, the American platform framing technique had a chance to enter the timber construction market as the forestry industry did not have a vision of collaborating particularly with architectural and structural designers to compete with concrete practices in Finland.

While the resulting pilot projects were successful, regulatory, and labor issues and logistical challenges combined with the disconnect between engineers and product manufacturers, the forestry industry's inability to provide the necessary technical assistance towards wood construction standards, and the lack of funding for further research and development, reduced the chance of wood to compete with the mature concrete industry [35].

The second wave of timber booms began in 2011 when an amendment to the Finnish fire code allowed wooden structures and facades to be used in projects, increasing the maximum allowable height of the building for wooden structures to 8-story.

2.2 Present

Regarding the log construction mentioned in the previous section, as is known, traditionally logs have been handcrafted from a single tree trunk, while modern logs are precise industrial products manufactured in plants by bonding together multiple parallels or cross lamellas of timber. As part of the global development of massive wooden construction, the use of industrial log construction has become more and more popular in Finland over the past decade (see **Figure 7**) [37] such that from just over 10% a decade ago, now about 30% of all new single-family homes have log structure [38].

Recent buildings using industrial logs show that this reputation also applies to larger construction, for example, school campuses (**Figure 8**). Additionally, in the early 2000s, due to the poor architectural quality of industrially produced log buildings, there were attitudes among designers and construction officials towards the use of logs in urban or suburban contexts, however, particularly in the last decade, the perception that log structures have an untapped potential for architectural expression has positively changed the perspective of professionals [39].

Wooden multi-story construction has been on the Finnish national policy agenda since the 1990s and there are high expectations for its potential market growth [40]. Additionally, in particular, due to the revision made in the Finnish fire code in 2018, it has been possible to design and construct residences, dormitories, hotels, nursing homes, offices with wooden structural systems up to 8-story, and buildings with more than 8-story, functional fire design analysis is applied in Finland.

Finland has the second-highest proportion of multi-story buildings in Europe after Spain, and about 47% of Finnish housing units are located in multi-story buildings [41]. However, the market share of timber multi-story apartments constructed was only 1% in 2010, and the share increased to 10% by 2015 [42]. By March of 2022, 130 two-story timber apartment buildings have been built in Finland, a total of 4150 apartments [43, 44].

Figure 7.
A four-story log apartment, Finland (photo by Hüseyin Emre Ilgın).

Figure 8.
Pudasjärvi log school campus, Finland (photo by Hüseyin Emre Ilgın).

The American platform-frame system, based on floor-by-floor stud frame construction, was mostly used for the construction of Finland's earliest residential buildings. Nowadays, in Finland, timber apartments are executed with three different structural solutions: a volumetric modular system, a load-bearing large element system, and a post-beam system, and among them, the most popular way of building wooden apartments is to use of volumetric modular element designs based on CLT [45]. On the other hand, these elements can also be applied as a rigid structure. Furthermore, timber-concrete composite board structures are primarily utilized on the intermediate floors due to their advantage in sound insulation.

Besides wooden construction in Finland, interest in high-rise construction has also risen over the past decade, which is mostly related to the urbanization trend in Finnish major cities as in other metropolises of the world [46–50]. In this sense, multi-story timber construction has been endorsed in Finland since the 1990s [51], and multi-story and tall buildings are considered the biggest opportunity for growth in wooden construction [52] with national policy support [53], as in the 14-story Lighthouse Joensuu (**Figure 3**) and 13-story HOAS Tuuliniitty (**Figure 4**), and the 8-story high Puukuokka 1.

On the other hand, due to the separation of the market by construction systems, difficulties arose when potential industry partners tried to enter the market, as the solution for each construction system was often different from the others. This challenge hindered the progress of the industry by discouraging potential competitors. Various strategies have been documented and introduced concerning the current market situation, both from a national programming perspective and as an internal review of possible policies.

Running various programs across the country to focus on the use of natural resources, from micro to macro scale, the Finnish government has been a supporter of the timber industry in general, putting wooden apartments on the national programming agenda. Alongside efforts to standardize construction systems, supporting activities in the industry have been undertaken by individual and government agencies.

Moreover, according to studies such as policy gap analysis of programs promoting the use of timber in construction in the Finnish context [54], the following are considered among the main obstacles and challenges: (i) demand for stricter fire safety measures compared to traditional building materials; (ii) lack of support from municipalities on tenures for new buildings; (iii) different practices and additional fee demands of insurance companies for timber structures; (iv) lack of knowledge about carbon footprint calculation methods, evaluation of operating and maintenance costs; (v) lack of suitable tools for implementing wood construction projects in BIM; (vi) training offer gap causing a shortage of available experts in the field; and (vii) skepticism about the durability of the material.

Overall, in the rapidly and constantly changing building construction industry, sustainable approaches often use specific materials and technologies to support architectural design. These strategies are also significantly influenced by the characteristics of the available market margin. Every major component in the market value chain must be scrutinized to give a healthy impetus to practical and profitable solutions in the industry. While Finland leads the way in joining the world race in environmentally-friendly applications, certain conditions in the Finnish construction sector tend to aggressively hinder progress. More specifically, the targeted level of using wood as the main building material in medium and large-scale projects has not been reached yet [35].

2.3 Future

As noted earlier, there is strong governmental support for timber construction in Finland, which is also defined in various national strategies and programs such as the Government Programme, the National Energy and Climate Strategy, the National Forest Programme, and the Finnish Bioeconomy Strategy, which aimed at increasing the share of long-term carbon storage products and applications. For example, The Wood Building Programme, which sets one of its goals as rising the market share of timber structures in public buildings to 30% in 2022 and 45% in 2025, has five focus areas: increasing the use of timber in urban development, endorsing the use of timber in public buildings, increasing the construction of large timber structures, reinforcing local skill bases, and encouraging exports [55].

In line with the government policy mentioned above, by focusing on the impact of business activities, for example, building construction industry, on climate and natural sources, ecological awareness has increased significantly in the last two decades and environmental degradation has been defined as a global problem (e.g., [56–58]). This important global rising awareness has led to the development of new and more environmentally friendly timber-based solutions, especially in the Finnish wood construction industry as the future vision. In this context, many research projects (e.g., the DoMWoB project/Dovetailed Massive Wood Board Elements for Multi-Story Buildings—see Acknowledgments and Funding) (**Figure 9**) [42, 59] are being carried out as in other EU countries (e.g., [60]).

In addition, as in other Scandinavian countries, the rise of wooden multi-story construction in Finland has become the most prominent new construction-related business opportunity in the emerging bio-economy. Similarly, the construction of tall timber buildings (≥9-story) seems to be gaining momentum, driven by decarbonization, forest management and timber life cycle, urbanization and densification, productivity in the construction industry, and benefits of using timber indoors [61, 62]. Moreover, in Finland, as part of the rise of the environmentally friendly building

Figure 9.
Manufacture of dovetail massive wood board element at Vocational College Lapland (Ammattiopisto Lappia), Kemi, Finland (photo by Hüseyin Emre Ilgın).

concept, the future of wooden construction can be shown as hybrid buildings, where other materials are used together and benefit most, either structural members (such as wood and steel or concrete combinations) or cross-section-based level (such as wood and plastic) [63]. As in the cases of the 25-story and 87 m high Ascent (Milwaukee, under construction), the 24-story and 84 m high HoHo (Vienna, 2020), and the 18-story and 58 m high Brock Commons Tallwood House (Vancouver, 2017), hybridization using a reinforced concrete core target better structural safety and performance, which becomes more and more important with increasing building height.

3. Conclusions

This study identifies, combines, and consolidates information about massive wood construction in Finland from past, present, and future perspectives. Finland has a long history of using massive wood in construction, starting with thousands of years of log building techniques. Wood-based solutions have traditionally held a strong position in Finland's construction industry and account for approx. 40% of all building materials. Today almost 90% of Finland's detached houses are timber-framed, and a quarter of them are made from industrial glue logs. Wood is also used on construction sites in structures, windows, doors, and finished surfaces, as well as in formwork construction, among other uses. Apartment buildings began to be made of wood, especially CLT and LVL mostly with volumetric elements. In addition, the possibilities of using wood have been expanded to include renovations and extensions of suburban concrete apartments. There are significant activities, initiatives, and legalization in support of wooden structures concerning current European regulations emphasizing the use of wood as a sustainable architectural building material for the future in Finland.

(a) (b)

Figure 10.
Preparation of dovetail specimens for fire resistance test at Tampere University Fire Laboratory, Tampere, Finland. (a) Drilling and (b) thermocouple insertion (photos by Hüseyin Emre Ilgın).

Overall, the global economy engine naturally shifted the focus of Finnish construction technology to viable solutions, which means that concrete's low return on value hinders the use of one of the defining features of Finland's global image—the vast forest resources are not fully utilized internally as they should be. In this sense, because of environmental considerations, there is a rising interest in the use of timber and the advancement of wooden structural elements. This has led to a wide variety of EWPs used in advanced ways to replace conventional construction materials, for example, steel and reinforced concrete, and enhance the appeal of wood construction, thus leading to the quest for groundbreaking and environmentally friendly EWP solutions (e.g., dovetail massive wood board elements) (**Figure 10**) for the future of timber in Finland. Currently, although the uptake of for example dovetail massive wood board elements for industrial applications is very limited, with new projects to be developed, it can be used more in the construction of multi-story and even tall buildings. In order to contribute to environmentally friendly construction and low embodied energy and carbon buildings, more research is needed to develop innovative and sustainable EWPs that are nontoxic, low-cost, recyclable with well-designed structural features and life cycle assessments.

This study will assist and guide Finnish key professionals in the design and implementation of timber buildings, highlighting the status and future directions of massive timber construction.

Acknowledgements

This project has received funding from the European Union's Horizon 2020 research and innovation program under the Marie Skłodowska-Curie grant agreement No [101024593].

Funding

This project has also received funding (60,000 EUR) from the Marjatta and Eino Kolli Foundation for funding the technical performance tests including fire safety, structural, moisture transfer resistance and air-tightness, and sound insulation.

Marjatta ja Eino Kollin

SÄÄTIÖ

Lisää mahdollisuuksia

Author details

Hüseyin Emre Ilgın* and Markku Karjalainen
Tampere University, Tampere, Finland

*Address all correspondence to: emre.ilgin@tuni.fi

IntechOpen

© 2022 The Author(s). Licensee IntechOpen. This chapter is distributed under the terms of the Creative Commons Attribution License (http://creativecommons.org/licenses/by/3.0), which permits unrestricted use, distribution, and reproduction in any medium, provided the original work is properly cited.

References

[1] Soikkeli A, Koiso-Kanttila J. Kärsämäki church in Finland—Modern language of form combined with old techniques and craftsmanship. In: Lourenço P, Roca P, Modena C, editors. Proceedings of the 5th International Conference [on] Structural Analysis of Historical Constructions: Possibilities of Numerical and Experimental Techniques, New Delhi. New York City: Macmillan; 2006. pp. 479-486

[2] Heikkilä J, editor. Massive Wood Architecture. Oulu: Department of Architecture, Oulu University Press Publication B21; 2002

[3] Häkkänen L, Ilgın HE, Karjalainen M. The current state of the Finnish cottage phenomenon: Perspectives of experts. Buildings. 2022;**12**(3):260

[4] Häkkänen L, Ilgın HE, Karjalainen M. Cottage culture in Finland: Development and perspectives. Encyclopedia. 2022;**2**(2):705-716

[5] Sinkko T, Jallinoja M, Räty T. Laminated log wall structures of Norway spruce and Scots pine, environmental product declaration. Building Information Foundation RTS. 2019. Available from: https://epd.rts.fi/system/epd_products/attachments/000/000/085/original/RTSEPD_31-19_SuomenHirsitaloteollisuus_LaminatedLogWallStructures_ver3.pdf? [Accessed: 16 April 2022]

[6] Mölsä S. Hirsitalojen ja muuttovalmiiden pientalojen suosio kasvussa. Rakennuslehti. 2019. Available from: https://www.rakennuslehti.fi/2019/04/hirsitalojen-ja-muuttovalmiiden-pientalojensuosio-kasvussa/ (in Finnish) 1568203293 [Accessed: 16 April 2022]

[7] Lakkala M, Luusua A, Pihlajaniemi J. Finnish perceptions of log and log architecture. Scandinavian Journal of Forest Research. 2020;**35**(5-6):296-307

[8] Hurmekoski E. Long-term outlook for wood construction in Europe. In: Dissertationes Forestales 211. Joensuu, Finland: School of Forest Sciences, Faculty of Science and Forestry, University of Eastern Finland; 2016

[9] Hurmekoski E, Jonsson R, Nord T. Context, drivers, and future potential for wood-frame multi-story construction in Europe. Technological Forecasting and Social Change. 2015;**99**:181-196

[10] Karjalainen M, Ilgın HE, Yli-Äyhö M, Soikkeli A. Complementary Building Concept: Wooden Apartment Building: The Noppa toward Zero Energy Building Approach. London, UK: IntechOpen; 2021

[11] Karjalainen M, Ilgın HE. The change over time in Finnish residents' attitudes towards multi-story timber apartment buildings. Sustainability. 2021;**13**:5501

[12] Ilgın HE, Karjalainen M, Koponen O, Soikkeli A. A Study on Contractors' Perception of Using Wood for Construction. London, UK: IntechOpen; 2022

[13] Karjalainen M, Ilgın HE, Tulonen L. Main design considerations and prospects of contemporary tall timber apartment buildings: Views of key professionals from Finland. Sustainability. 2021;**13**:6593

[14] Toppinen A, Sauru M, Pätäri S, Lähtinen K, Tuppura A. Internal and external factors of competitiveness shaping the future of wooden multistory

construction in Finland and Sweden. Construction Management and Economics. 2019;**37**(4):201-216

[15] Lazarevic D, Kautto P, Antikainen R. Finland's wood-frame multi-storey construction innovation system: Analysing motors of creative destruction. Forest Policy and Economics. 2020;**110**:101861

[16] The National Building Code of Finland—Structural Fire Safety, Decree of the Ministry of the Environment. 2017. Available from: https://ym.fi/en/the-national-building-code-of-finland [Accessed: 16 April 2022]

[17] Soikkeli A, Ilgın HE, Karjalainen M. Wooden additional floor in Finland. Encyclopedia. 2022;**2**(1):578-592

[18] Energy and Climate Strategy, Finnish Ministry of Economic Affairs and Employment. Available from: https://tem.fi/en/energy-and-climate-strategy#:~:text=Finland's%20long%2Dterm%20goal%20is,climate%20policies%20are%20closely%20connected [Accessed: 16 April 2022]

[19] Guidelines on State Aid for Climate, Environmental Protection and Energy. European Commission; 2022. Available from: https://ec.europa.eu/commission/presscorner/detail/en/qanda_22_566 [Accessed: 16 April 2022]

[20] Wood Building Programme, Finnish Ministry of Environment. Available from: https://ym.fi/en/wood-building [Accessed: 16 April 2022]

[21] Karjalainen M, Ilgın HE, Somelar D. Wooden Extra Stories in Concrete Block of Flats in Finland as an Ecologically Sensitive Engineering Solution, Ecological Engineering—Addressing Climate Challenges and Risks. London, UK: IntechOpen; 2021

[22] Karjalainen M, Ilgın HE, Somelar D. Wooden additional floors in old apartment buildings: Perspectives of housing and real estate companies from Finland. Buildings. 2021;**11**:316

[23] Karjalainen M, Ilgın HE, Metsäranta L, Norvasuo M. Wooden Facade Renovation and Additional Floor Construction for Suburban Development in Finland. London, UK: IntechOpen; 2022

[24] Karjalainen M, Ilgın HE, Metsäranta L, Norvasuo M. Residents' attitudes towards wooden facade renovation and additional floor construction in Finland. International Journal of Environmental Research and Public Health. 2021;**18**:12316

[25] Karjalainen M, Ilgın HE, Metsäranta L, Norvasuo M. Suburban residents' preferences for livable residential area in Finland. Sustainability. 2021;**13**:11841

[26] Ilgın HE, Karjalainen M. Perceptions, Attitudes, and Interest of Architects in the Use of Engineered Wood Products for Construction: A Review. London, UK: IntechOpen; 2021

[27] Ilgın HE, Karjalainen M, Pelsmakers S. Finnish architects' attitudes towards multi-storey timber-residential buildings. International Journal of Building Pathology and Adaptation. 2021 [ahead-of-print]

[28] Ilgın HE, Karjalainen M, Pelsmakers S. Contemporary tall residential timber buildings: What are the main architectural and structural design considerations? International Journal of Building Pathology and Adaptation. 2022 [ahead-of-print]

[29] Ilgın HE, Karjalainen M, Koponen O. Review of the Current State-of-the-Art

of Dovetail Massive Wood Elements. London, UK: IntechOpen; 2021

[30] Ilgın HE, Karjalainen M, Koponen O. Dovetailed massive wood board elements for multi-story buildings. In: Proceedings of the LIVENARCH VII Livable Environments & Architecture 7th International Congress OTHER ARCHITECT/URE(S), Trabzon, Turkey, 28-30 September 2021, Volume I. 2021. pp. 47-60

[31] Definitions of Finnish Log Construction, The Finnish Timber Council (Puuinfo). Available from: https://puuinfo.fi/puutieto/timber-construction/definitions-of-finnish-log-construction/?lang=en [Accessed: 16 April 2022]

[32] Heikkilä J, Suikkari R. Log Structures in Finnish Architecture—Continuing the Tradition. 2017. Available from: http://www.arcchip.cz/w11/w11_heikkila.pd [Accessed: 16 April 2022]

[33] Hall J. Feasibility of exporting Finnish log homes to satisfy New Zealand building demand conditions [MSc thesis]. Jyväskylä, Finland: International Business, Jyväskylä University of Applied Sciences; 2017

[34] Korvenmaa P. The Finnish wooden house transformed: American prefabrication, war-time housing and Alvar Aalto. Construction History. 1990;**6**:47-61

[35] Sun J. Mid-rise timber construction in Finland: A study on material, technology and market maturity [Bachelor's thesis]. Helsinki, Finland: Civil Engineering, Sustainable Building Engineering, Metropolia University of Applied Sciences

[36] Nordic Timber Council. Traditional Finnish Timber Construction. Available from: http://www.nordictimber.org/traditional-finnish-timber-construction [Accessed: 16 April 2022]

[37] Lakkala M, Pihlajaniemi J, editors. Modernihirsikaupunki:tutkimushankkeen loppuraportti, Arkkitehtuuri B. Oulu, Finland: Oulun yliopisto; 2019 (in Finnish)

[38] Jussila A. Hirsiomakotitalojen markkinaosuus on edelleen kasvussa. 2020. Available from: https://www.suomirakentaa.fi/ajankohtaista/uutiset-1/hirsiomakotitalojen-markkinaosuuson-edelleen-kasvussa 566 [Accessed: 16 April 2022] (in Finnish)

[39] Lakkala M, Pihlajaniemi J. Tectonics and architectonic quality in recently published Finnish log architecture: Corresponding architects' perceptions. Frontiers of Architectural Research. 2021;**10**(4):741-757

[40] Vihermäki H, Toppinen A, Toivonen R. Intermediaries to accelerate the diffusion of wooden multi-storey construction in Finland. Environmental Innovation and Societal Transitions. 2020;**36**:433-448

[41] Karjalainen M. Study of the Finnish multi-story timber frame apartment buildings 1995-2018. In: Proceeding of the 6th International Conference S. ARCH-2019 5-7 March 2019, Havana, Cuba. 2019

[42] Toppinen A, Röhr A, Pätäri S, Lähtinen K, Toivonen R. The future of wooden multistory construction in the forest bioeconomy—A Delphi study from Finland and Sweden. Journal of Forest Economics. 2018;**31**:3-10

[43] Karjalainen M, Ilgın HE. A statistical study on multi-story timber residential buildings (1995-2020) in Finland. In: Proceedings of the LIVENARCH VII

Livable Environments & Architecture 7th International Congress OTHER ARCHITECT/URE(S), Trabzon, Turkey, 28-30 September 2021, Volume I. 2021. pp. 82-94

[44] Wood Magazines, Media Kit 2022, The Finnish Timber Council (Puuinfo). Available from: https://puuinfo.fi/puulehti/media-kit-2022-wood-magazine/?lang=en [Accessed: 16 April 2022]

[45] Tulonen L, Karjalainen M, Ilgın HE. Tall Wooden Residential Buildings in Finland: What Are the Key Factors for Design and Implementation? London, UK: IntechOpen; 2021

[46] Ilgın HE. A study on interrelations of structural systems and main planning considerations in contemporary supertall buildings. International Journal of Building Pathology and Adaptation. 2022 [ahead-of-print]

[47] Ilgın HE. Space efficiency in contemporary supertall residential buildings. Architecture. 2021;**1**(1):25-37

[48] Ilgın HE. Space efficiency in supertall office buildings. Journal of Architectural Engineering. 2021;**27**(3):4021024

[49] Ilgın HE, Ay BO, Gunel MH. A study on main architectural and structural design considerations of contemporary supertall buildings. Architectural Science Review. 2021;**64**(3):212-224

[50] Ilgın HE. Potentials and limitations of supertall building structural systems: Guiding for architects [Ph.D. dissertation]. Ankara, Turkey: Department of Architecture, Middle East Technical University; 2018

[51] Lazarevic M, Mäenpää D, Ovaska I, Peck P, Rodhe H, Temmes A, et al. Renewal of Forest Based Manufacturing Towards a Sustainable Circular Bioeconomy: Reports of the Finnish Environment Institute 13/2017. Helsinki, Finland: Finnish Environment Institute; 2017

[52] Karjalainen M. Status and possibilities of timber construction in Finland. In: Lilja K, editor. Wood-Based Bioeconomy Solving Global Challenges. Ministry of Economic Affairs and Employment of Finland [MEAE 2/2017]: Helsinki, Finland; 2017. pp. 35-39

[53] Vihemäki H, Ludvig A, Toivonen R, Toppinen A, Weiss G. Institutional and policy frameworks shaping the wooden multi-storey construction markets: A comparative case study on Austria and Finland. Wood Material Science & Engineering. 2019;**14**(5):312-324

[54] Maniak-Huesser M, Tellnes LGF, Zea Escamilla E. Mind the gap: A policy gap analysis of programmes promoting timber construction in nordic countries. Sustainability. 2021;**13**(21):11876

[55] Wood Construction is Being Promoted in Finland. Finnish Ministry of Agriculture and Forestry. Available from: https://mmm.fi/en/en/forests/use-of-wood/wood-construction [Accessed: 16 April 2022]

[56] Sotayo A, Bradley D, Bather M, Sareh P, Oudjene M, El-Houjeyri I, et al. Review of state of the art of dowel laminated timber members and densified wood materials as sustainable engineered wood products for construction and building applications. Developments in the Built Environment. 2020;**1**:1-11

[57] Salvadori V. Multi-storey timber-based buildings: An international survey of case-studies with five or more storeys over the last twenty years [PhD dissertation]. Vienna, Austria: Technische Universität Wien; 2021

[58] Svatoš-Ražnjević H, Orozco L, Menges A. Advanced timber construction industry: A review of 350 multi-storey timber projects from 2000-2021. Buildings. 2022;**12**(4):404

[59] Maurya PK, Ali SA, Ahmad A, Zhou Q, Castro JS, Khan E, et al. An introduction to environmental degradation: Causes, consequence and mitigation. In: Environmental Degradation: Causes and Remediation Strategies. Haridwar, India: Agro Environ Media, Agriculture and Environmental Science Academy; 2020

[60] Rinne R, Ilgın HE, Karjalainen M. Comparative study on life-cycle assessment and carbon footprint of hybrid, concrete and timber apartment buildings in Finland. International Journal of Environmental Research and Public Health. 2022;**19**:774

[61] Sijakovic M, Peric A. Sustainable architectural design: Towards climate change mitigation. Archnet-IJAR: International Journal of Architectural Research. 2021;**15**(2):385-400

[62] Ilgın HE, Karjalainen M. Preliminary design proposals for dovetail wood board elements in multi-story building construction. Architecture. 2021;**1**:56-68

[63] Ilgın HE, Karjalainen M, Koponen O. Various Geometric Configuration Proposals for Dovetail Wooden Horizontal Structural Members in Multistory Building Construction. London, UK: IntechOpen; 2022

Chapter 2

Tallest Timber Buildings: Main Architectural and Structural Design Considerations

Hüseyin Emre Ilgın and Markku Karjalainen

Abstract

Since the end of the twentieth century, the question of how to deal with the increasing scarcity of resources has been at the center and the need for renewable materials has come to the fore, especially in the construction sector. A possible solution to these environmental challenges is represented by the development of engineered timber products, which allowed the realization of tall timber structures. Their main drivers are decarbonization, forest management, and timber life cycle, urbanization, and densification, productivity in the construction industry, and the benefits of using timber indoors. In this context, this chapter will analyze data from the 10 tallest timber building cases to enhance the understanding of contemporary trends. Data are collected through literature surveys and case studies to analyze the main architectural and structural design concerns to contribute to the knowledge about the growing tall timber structures around the world. By revealing up-to-date features of the tallest timber towers, it is thought that this chapter will contribute to aiding and directing key construction professionals such as architects, structural engineers, and contractors, in the design and construction of future tall timber building developments.

Keywords: timber/wood, engineered timber/wood products, tall building, timber construction, architectural design considerations, structural design considerations, dovetail massive wooden board elements

1. Introduction

The utilization of timber in the construction sector has been revived since the mid-1990s [1, 2], and particularly in the last 10 years [3, 4], due to environmental concerns, urbanization challenges, and productivity in the construction industry [5–7]. Since the end of the twentieth century, the question of how to deal with the increasing scarcity of resources has been at the center and the need for renewable (building) materials has come to the fore, especially in the building construction industry [8]. A potential solution to these challenges is the development of engineered timber products (ETPs) that enable the erection of tall timber buildings [9] as in the case of the 18-story and 85 m high Mjøstårnet (Brumunddal, 2019).

 IntechOpen

CO_2 has been a game-changer since 1970, sparking a revolution in the way buildings are built. With the successful implementation of issues such as efficiency and passive standards in just a few years, there has been an increased emphasis on sustainability during and after the construction site [10]. Furthermore, today, the construction industry accounts for approximately 40% of annual greenhouse gas emissions, 40% of global resource consumption, 40% of energy use, and 50% of global waste, timber is a valuable alternative material [11, 12].

In this sense, the use of timber can enable the construction industry to avoid significant greenhouse gas emissions associated with unsustainable material use, as it is a natural carbon sink [13]. In other words, the fact that it is a renewable building material that can store CO_2 compared with steel and concrete, which are traditional building materials, has brought timber to an important point as a construction material [14, 15].

On the other hand, simultaneously, the world population doubled in less than a century, and for the first time in history, more people lived in cities than in the countryside [16]. The overall effect of this high density of people in cities forced buildings to rise. However, combined with the chronically low productivity of the construction sector since the 1990s and the high demand for new buildings in the future [17], there may be other challenges to reducing greenhouse gas emissions. The assessment of a skilled and aging workforce and slow construction time, among other factors, are significant challenges for both established and future companies [18]. Prefabrication is recommended as the best way to improve productivity, and timber is perfectly suited for this as it is light and easy to work with [19, 20].

Latest technical developments in ETPs (e.g., [21]) and systems, as well as regulatory procedures in fire codes, other building codes, and various government regulations initiatives, have allowed timber construction to reach new heights [22]. Multistory construction is a new and promising business with high potential to support the bioeconomy [23] as in the case of the 25-story and 87 m high Ascent (Milwaukee, under construction) (**Figure 1**). Besides the potential for substantial

Figure 1.
Ascent (image courtesy of Jason Korb/Korb + Associates Architects).

environmental and economic life cycle advantages can contribute to social sustainability in the processing of materials, as in both primary production and timber-based value chains [24].

In the literature, numerous surveys present the technical features of ETPs, their use in building construction, and diverse technical solutions (e.g., [25–28]). Several surveys focus on timber as a construction material from the viewpoints of key specialists (e.g., [29–32]) and users or inhabitants (e.g., [33, 34]); whereas there is a very limited number of comprehensive comparative design studies on architectural and structural parameters of multistory and tall timber buildings (e.g., [35–37]).

This chapter aims to identify, organize, and combine the data about the tallest timber buildings from the primary architectural and structural aspects to enhance understanding of the design and construction of these towers. To accomplish this goal, data were collected from the 10 tallest timber buildings under construction and completed.

The scope of the chapter is limited to the information available and uses key points to provide a representative understanding of contemporary trends in tallest timber buildings: general information (building name, location, height, number of stories, completion, gross floor area, amount of timber used), architectural and structural design parameters (building form, core type, structural system, and material). It is thought that this study will contribute to aiding and directing architects in the design and construction of future tallest timber towers.

2. Materials and methods

The chapter was mainly conducted through a literature review including peer-reviewed research, official documents and reports, fact sheets, architectural and structural magazines, and other Internet sources. Additionally, case studies were used to identify, gather, and combine the data about the tallest timber buildings to examine the architectural and structural perspectives. The study sample included 10 tallest timber buildings under construction and completed, in a variety of countries (two from Norway, two from Finland, two from Canada, one from Austria, one from the Netherlands, one

#	Name	City (country)	Height (m)	# of stories	Completion date	Gross floor area	Amount of timber used*
1	Ascent	Milwaukee (USA)	87	25	UC	30,136 m^2	NA
2	Mjøstårnet	Brumunddal (Norway)	85	18	2019	11,300 m^2	2600 m^3/GL (structural timber)
3	HoHo	Vienna (Austria)	84	24	2020	25,000 m^2	4350 m^3 (entire construction)
4	HAUT	Amsterdam (Netherlands)	73	22	2022	14,500 m^2	2000 m^3 (entire timber)
5	Brock Commons Tallwood House	Vancouver (Canada)	58	18	2017	15,115 m^2	1973 m^3/CLT 260 m^3/GLPSL
6	Treet	Bergen (Norway)	49	14	2015	7140 m^2	550 m^3/GL 385 m^3/CLT

#	Name	City (country)	Height (m)	# of stories	Completion date	Gross floor area	Amount of timber used*
7	Lighthouse Joensuu	Joensuu (Finland)	48	14	2019	5935 m^2	2000 m^3 (entire construction)
8	HOAS Tuuliniitty	Tuuliniitty (Finland)	42	13	2021	7584 m^2	NA
9	Origine	Quebec (Canada)	41	13	2017	13,124 m^2	3111 m^3 (mass timber)
10	Trafalgar Place	London (UK)	36	10	2015	16,661 m^2	750 m^3 (timber volume)

*Note on abbreviation: 'UC' indicates under construction; 'NA' indicates not available; 'CLT' indicates cross-laminated timber; 'GL' indicates glue-laminated timber; 'PSL' indicates parallel strand lumber. *Different levels and kinds of data for "the amount of timber" e.g. structural timber, entire construction, or only CLT were given by various references.*

Table 1.
10 tallest timber buildings.

from the United Kingdom, and one from the United States) as seen in **Table 1**. In the study, a "tall building" was defined as a building with over eight story [22].

In terms of functionality, tall buildings can be classified as single-use or mixed-use. In this study, hotel, residence, and office were considered as primary functions, whereas their combinations were considered mixed-use. Taking into account existing literature (e.g., [36–43]), the classifications based on their structural behavior under lateral loads by Ilgın [44–46] and Ilgın et al. [47] were used in this paper due to its more comprehensive and clearer structures (see **Table 2**).

Core	Building form	Structural system	Structural material
Central core	Prismatic form	Shear-frame system	Steel
• Central	Setback form	• Shear trussed frame	Reinforced concrete
• Central split	Tapered form	• Shear walled frame	Composite
Atrium core	Twisted form	Mega core system	
• Atrium	Leaning/tilted form	Mega column system	
• Atrium split	Fee form	Outriggered frame system	
External core		Tube system	
• Attached		• Framed-tube	
• Detached		• Trussed-tube	
• Partial split		• Bundled tube	
• Full split			
Peripheral core			
• Partial peripheral			
• Full peripheral			
• Partial split			
• Full split			

Table 2.
Core, building form, structural system, and structural material classifications.

3. Findings: main architectural and structural design considerations

As can be seen in **Table 3**, the case study buildings were designed mostly for residential purposes, and the two mixed-use cases also included residential use. Additionally, central core arrangement was the dominant core typology (only one case with peripheral core). The benefits of a central core are factors, e.g., structural contribution, compactness, making the exterior facade open to light and scenery, and facilitating fire escape, which can aid in the dominant formation of this typology.

Prismatic forms were the most common and occurred in eight case studies including HoHo (**Figure 2**). The reason why prismatic forms are common may be due to ease of workmanship, practicability, and efficient use of interior space (especially in rectangular floor plans) compared with complicated forms.

The advantages of shear wall systems in buildings up to approximately 35 stories such as construction speed, suitability for prefabrication, and sufficient rigidity to withstand lateral loads may be the reasons behind this occurrence [48] as in the case of the 22-story and 73 m high HAUT (Amsterdam, 2022) (**Figure 3**) with a concrete

#	Name	Function	Core type	Form	Structural system	Structural material	Structural description
1	Ascent	R	Central	Prismatic	Shear-walled frame	Composite	Core: RC Column: GL
2	Mjøstårnet	R/H/O	Central	Prismatic	Trussed-tube	Timber	Nonstructural core: CLT Column: GL exterior brace: GL
3	HoHo	R/H/O	Central	Prismatic	Shear-walled frame	Composite	Core: RC Column: GL
4	HAUT	R	Central	Free	Shear wall	Composite	Core: RC Shear wall: CLT
5	Brock Commons Tallwood House	R	Central	Prismatic	Shear-walled frame	Composite	Core: RC Column: GL and PSL
6	Treet	R	Central	Prismatic	Trussed-tube	Timber	Nonstructural core: CLT exterior braces, belt, outrigger: GL
7	Lighthouse Joensuu	R	Central	Prismatic	Shear wall	Timber	Core and shear wall: LVL
8	HOAS Tuuliniitty	R	Central	Prismatic	Shear wall	Timber	Core and shear wall: CLT
9	Origine	R	Central	Free	Shear wall	Timber	Core and shear wall: CLT
10	Trafalgar Place	R	Peripheral	Prismatic	Shear wall	Timber	Core and shear wall: CLT

Note on abbreviations: 'R' indicates residential; 'H' indicates hotel; 'O' indicates office; 'RC' indicates reinforced concrete.

Table 3.
Tallest timber buildings by function, core type, form, structural system, and structural material.

Figure 2.
HoHo (photo courtesy of DERFRITZ).

core and CLT shear walls. Additionally, Mjøstårnet (**Figure 4**) and Treet took the advantage of trussed-tube system, in which exterior multistory GL trusses handle the horizontal and gravity loads to ensure the required rigidity of the structure and the CLT core has a nonstructural function [49, 50].

On the other hand, the interstory drift between adjacent floors of upper stories in shear wall systems and the interstory drift between adjacent floors of lower stories in rigid frame systems are problematic issues, but shear frame systems (namely shear trussed frame and shear-walled frame systems) offer a solution where both systems compensate for each other's disadvantages as in the case of the 18-story and 58 m high Brock Commons Tallwood House (Vancouver, 2017) (**Figure 5**).

In terms of structural material, CLT was the structural material commonly used in 10 selected cases (**Table 3**). In the buildings where composite/hybrid systems were employed, concrete was utilized in all four cases. Additionally, in all case studies, the ground floor or podium was made of concrete and had a reinforced concrete core. Moreover, among them, in Ascent, mass timber residential floors were built over 5-story-concrete parking. Concrete podium construction has many advantages, including ground-level housing facilities and services, offering high clearances in public areas and large openings, and creating fireproof zones for primary mechanical

Figure 3.
HAUT (photo courtesy of Jannes Linders).

Figure 4.
Mjøstårnet (photo courtesy of Voll Arkitekter AS + Ricardo Foto).

and electrical components [51]. Furthermore, the reason for employing concrete core: (i) to provide the lateral rigidity and strength of the structure to a great extent; (ii) to take advantage of the natural resistance of concrete against fire; (iii) to benefit from

Figure 5.
Brock Commons Tallwood House (photo by Michael Elkan and courtesy of Acton Ostry Architects).

its advantage in damping wind-induced building sway, which is one of the commonly confronted issues in high-rise buildings [52].

4. Concluding remarks

Driven predominantly by decarbonization, forest management, and timber life cycle, urbanization and intensification, and productivity in the construction industry, tall timber buildings have been at the forefront of construction practices in the global urban context for over one decade with an ever-increasing trend of height. It is thought that the analysis of the key architectural and structural design concerns of the 10 tallest buildings (one is under construction) will contribute to the planning of future timber buildings that will push the height limits.

The tallest timber buildings were mostly designed as residential. Central core arrangement was the dominant core typology. Prismatic forms were most widely used. Shear wall systems were preferred in five cases. In terms of structural material, six cases used pure wood, mostly CLT, while others opted for composite, usually concrete.

Rules, expectations, requirements, and typologies for tall wooden buildings, whose design dynamics are associated with technological developments and new construction techniques, have not yet been clarified. The diversity in the design and construction methods of these structures is still evolving to meet various building codes, market demands, contexts, and environments. This chapter has given the most up-to-date information on this pioneer building typology.

This report also has its limitations, since the empirical data presented in this chapter were limited to 10 buildings, it seems difficult to generalize about timber tall buildings of the future. On the other hand, given the increase in the number of tall timber buildings erected, further research can be conducted with larger sample groups to obtain broader generalizations and new information.

Additionally, the increase in global environmental awareness strengthens the attractiveness of timber construction, which leads the search for innovative and environmentally friendly engineered timber product solutions such as the DoMWoB

(a)

(b)

Figure 6.
(a) Dovetail massive wood board prototype manufactured at Vocational College Lapland (Ammattiopisto Lappia), Kemi, Finland; (b) Fire test specimens mounted to supporting construction made of aerated concrete blocks at Tampere University Fire Laboratory, Tampere, Finland (photos by Hüseyin Emre Ilgın).

project (Dovetailed Massive Wood Board Elements for Multi-Story Buildings); see Acknowledgments and Funding (**Figure 6**) [53] in the future. Although for example, the uptake of dovetail massive timber elements for industrial applications is very limited at the moment, with new research projects to be developed, these elements can be used more in multistory and even tall building construction.

Acknowledgements

This project has received funding from the European Union's Horizon 2020 research and innovation program under the Marie Skłodowska-Curie grant agreement No [101024593].

Funding

This project has also received funding (60,000 EUR) from the Marjatta and Eino Kolli Foundation for funding the technical performance tests including fire safety, structural, moisture transfer resistance and air-tightness, and sound insulation.

Author details

Hüseyin Emre Ilgın* and Markku Karjalainen
Tampere University, Tampere, Finland

*Address all correspondence to: emre.ilgin@tuni.fi

IntechOpen

© 2022 The Author(s). Licensee IntechOpen. This chapter is distributed under the terms of the Creative Commons Attribution License (http://creativecommons.org/licenses/by/3.0), which permits unrestricted use, distribution, and reproduction in any medium, provided the original work is properly cited.

References

[1] Mayo J. Solid Wood—Case Studies in Mass Timber Architecture, Technology and Design. London, Routledge; 2015

[2] Tulonen L, Karjalainen M, Ilgın HE. Tall Wooden Residential Buildings in Finland: What Are the Key Factors for Design and Implementation? IntechOpen: London, UK; 2021

[3] Krötsch S, Müller L. The development of multi-storey timber construction. In: Kaufmann H, Krötsch S, Winter S, editors. Manual of Multi-Storey Timber Construction. Munich, Germany: Detail Business Information; 2018

[4] Karjalainen M, Ilgın HE, Tulonen L. Main design considerations and prospects of contemporary tall timber apartment buildings: Views of key professionals from Finland. Sustainability. 2021;**13**:6593

[5] United Nations. World Urbanization Prospects: 2018: Highlights. New York, NY, USA: United Nations; 2019

[6] Ilgın HE, Karjalainen M. Perceptions, Attitudes, and Interest of Architects in the Use of Engineered Wood Products for Construction: A Review. IntechOpen: London, UK; 2021

[7] Kuzman MK, Sandberg D. A new era for multi-storey timber buildings in Europe. In: New Horizons for the Forest Products Industry, Proceedings of the 70th Forest Products Society International Convention; 26-29 June 2016; Portland, OR, USA. Ljubljana, Slovenia: University of Ljubljana, Biotechnical Faculty, Department of Wood Science and Technology; 2016

[8] Karjalainen M, Ilgın HE, Metsäranta L, Norvasuo M. Residents' Attitudes towards wooden facade renovation and additional floor construction in Finland. The International Journal of Environmental Research and Public Health. 2021;**18**:12316

[9] Ilgın HE, Karjalainen M, Koponen O, Soikkeli A. A Study on Contractors' Perception of Using Wood for Construction. IntechOpen: London, UK; 2022

[10] Salvadori V. Multi-storey timber-based buildings: An international survey of case-studies with five or more storeys over the last twenty years [PhD dissertation]. Vienna, Austria: Technische Universität Wien; 2021

[11] Rinne R, Ilgın HE, Karjalainen M. Comparative study on life-cycle assessment and carbon footprint of hybrid, concrete and timber apartment buildings in Finland. International Journal of Environmental Research and Public Health. 2022;**19**:774

[12] Karjalainen M, Ilgın HE, Somelar D. Wooden Extra Stories in Concrete Block of Flats in Finland as an Ecologically Sensitive Engineering Solution, Ecological Engineering—Addressing Climate Challenges and Risks. IntechOpen: London, UK; 2021

[13] Ilgın HE, Karjalainen M, Koponen O. Dovetailed massive wood board elements for multi-story buildings. In: Proceedings of the LIVENARCH VII Livable Environments & Architecture 7th International Congress Other Architect/ure(s); 28-30 September 2021; Trabzon, Turkey. Vol. I. pp. 47, 2021-60

[14] Ilgın HE, Karjalainen M, Koponen O. Review of the Current State-of-the-Art of Dovetail Massive Wood Elements. IntechOpen: London, UK; 2021

[15] Häkkänen L, Ilgın HE, Karjalainen M. Cottage culture in Finland: Development and perspectives. Encyclopedia. 2022;**2**(2):705-716

[16] United Nations World. Population Prospects—The 2017 Revision: Key Findings and Advance Tables. New York, NY, USA: Department of Economic and Social Affairs Population Division; 2017. pp. 1-46

[17] Changali S, Mohamman A, van Nieuwland M. The Construction Productivity Imperative. New York, NY, USA: McKinsey Productivity Sciences Center; 2015

[18] McKinsey & Company. Reinventing Construction: A Route to Higher Productivity. Singapore: McKinsey Productivity Sciences Center; 2017

[19] Karjalainen M, Ilgın HE, Somelar D. Wooden additional floors in old apartment buildings: Perspectives of housing and real estate companies from Finland. Buildings. 2021;**11**:316

[20] Soikkeli A, Ilgın HE, Karjalainen M. Wooden additional floor in Finland. Encyclopedia. 2022;**2**(1):578-592

[21] Nazrul IM, Rahman F, Das AK, Hiziroglu S. An overview of different types and potential of bio-based adhesives used for wood products. International Journal of Adhesion and Adhesives. 2022;**112**:102992

[22] Ilgın HE, Karjalainen M, Pelsmakers S. Contemporary tall residential timber building: What are the main architectural and structural design considerations? International Journal of Building Pathology and Adaptation. 2022. Ahead-of-print

[23] Ilgın HE, Karjalainen M, Pelsmakers S. Finnish architects' attitudes towards multi-storey timber-residential buildings. International Journal of Building Pathology and Adaptation. 2021. Ahead-of-print

[24] Toppinen A, Röhr A, Pätäri S, Lähtinen K, Toivonen R. The future of wooden multistory construction in the Forest bioeconomy—A Delphi study from Finland and Sweden. Journal of Forest Economics. 2018;**31**:3-10

[25] Siahkamari M, Emmanuel S, Hodge DB, Nejad M. Lignin-Glyoxal: A fully biobased formaldehyde-free wood adhesive for interior engineered wood products. ACS Sustainable Chemistry & Engineering. 2022;**10**(11):3430-3441

[26] Ilgın HE, Karjalainen M. Preliminary design proposals for dovetail Wood Board elements in multi-story building construction. Architecture. 2021;**1**:56-68

[27] Karjalainen M, Ilgın HE, Yli-Äyhö M, Soikkeli A. Complementary Building Concept: Wooden Apartment Building: The Noppa toward Zero Energy Building Approach. IntechOpen: London, UK; 2021

[28] Hua LS, Chen LW, Antov P, Kristak L, Md TP. Engineering wood products from eucalyptus spp. Advances in Materials Science and Engineering. 2022;**2022**

[29] Karjalainen M, Ilgın HE, Metsäranta L, Norvasuo M. Wooden Facade Renovation and Additional Floor Construction for Suburban Development in Finland. IntechOpen: London, UK; 2022

[30] Gagnon B, Tanguay X, Amor B, Imbrogno AF. Forest products and circular economy strategies: A Canadian perspective. Energies. 2022;**15**(3):673

[31] Karjalainen M, Ilgın HE, Metsäranta L, Norvasuo M. Suburban residents' preferences for livable

residential area in Finland. Sustainability. 2021;**13**:11841

[32] Häkkänen L, Ilgın HE, Karjalainen M. The current state of the Finnish cottage phenomenon: Perspectives of experts. Buildings. 2022;**12**(3):260

[33] Karjalainen M, Ilgın HE. The change over time in Finnish residents' attitudes towards multi-story timber apartment buildings. Sustainability. 2021;**13**:5501

[34] Harju C. The perceived quality of wooden building materials—A systematic literature review and future research agenda. International Journal of Consumer Studies. 2022;**46**(1):29-55

[35] Karjalainen M, Ilgın HE. A statistical study on multi-story timber residential buildings (1995-2020) in Finland. In: Proceedings of the LIVENARCH VII Livable Environments & Architecture 7th International Congress Other Architect/ure(s); 28-30 September 2021; Trabzon, Turkey. Vol. I. pp. 82, 2021-94

[36] Svatoš-Ražnjević H, Orozco L, Menges A. Advanced timber construction industry: A review of 350 multi-storey timber projects from 2000-2021. Buildings. 2022;**12**(4):404

[37] Kuzmanovska I, Gasparri E, Tapias Monné D, Aitchison M. Tall timber buildings: Emerging trends and typologies. In: Proceedings of the World Conference on Timber Engineering; 20-23 August 2018; Seoul, Korea.

[38] Gunel MH, Ilgın HE. A proposal for the classification of structural systems of tall buildings. Building and Environment. 2007;**42**(7):2667-2675

[39] Salvadori V. Worldwide Structural Survey of 197 Multi-Storey Timber-Based Buildings From 5 to 24 Storeys. In: Proceedings of the Conference: WCTE 2021—World Conference on Timber Engineering; 9-12 August 2021; Santiago del Chile, Chile

[40] Erikshammar J. Activity: Wood-Based Product Platforms: An Industrial Application of Industrialized House-Building, An Industrial Application of Industrialized House-Building. Reading, UK: University of Reading; 2014

[41] Brege S, Stehn L, Nord T. Business models in industrialized building of multi-storey houses. Construction Management and Economics. 2014;**32**:208-226

[42] Ilgın HE. Potentials and limitations of supertall building structural systems: Guiding for architects [Ph.D. dissertation]. Ankara, Turkey: Department of Architecture, Middle East Technical University; 2018

[43] Hurmekoski E, Jonsson R, Nord T. Context, drivers, and future potential for wood-frame multi-story construction in Europe. Technological Forecasting and Social Change. 2015;**99**:181-196

[44] Ilgın HE. Space efficiency in contemporary supertall office buildings. Journal of Architectural Engineering. 2021;**27**(3):4021024

[45] Ilgın HE. Space efficiency in contemporary supertall residential buildings. Architecture. 2021;**1**(1):25-37

[46] Ilgın HE. A study on interrelations of structural systems and main planning considerations in contemporary supertall buildings. International Journal of Building Pathology and Adaptation. 2022. Ahead-of-print

[47] Ilgın HE, Ay BÖ, Gunel MH. A study on main architectural and structural design considerations of contemporary supertall buildings. Architectural Science Review. 2021;**64**(3):212-224

[48] Gunel MH, Ilgın HE. Yüksek Bina: Tasıyıcı Sistem ve Aerodinamik Form, Turkey (in Turkish). Ankara: METU Faculty of Architecture Press; 2014

[49] Abrahamsen R. Mjøstårnet—Construction of an 81 m tall timber building, 23. Internationales Holzbau-Forum IHF 2017, 06-08.12. Germany: Garmisch-Partenkirchen; 2017

[50] Malo KA, Abrahamsen RB, Bjertnæs MA. Some structural design issues of the 14-storey timber framed building "Treet" in Norway. European Journal of Wood and Wood Products. 2016;**74**(3):407-424

[51] Harte AM. Mass timber—The emergence of a modern construction material. Journal of Structural Integrity and Maintenance. 2017;**2**(3):121-132

[52] Gunel MH, Ilgın HE. Tall Buildings: Structural Systems and Aerodynamic Form. London and New York: Routledge; 2014

[53] Ilgın HE, Karjalainen M, Koponen O. Various Geometric Configuration Proposals for Dovetail Wooden Horizontal Structural Members in Multistory Building Construction. IntechOpen: London, UK; 2022

Chapter 3

Sustainable Wooden Skyscrapers for the Future Cities

Amjad Almusaed and Asaad Almssad

Abstract

At the time of writing, energy-saving and eco-friendly building materials have gained acceptance, recognition, and a strong foothold in the construction sector. There is an appreciable degree of congruence in the development of green buildings and bio-based building materials, making it imperative to promote and sustain the application of such materials. Wood is endowed with a host of favorable properties sought after in a building material—its organic warmth, softness, ability to control indoor moisture levels and act as a good insulator, malleability, and workability, to name a few. Wooden buildings blend perfectly into the surrounding landscapes much better than their counterparts. It facilitates design for lightweight and strength, is a renewable resource, and accords stability and seismic resistance to structures. The focus of this chapter is on wooden skyscrapers which promise to be a greener and eco-friendlier option vis-à-vis the conventional concrete high-rises.

Keywords: bio-based materials, eco-friendly building materials, sustainable buildings, wooden skyscrapers

1. Introduction

Modern architecture is changing the face of megacities, creating a more comfortable and prosperous environment for life. Leading architects are increasingly choosing those forms and materials that increase the energy efficiency of future buildings. Futuristic buildings coexist with the legacy of the past and harmoniously fit into the style of the area. And the plasticity of their facades reflects the dynamism of modern cities. These projects differ from traditional buildings not only in their architectural appearance but also in their rich infrastructure. In addition, they often embody the most daring and progressive ideas of their time. We are constantly in contact with building materials. Metal handles, wooden walls, and glass windows would create a completely different atmosphere if the handles were, say, glass, the walls were metal, and the windows were wooden.

And yet, before embarking on a detailed design of the future building, it makes sense to determine its style at least approximately. If it will be a fusion-style building (some experts consider the term "eclectic" already obsolete), then such a decision should not be spontaneous, but meaningful and justified. It is worth understanding what elements of which styles the country house will combine, whether one

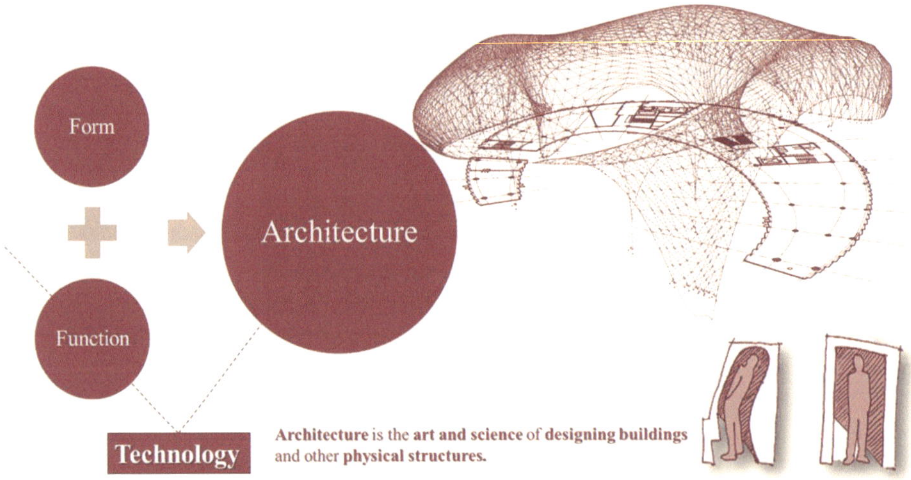

Figure 1.
The modern architecture between form and functions.

component will dominate the others, how harmony can be achieved in the resulting exterior, and so on. Separately, you need to think about the materials and technologies that will be used in the construction process: how to emphasize the creative idea with their help and facilitate its implementation, what new and unexpected esthetic solutions the material or technology itself can offer the architect (**Figure 1**). The material is as important to the building as its form, function, and location.

In the circular bio-economies which will gradually entrench themselves in many parts of the world, wood, as a renewable material of construction, will reign again as a dominant material in anthroposphere structures, supplanting the now-prevalent nonrenewable materials. Wood wastes generated in the forestry sector will lend themselves to being reworked and recycled back into the anthroposphere [1, 2]. It is not just the fact that it is renewable and abundant which makes wood a favorite in the architecture, building, and construction (ABC) sector of a circular bioeconomy. It is strong and light, has good thermal insulation properties [3], has the ability to resist shock loads without getting damaged, and dampens vibrations (thus resisting seismic shocks). It is highly malleable and workable and lends itself well to gluing, being joined by fasteners, etc. In Europe, wood found used in the past as the main building material for temples, towers owned by appanage princes, and peasants' farmsteads and is more common within Europe, in Scandinavia. Many Finnish, Norwegian, and Swedish citizens expressed different views on the acceptability of the use of wood than their fellow-Europeans in Austria, Denmark, Germany, and the United Kingdom [4].

Expanding the scope of use of wood and finding creative and innovative ways of incorporating wood waste back into the anthroposphere supports the paradigms of circular bio-economies [5]. If the processing turns out to be complex, the wood itself can be modified and conferred with improved properties. Modified wood is a new material in which its anatomical structure is preserved, while its physical and mechanical properties are significantly improved. Various types of modified wood are used not only as substitutes but also as full-fledged, promising composite materials. The static flexural strength of Wood-Based Laminate Constructions comes in handy as they frequently experience static flexural and compressive deformation during service [6].

The mechanical properties of wood depend on a host of factors, the most important of which are the nature of the load, the direction in which it acts on the fibers, the speed and the duration of the load, as well as the structural defects in the wood, effects of humidity, etc. The mechanical and deformation characteristics are determined in the laboratory on small specimens made of defect-free wood, thus obtaining the standard strengths of the ideal wood under short loads. The modulus of rupture (MOR) and modulus of elasticity (MOE) are determined using nondestructive (NDT), semi-destructive (SDT), and destructive (DT) test methods [7]. The moisture content is also determined, as it must be remembered that variations in moisture content cause local swelling or shrinkage, thereby changing the distribution of stresses and impacting the strength and bearing capacity adversely [8]. Variation in the quality of wood is common, both within the same species and across different species; and the sources of such variations are diverse. It is found that most of the mechanical properties of the glued wood elements are superior to those of the wood in the component elements. This may be reasoned out as follows:

- Reduction of adverse effects due to eccentric defects, such as knots, which introduce bending stress on individual parts [9].

- Reduction of the weakening effect of nodes, by consolidation introduced by adjacent elements.

- Ensuring a more homogeneous element with a positive effect on the resistances and on the general density, which is very close to the average density of the component elements.

2. ABC[1] and wood

Wood, it goes without saying, is one of the oldest building materials. Houses, towers, and bridges of yore were built with wood. Special wooden structures—circles—were used in the construction of ancient arches [10]. Centuries of experience and scientific research have shown that during normal operation of wooden structures, their service life is measured in centuries. An example of this is the oldest wooden bridge in Europe—the Chapel Bridge in Lucerne, dating back to 1330. The use of wood and its derivatives in construction and especially for insulation and finishing depends to a large extent on its favorable thermal properties. By virtue of its low coefficient of thermal conductivity vis-à-vis other materials of construction, even a light/thin wood frame wall may provide a structure with adequate mechanical properties and an acceptable level of thermal insulation [11]. The interest in "zero-energy" or "low-energy," or "climate-positive" constructions with a reduced demand for externally supplied heat energy has entrenched itself in academic, research, and ABC circles and is sure to be fueled into the future [12]. Talking of thermal conductivity,

[1] ABC stands for Architecture, Building and Construction …. used here as a pun to make the sub-heading attractive.

the coefficient λ of dry wood (at a moisture content below 20%), ranges between 0.14 and 0.21 W/m.K. It is noteworthy that thermal conductivity in a direction perpendicular to the fibers is lower than in a direction parallel to them (which is quite intuitive). It is dependent on the density and the moisture content of the wood. For densities in the range of 300–800 kg / m^3, and moisture content lower than 40%, when heat flows perpendicular to the fibers, the thermal conductivity coefficient can be calculated as shown in Eq. (1):

$$\lambda_0 = [237 + 0.02\rho_0(1 + 2\omega)]10^{-4} \quad (1)$$

where

- λ_o—coefficient of thermal conductivity (W / m.K)
- ρ_o—wood density (kg / m^3).
- ω—moisture content (%).

Experimental tests have shown that in the temperature range from 20–100°C, the thermal conductivity coefficient can be determined by the relation shown in Eq. (2):

$$\lambda = \lambda_0\left[1 + \left(1.1 - 10^{-4}\rho\right)(\Theta_w - 20)/100\right] \quad (2)$$

where

- λ—thermal conductivity coefficient at temperature Θ_w (W/m.K)
- λ_o—thermal conductivity coefficient determined with the aid of Eq. (1).
- ρ—density of wood determined at 20°C.

Among other things, sustainable construction is a strategy adopted these days to move steadily, surely, and slowly toward the goal of net-zero greenhouse gas emissions. Focusing merely on the use-phase and urging consumers to reduce their energy usage is necessary but not sufficient. It is here that a material like wood, adopted in the design stage itself, complements the efforts which the inhabitants of buildings would also make [13].

Like all materials in general, wood expands and contracts in response to temperature variations. This variation, which is expressed in terms of the coefficient of thermal expansion αT is not essentially the same along the three axes—longitudinal, tangential, and radial. Its value in the longitudinal direction (parallel to the fibers) lies between 3E6 and 6E6, while it is much higher in the tangential and radial directions perpendicular to the fibers—between 10E6 and 15E6. If one compares the coefficient of longitudinal thermal expansion of wood with those of steel and concrete (materials which wood can replace in structures), then wood is much lower. This implies that thermal expansion joints are not required for wooden constructions. This is also bolstered by the fact that temperature changes lead to variations in moisture content (water evaporating when it gets warmer, for instance), leading to contractions (or swelling) in directions opposite to the thermally induced deformations [2]. The specific heat (c) for wood (moisture content below 20%) is about 5.07 W/kg.K. It must be noted that the specific heat is quite sensitive to the moisture content of the wood:

$$c = 1.16(0.324 + u)/(1 + u)[w/kg \bullet K] \tag{3}$$

Part 1.2 of the EUROCOD 5 standard proposes the calculation of specific heats, for a humidity ω and a wet bulb potential temperature, $\Theta_w$with the relation [14]:

$$c = (c_\theta + \omega_{cap})/((1 + \omega) for \Theta_w \leq 1000^\circ C \tag{4}$$

$$c = c_\theta \text{ for } \Theta_w > 1000^\circ C \tag{5}$$

where.
$c_\Theta = 1110 + 4.2\ \Theta_w$ (specific heat as a function of temperature).
$c_{water} = 4200$ J / kg K (specific heat of water).

2.1 Quality of wood

The market imposes several quality requirements on products made of wood. Every sector which finds use for wood has its own range of specifications when it comes to wood species and quality [15]. Wood demanded by the construction sector, thereby, is categorized into different quality classes, and the prices are proportional to the quality [16]. In the current international calculation standards for building structural elements, quality classes are associated with predefined values of mechanical strength at different stresses, or physical characteristics:

- *Change—generating tissue*: This consists of a single layer of cells located between the bark and wood, which causes an increase in thickness [17]. A new growth ring is added annually to the trunk of the tree, and the number of rings indicates the age of the tree.

- *Intercellular canals:* These are structural elements which can be resinous-to-resinous, gumiferous, or deciduous [18]. The resin channels contain only resins, while the rubber equivalents contain gums, resins, and oils.

- *Load-bearing capacity:* The property of a construction system or its element is able to withstand loads imposed by other elements of the structure/construction. This is dependent on the geometric characteristics of the section size that determine the load-bearing capacity and deformability [19].

The behavior of wooden structures over time needs to be monitored. Wooden structures are used in building coverings, agricultural construction, and rooms where there is a likelihood of exposure to aggressive chemicals [20]. Wooden structures are also widely used by landscape architects in the construction of pavilions, gazebos, bridges in parks, gardens, and other natural ensembles. In construction, coniferous wood is most often used [21, 22]. Elements of wooden structures are connected to each other by means of glue (glued structures) or with the help of nails, dowels, and other fasteners. The most widespread are glued structures—this technology allows you to create strong and durable elements of almost any shape and size.

3. SWOT[2] for skyscrapers in modern cities

Skyscrapers, being tall, inevitably become an important part of the cityscape. The world's most iconic skyscrapers have silhouettes which people instantly recognize, like the peak of a popular mountain or the familiar face of a friend. It is unlike a sculpture or painting; in that it cannot be the work of a single artist. It is a product of teamwork, resulting from numerous collaborative exercises among architects and CEOs, steel-workers and engineers, bankers, and billionaires [23]. Architects mull over what a freestanding skyscraper would look like and how it would look alongside, behind, or in front of the surrounding buildings. All buildings together constitute the skyline of a city. Quite like the different buildings that make them up, the skylines of different cities are also different from each other, in general. Skyscrapers can be considered as reflections of the culture and values of the inhabitants of the city they belong to, and on account of their massiveness and by the tower over all other structures in their vicinity, they end up attracting attention invariably, and defining the city or becoming almost synonymous with it [24, 25]. The Makkah Royal Clock Tower in Mecca (Saudi Arabia), for instance, has a large clock which shows time—an important factor for Muslims—and is easily visible to the people of the city. Taipei 101, in Taipei (Taiwan), was designed in eight sections because "8"is a lucky number in China—the Chinese word for this number is homophonic with the word for prosperity. High-rise buildings must not only be viewed from an urban planning and architectural perspective, as the sociological perspective provides useful insights into the history of urban development. Towers, skyscrapers, and high-rises have been added to the cityscapes of the world over the last 100 years, to facilitate efficient land use and in response to the rising rate of urbanization worldwide. The earlier design approaches of high-rises were sheathed in the traditional fake clothing of postmodernity. However, the development of modern architecture was more inclined to modular repetitions and broad abstractions integrated into the international style [26]. The typical American high-rise construction developed from the 1880s onward, beginning in Chicago and New York. Chicago was, at that time, an important industrial and commercial city, next only to New York. Sustainable skyscrapers, while making economical use of available land, facilitate energy-saving and provide comfortable habitation for the urban denizens.

Veritably, they are the icons of modern cities. They inspire man to aspire for greater goals and keep aiming higher (readers may wish to read Ayn Rand's The Fountainhead to understand the "spirit of the skyscraper," so to say) [27]. The timid out-of-towner can suitably palpitate on entering the bright lobby, while Superman or Superwoman can aspire to the executive floor or even higher! [28]. Although people have mixed reviews of skyscrapers, it is undeniable that skyscrapers have played an important role in strengthening the vertical development of cities, preventing excessive horizontal expansion, multiplying the capacity of a city's population, and shortening the distances people travel. It can be reiterated here that they have dominated the cityscapes ever since they came into being, visible to one and all, from both near and far [29]. However, if the race of skyscrapers were even a thousand times a vanity fair, their construction would not cease to be the most difficult engineering problem. There are parallel directions of development in the world. It starts with the development of large territories, including industrial zones, dilapidated

[2] Strengths, weaknesses, opportunities, and threats.

housing stock, and places that are now turned off from the city's work. In such cases, the urban planning task becomes primary—creating the right balance of the territory, an effective street-and-road network, transport accessibility, social infrastructure, and parks. Here, of course, there is really no desire for high-density development. The main goal is to include the place in the city's "work" and activate it by creating jobs and infrastructure [30].

3.1 New code in an UN-sustainable building standard

The rapid urbanization of the planet and the imminent challenges of climate change compel us to reconsider the purpose and form of development of cities. Last year, the participants of the Third International Conference on Housing and Sustainable Development, organized by the UN-Habitat Center, adopted a new urbanization plan. Sustainable urban development means that we must make them comfortable not only for ourselves but also for future generations—including protecting them from the adverse impacts of climate change [31]. Yet, at the same time, cities themselves "contribute" to global warming by being the fount of greenhouse gas emissions.

In order to control the contribution of cities to global warming, energy efficiency is the watchword. New building construction should occur by new norms and standards that ensure energy efficiency, while ensuring comfort for residents, with a salubrious indoor climate [32]. City administrations must prioritize investments in public transportation, while residents themselves must take initiatives to drive less and walk or use their bicycles more. Greening the city is of paramount importance, with the setting-up of parks, planting trees adjacent to sidewalks, and preserving any sylvan surroundings which may exist near the cities as these are carbon-sinks—veritably, the lungs of the city. Development must be harmonious, without anything "good" being overly compromised to augment another. The focus must be on the resident, not on accommodating more and more people in the city come what may, and not certainly on increasing the profit margins of the builders.

3.2 Examples of sustainable wooden skyscrapers

Wooden structures remind one, at first thought of small, idyllic cottages in the "middle of nowhere" (in the "woods," so to say), but wood will soon become the material of choice, as mentioned earlier for more and more structures in urban settings too. As referred to earlier in the chapter, wooden buildings in cities have been around in Scandinavia for quite some time, with Norway boasting of perhaps the tallest wooden building on date [33]. The penchant for including more and more wood in the housing stock of cities has now spread to other countries in Europe, Asia, and the USA. Of course, when one talks of skyscrapers built with wood, it must be remembered that it is always along with other materials like concrete. This ensures that some necessary properties like fire resistance and vibration damping are not unduly compromised. Concrete though is not environmentally friendly and is associated with high greenhouse gas emissions, with carbon dioxide being emitted not just owing to combustion of fossil fuels upstream but also released from the calcium carbonate which is the principal raw material for cement [34]. Researchers have been seeking solutions to tide over this issue, and there should be some on the horizon soon.

A solid wooden beam is covered with a thick, solid, white layer on top. Dry wood is not damaged by exposure to corrosive gases and chemicals, and in that regard, scores over metals and concrete. One however has to reckon with hygroscopicity, structure heterogeneity, and inflammability. The last-named property has been responsible for the destruction of several wooden structures constructed in the past.

3.2.1 Skellefteå cultural center: Sweden: 2019

The Swedish city of Skelleftea inaugurated a 20-story "skyscraper" built entirely of wood and other sustainable materials in September this year, the publication said. Construction has an important role to play: to provide environmentally sustainable alternatives. Skelleftea is a community of 30,000 people, just 200 kilometers south of the Arctic Circle. As the forestry sector is very well developed in this part of the world, the authorities resorted to wood. It is, in a way, as far as Scandinavia is concerned, as mentioned earlier, a kind of a déjà vu, a return to the past [35].

The 75-meter-high building is a cultural center that houses 6 theaters, several art exhibitions, a library, and a hotel with over 200 rooms (**Figure 2**). Above all, however, the role of the building is to abate pollution in the area. "The original idea was not a simple 20-story house in Skelleftea, but a strategy that meant that Skelleftea not only survived, but also developed." The building is built with the help of over 12,000 cubic meters of timber, extracted from the immediate vicinity of the town, thus reducing transportation costs and, implicitly, pollution [36]. The cultural center is based on laminated wood pillars, thus completely avoiding the use of cement. The cement industry is responsible for about 7 percent of global carbon emissions, according to the International Energy Agency (as also mentioned earlier, carbon dioxide is emitted from calcium carbonate, in addition to from the fossil fuels which may be used as heat energy sources). The building is equipped with solar panels, storage batteries, and solar-powered heating systems. Even the building's fire sprinkler system, which usually runs on fossil fuel elsewhere, is powered by renewable

Figure 2.
The design of the Skellefteå cultural center.

energy. The remaining energy, stored in the batteries, is then supplied to other usage points in the city, making the skyscraper a so-called prosumer.

3.2.2 Trätoppen "tree top" Stockholm: Sweden: Proposed

This is a 40-story, 133-meter-tall, 35-meter wide, and 18-meter-deep wooden skyscraper with 850-square-meter apartments per floor, which could well become the tallest building in the Swedish capital city. The facades' original "digital" decor is inspired by the numbers in the old car park, showing which floor the driver is on Treetop, which translates as "top of the tree." This 40-story building will stand out surely as one of the many icons in Stockholm and will surely attract tourists who come to the city (**Figure 3**). It will be 25% lighter in mass than a similar skyscraper built with reinforced concrete and will necessitate a smaller and "shallower" foundation [37]. There, however, are challenges related to lack of durability which have to be overcome [38]. In recent years, significant advances have been made in wood-based composite materials, such as cross-laminated wood (CLT panel), consisting of cross-located sawn softwood and hardwood with fibers glued at a certain angle. And just as carbon fiber composites are used to make race cars, planes, and golf clubs stronger, CLT adds durability to wood structures.

3.2.3 Mjøsa tower: Norway: 2019

The 18-story Mjøsa Tower or Mjøstårnet (the tower of Lake Mjøsa) in Brumunddal, Norway, which is 85.4 meters tall. The base cross section of the building is a 37.5 x 17 meters rectangle and approximately 11,300 m^2. Adjacent to it is a 4700 m^2 swimming pool, also with a wooden structure (**Figure 4**). The supporting structure is made entirely of glulam beams and pillars, while the balconies, stairwell, and elevator are made of X-Lam structural wood panels. To maximize the project's environmental sustainability, the wood used was obtained from local forests and two new

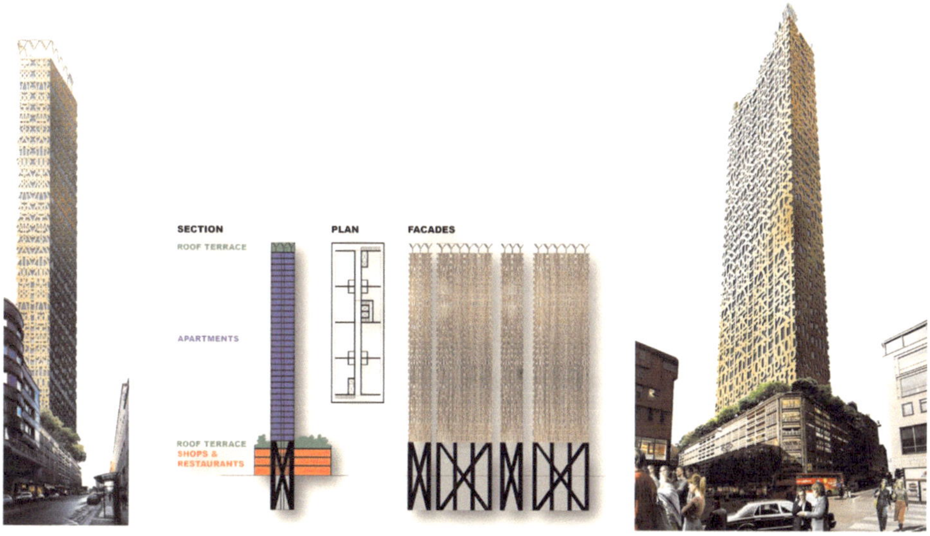

Figure 3.
The "Trätoppen" tower in Stockholm—Sweden (proposed project).

Figure 4.
The "Mjøsa" tower in Norway.

trees were planted for each one cut down, reflecting the high Scandinavian standards of management in the forestry sector. Fire safety is taken care of, in this skyscraper [39]. Untreated solid wood creates its own fire-resistant surface as the outer layer chars in a fire, making the wood immune to further fire-induced damage. Fire safety regulations state that a building must withstand a full fire for at least 2 hours without collapsing. The floors of the first 11 floors are made of wood, while the floors of the last 7 floors of the tower are reinforced with concrete. Now, higher one is in a building, be the building made of concrete or wood, it sways. In the case of the Mjøsa Tower, the weight of the concrete on the upper floors dampens the tendency to sway, restricting it in the topmost floor to about 14 centimeters.

The facility includes home offices, a hotel, and apartments. The construction project is a testament to how more massive and less environmentally friendly concrete can be replaced with wood. This high-rise Mjøsa Tower was built from glued laminated timber, cross-laminated timber, and Kerto LVL [40]. To achieve the required load-bearing capacity, cross-glued Kerto-Q laminated veneer lumber panels are also used as the material for the floors. The plates are characterized by their robustness and resilience. The construction time thereby has decreased by 35–40% vis-à-vis working with cast-in-place concrete, thanks to the lightness of wood [41].

3.2.4 Multi-story wooden building "Treet" (Bergen, Norway): 2015

The building was recently built in the Norwegian city of Bergen—a 14-story, 52.8 meter-tall, 62-apartment high-rise residential building called *Treet* (which translates as "Tree"). The previous tallest wooden building was the 32-meter-tall Forte building in Melbourne, Australia. The load-bearing structures of the building are mainly made of glued laminated timber, a building material made by longitudinally gluing wooden boards (lamellas) with waterproof glue. Concrete was only used for the three main floors, which served as platforms for four tiers of stacked modular sections [42].

Treet, located near the Paddleford Bridge, is constructed as a wooden building with glulam beams as the outer and inner skeletons and has 14 floors above the plinth in

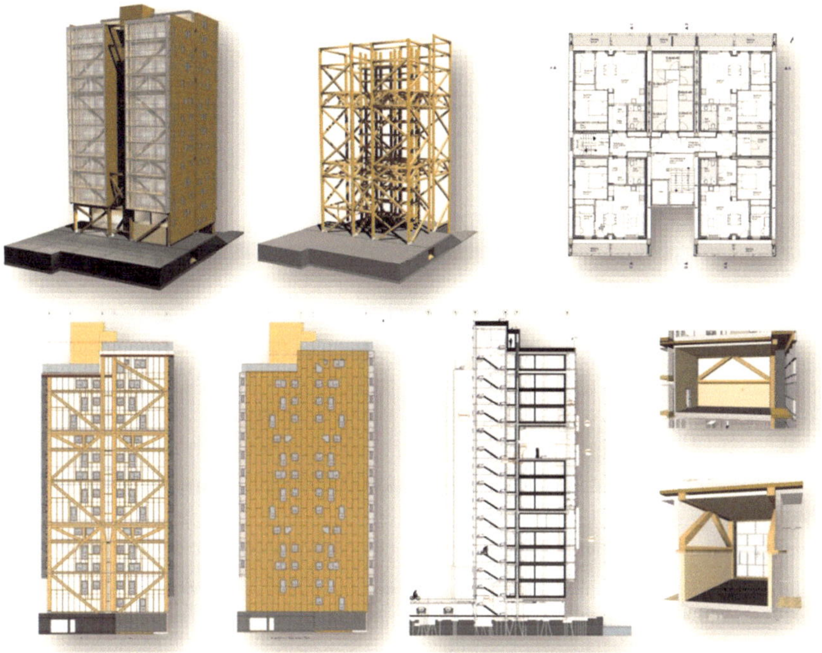

Figure 5.
The conceptual and execution phases of a "Treet" building.

concrete which includes parking spaces and the main technical installations. The 5th and the 10th floors of the building are more securely attached to the glulam beam skeletal structure, to dampen swaying when it is windy (**Figure 5**). The other floors consist of prefabricated modules. The main difficulty was to find a place for all the engineering systems. About 180 mm of space was allocated under the ceiling, in which it was necessary to fit the sprinklers and ventilation and lighting systems [42]. Therefore, when prefabricating the modules, the margin for error was very small. A special glued beam capable of withstanding fire for 90 minutes was used, without compromising the structural integrity in any way. Refractory paint was used for finishing work. In addition, the building was designed in accordance with stringent standards governing energy consumption in passive houses, which necessitated extra attention to be given to heat recovery in HVAC systems and associated piping. Separate sprinkler placement drawings were required, as they had to be installed in the balconies.

3.2.5 HoHo tower: Vienna: 2018

The new 84-meter high 24-story HoHo tower in Vienna, Austria, which will be the tallest wooden building in the world, has been underway for over a year. Approximately 76% of the structure will be wooden [43].

Vienna is a city with numerous baroque buildings and architecture from the era of Grinders.

The HoHo skyscraper will house apartments and offices, spa and wellness centers, restaurants, and one hotel (**Figure 6**). Constructing such a tall structure in wood requires meticulous planning, a team of creative designers, architects and engineers,

Figure 6.
The HoHo tower in Vienna.

and appropriate building infrastructure This tower in Vienna is an exemplar of eco-friendliness and economy [43].

In HoHo, massive cross-laminated wood elements and prefabricated concrete panels are combined. A deliberately "simple" system uses the laying of four prefabricated serial building elements: supports, ceilings, and facade elements. The novel wood-concrete composite ceiling elements reduce the proportion of steel fasteners in the construction. Prefabrication of wooden structures takes place under controlled conditions. The supports, in turn, form a single mounting element with similar prefabricated solid wood exterior wall modules. This modular design approach [44] decreases the working time on the construction site. It facilitates the avoidance of problems associated with adverse weather conditions and long drying periods. However, one needs to bear in mind that the visible wooden surfaces need to be handled carefully, as they would form the inner envelope for the houses and are meant to contribute to a feeling of coziness and not detract therefrom. The way space is engineered within the building is flexible and can be changed any time, without incurring high costs and extra effort. This contributes directly to the durability of the building.

3.2.6 W350 project: Japan: proposed

This project is a proposed wooden skyscraper in downtown Tokyo (Japan), which was announced in 2018. The Timber Interface consists of wood with a small cross section; thus, it can be used for renewing installations with a short lifespan, daily cleaning of windows, and general maintenance of buildings (**Figure** 7). About 70% of Japan's land is forested, and 40% of the forested area, i.e., approximately 30% of the land, is artificially forested. The well-managed practice of tree planting, logging, building production, and replanting has favored the national environment of Japan's lands, climate, cities, and forests, maintaining forestry and the surrounding area [45].

The "W350 Plan" is an R&D concept that aims to further advance this technology and realize an "environmental wooded city with the goal of reducing the total greenhouse gas emissions of "embodied carbon" during the construction phase of the life cycle, to curb climate change [46]. Many companies work to develop refractory materials and genome selection breeding to realize a highly durable and comfortable building space using wood. The skyscraper will be 90% wood, the rest being steel which will serve the purpose of providing the skyscraper with wind and seismic

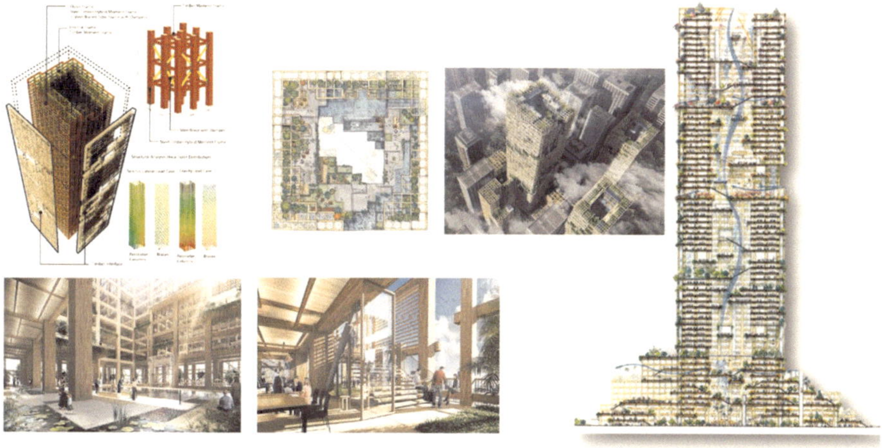

Figure 7.
The futurist tower "W350 project" in Japan.

resistance. Wood too, for that matter, is known to be resistant to seismic shocks. The project requires 185,000 cubic meters of timber and plans to revitalize forestry and timber demand in Japan [47]. In addition to esthetics, the choice of wood is intended to "turn the city into a forest." Wooden structures are also easier—when compared to concrete structures—to repair or replace if they collapse. It is estimated that the costs for fashioning wooden structures and incorporating them in buildings will continue to decrease due to technological advancement.

Eight years ago, a law was passed in Japan that requires construction companies to use wood in public institutions smaller than three stories [48]. There are other such constructions globally, although not as tall as the one proposed for construction in Japan. There is an 18-story wooden office building in Minneapolis and a 16-meter-tall student apartment building in Vancouver. Sumitomo Forestry, which develops businesses that utilize wood such as housing and building materials, has said that it looks forward to utilizing a lot of wood in the building and construction sector over time, in Japan.

3.2.7 The Chicago River beech tower—A vision of new building

It is a collaborative research effort aimed at identifying challenges and opportunities for the design of increasingly high-mass timber structures. The Chicago River Beech Tower is an 80-story, 300-duplex-unit residential building, which just about stays within the upper range established for residential towers in the city [49] (**Figure 8**). While the River Beech Tower structure is well balanced, an increase in material volume was expected as the design progressed.

The River Beech Tower aims to provide the understanding necessary to design and build large buildings using next-gen engineered wood structures.

4. Results and conclusions

Climate change has been a key driver in the resurgence of wooden structures in building and construction in urban settings. Wood is a solid material made up of

Figure 8.
The Chicago River beech tower.

organic substances (cellulose, lignin, etc.) with carbon, hydrogen, and oxygen as the main constituent elements. From a microstructural point of view, it is made up of supporting and guiding tissues. The structure of the wood can be comprehensively studied by observing its cross section, the radial longitudinal section, and the tangential longitudinal section.

Wood has rarely been used in the construction of high-rises, but that is about to change, as the examples described in the chapter illustrate. Though it is inflammable and many old wooden buildings have been gutted down by fire, wood is essentially a carbon-sink (which stores up the carbon in it during its use phase as a building material for a long time), is hard and light, is easily workable, has very good acoustic and thermal properties, reduces the size and the cost of the foundations of a building, and provides occupants with a more comfortable and healthier indoor environment.

The wooden skyscrapers described, and those which may likely spring up in the years to come, in other cities of the world include many architectural functions such as offices, hotels, shops and residential units, garden roofs, terraces covered with greenery, water features, and huge interior spaces filled with natural light. The revolutionary construction is made of a durable material called glulam, which is made up of wooden planks that are glued together to form beams.

The use of wood essentially comes as a response to the need to rethink our approach to buildings in cities and pursuing the paradigm of zero-emission and energy-neutral buildings, toward the achievement of Sustainable Development Goal # 11—sustainable cities and communities. Indeed, they are not panaceas to all the challenges which humankind dwelling in cities faces on date, but surely, one step forward in the mitigation of and adaptation to the adverse effects of climate change.

Even if ultrahigh buildings are erected today for a different purpose—to display wealth, power, grandeur, and ambition, it would be wise to do that in a sustainable manner—and earn bonus points in the process!.

DOI: http://dx.doi.org/10.5772/intechopen.105809

Author details

Amjad Almusaed[1]* and Asaad Almssad[2]

1 Department of Construction Engineering and Lighting Science, Jonkoping University, Sweden

2 Faculty of Health, Science and Technology, Karlstad University, Sweden

*Address all correspondence to: amjad.al-musaed@ju.se

IntechOpen

© 2022 The Author(s). Licensee IntechOpen. This chapter is distributed under the terms of the Creative Commons Attribution License (http://creativecommons.org/licenses/by/3.0), which permits unrestricted use, distribution, and reproduction in any medium, provided the original work is properly cited.

References

[1] Jonsson R. Trends and possible future developments in global Forest-product markets—Implications for the Swedish Forest sector. Forests. 2011;**2**(1):147-167. DOI: 10.3390/f2010147

[2] Almusaed A, Yitmen I, Almsaad A, Akiner İ, Akiner ME. Coherent investigation on a smart kinetic wooden Façade based on material passport concepts and environmental profile inquiry. Materials (Basel). 2021;**14**(14): 3771. DOI: 10.3390/ma14143771

[3] Demin J. Effect of thermal insulation components on physical and mechanical properties of plant fibre composite thermal insulation mortar. Journal of Materials Research and Technology. 2020;**9**(6):12996-13013. DOI: 10.1016/j.jmrt.2020.09.009

[4] Viholainen N et al. Citizen views on wood as a construction material: results from seven European countries. Canadian Journal of Forest Research;**51** (5):647-659. DOI: 10.1139/cjfr-2020-0274

[5] Novitskaya L, Nikolaeva N, Galibina N, Tarelkina T, Semenova L. The greatest density of parenchyma inclusions in Karelian birch wood occurs at confluences of phloem flows. Silva Fennica. 2016;**50**(3):1461. DOI: 10.14214/sf.1461

[6] Almusaed A, Almssad A, Homod RZ, Yitmen I. Environmental profile on building material passports for hot climates. Sustainability. 2020;**12**(9): 3720

[7] Nowak T, Patalas F, Karolak A. Estimating mechanical properties of Wood in existing structures—Selected aspects. Materials. 2021;**14**(8):1941. DOI: 10.3390/ma14081941

[8] Erkan M, Kaya G. The effect of relative humidity and moisture to the durability of spruce and laminated timber. ITU A|Z. 2017;**14**(1):103-110. DOI: 10.5505/itujfa.2017.18480

[9] Estévez-Cimadevila J, Suárez-Riestra F, Otero-Chans D, Martín-Gutiérrez E. Experimental analysis of pretensioned CLT-glulam T-section beams. Advances in Materials Science and Engineering. 2018;**2018**:12. DOI: 10.1155/2018/1528792

[10] Homod RZ, Almusaed A, Almssad A, Jaafar MK, Goodarzi M, Sahari KS. Effect of different building envelope materials on thermal comfort and air-conditioning energy savings: A case study in Basra city, Iraq. Journal of Energy Storage. 2021;**34**:101975

[11] Ninikas K et al. Thermal behavior of a light timber-Frame Wall vs. a theoretical simulation with various insulation materials. Journal of Composites Science. 2022;**6**(1):22. DOI: 10.3390/jcs6010022

[12] Szymczak G et al. Influence of variable moisture conditions on the value of the thermal conductivity of selected insulation materials used in passive buildings. Energies. 2022;**15**(7): 2626. DOI: 10.3390/en15072626

[13] Gaujena B, Agapovs V, Borodinecs A, Strelets K. Analysis of thermal parameters of hemp fiber insulation. Energies. 2020;**13**(23):6385. DOI: 10.3390/en13236385

[14] Hopkin DJ, El-Rimawi J, Silberschmidt V, Lennon T. An effective thermal property framework for softwood in parametric design fires: Comparison of the Eurocode 5

parametric charring approach and advanced calculation models. Construction and Building Materials. 2011;**25**(5):2584-2595. DOI: 10.1016/j.conbuildmat.2010.12.002

[15] Michael H et al. The wood from the trees: The use of timber in construction. Renewable and Sustainable Energy Reviews. 2017;**68**:333-359. DOI: 10.1016/j.rser.2016.09.107

[16] Newton PF. Wood quality attribute models and their utility when integrated into density management decision-support systems for boreal conifers. Forest Ecology and Management. 2019; **438**:267-284. DOI: 10.1016/j.foreco.2019.01.053

[17] Ghislain B, Alméras T, Prunier J, et al. Contributions of bark and tension wood and role of the G-layer lignification in the gravitropic movements of 21 tropical tree species. Annals of Forest Science. 2019;**76**:107. DOI: 10.1007/s13595-019-0899-7

[18] Dünisch O, Baas P. On the origin of intercellular canals in the secondary xylem of selected Meliaceae species. IAWA Journal. 2006;**27**(3):281-297. DOI: 10.1163/22941932-90000155

[19] Hakro MR et al. Numerical analysis of piled-raft foundations on multi-layer soil considering settlement and swelling. Buildings. 2022;**12**(3):356. DOI: 10.3390/buildings12030356

[20] Moses J, Oludolapo A. Sustainable energy transition for renewable and low carbon grid electricity generation and supply. Frontiers in Energy Research. 2022. DOI: 10.3389/fenrg.2021.743114. Available from: https://www.frontiersin.org/articles/10.3389/fenrg.2021.743114/full

[21] Stauskis G. Re-pedestrianising open spaces through optimising mobility in urban landscape: Great importance of the small detail. Landscape Architecture and Art. 2018;**13**:56-63. DOI: 10.22616/J.LANDARCHART.2018.13.06

[22] Almusaed A. Introductory chapter: A general reading process on landscape architecture. In: Landscape Architecture—The Sense of Places, Models and Applications. London, United Kingdom: IntechOpen; 2018. DOI: 10.5772/intechopen.77971

[23] Jonathan Shaw. Skyscraper as Symbol; The Semiotics of Skyscrapers, Harvard Magazine. 2010. Available from: https://www.harvardmagazine.com/2010/05/skyscraper-as-symbol. [Accessed: April 18, 2022]

[24] Almusaed A, Almssad A. City Phenomenon between Urban Structure and Composition. In: Sustainability in Urban Planning and Design. London, United Kingdom: IntechOpen; 2019. DOI: 10.5772/intechopen.90443

[25] Kheir A-KMM, Ali AMM. Skyscrapers and placemaking: Supporting local culture and identity. International Journal of Architectural Research, Archnet-IJAR. 2012;**6**(2): 43-64. DOI: 10.26687/archnet-ijar.v6i2.83

[26] Zahiri N, Dezhdar O, Foroutan M. Rethinking of critical regionalism in high-rise buildings. Buildings. 2017;**7**(1): 4. DOI: 10.3390/buildings7010004

[27] Rand A. The Fountainhead, First Published by Bobbs Merrill in the USA. 1943. p. 753

[28] Graham S. Contemporary Skyscrapers Turning Nowhere into Somewhere, 91/2 | 2017 Gouverner la Ville Verticale : Entre Ville d'exception et Ville Ordinaire2017. DOI: 10.4000/geocarrefour.10129

[29] Ar VV. A study of challenges in designing and construction of skyscrapers. International Journal of Engineering Research & Technology (IJERT). 2019;**08**(12). DOI: 10.17577/ijertv8is120201

[30] Turok I, McGranahan G. Urbanization and economic growth: The arguments and evidence for Africa and Asia. Environment and Urbanization. 2013;**25**(2):465-482. DOI: 10.1177/0956247813490908

[31] Tang H-T, Lee Y-M. The making of sustainable urban development: A synthesis framework. Sustainability. 2016;**8**(5):492. DOI: 10.3390/su8050492

[32] Economidoua M et al. Review of 50 years of EU energy efficiency policies for buildings. Energy and Buildings. 2020; **225**(2020):110322. DOI: 10.1016/j.enbuild.2020.110322

[33] Steen-Olsen K, Wood R, Hertwich EG. The carbon footprint of Norwegian household consumption 1999–2012. Journal of Industrial Ecology. 2016;**20**(3):582-592. DOI: 10.1111/jiec.12405

[34] Mohammed S et al. 2012, trends and developments in green cement and concrete technology. International Journal of Sustainable Built Environment. 2012;**1**(2):194-216. DOI: 10.1016/j.ijsbe.2013.05.001

[35] Kai B. Rethinking Urban Connectivity; A Case of Skellefteå, kth royal Institute of Technology, School of Architecture and the Built Environment, Degree Project in Architecture; 2021

[36] Andersson A. 2020, Cultural centres from around 2020 : Knowledge, meetings and growth in Askersund, Värnamo, Skellefteå and Karlskrona, Uppsala University, Disciplinary Domain of Humanities and Social Sciences, Faculty of Arts, Department of ALM.URN: urn:nbn:se:uu:diva-416689

[37] Moynihan MC, Allwood JM. Utilization of structural steel in buildings. Proceedings Mathematical, Physical, and Engineering Sciences. 2014;**470**(2168):20140170. DOI: 10.1098/rspa.2014.0170

[38] Hart J, Pomponi F. More timber in construction: Unanswered questions and future challenges. Sustainability. 2020; **12**(8):3473. DOI: 10.3390/su12083473

[39] Born RO'. Life cycle assessment of large scale timber bridges: A case study from the world's longest timber bridge design in Norway. Transportation Research Part D: Transport and Environment. 2018;**59**:301-312

[40] Causevic A, Rustempasic N. Cross-laminated timber (CLT) application in multi-story buildings. Technics Technologies Education Management Journal. 2020;**15**(2):96-101

[41] Jarl EL, Gösta K. 2003, long-term changes of the crustacean zooplankton community in Lake Mjøsa. Journal of Limnology. 2003;**62**(2):143-150

[42] Abrahamsen RB, Malo KA. Structural design and assembly of "treet"—A 14-story timber residential building in Norway. New Zealand Timber Design Journal. 2014;**22**(3):3-10

[43] Zhao X, Zhang B, Kilpatrick T, Sanderson I. Numerical analysis on global serviceability Behaviours of tall CLT buildings to the Eurocodes and UK National Annexes. Buildings. 2021;**11**(3): 124. DOI: 10.3390/buildings11030124

[44] Leskovar Ž, Vesna, and Miroslav Premrov. A Review of Architectural and Structural Design Typologies of

Multi-Storey Timber Buildings in Europe. Forests. 2021;**12**(6):757. DOI: 10.3390/f12060757

[45] Harada H, Fukushima T, Hatori T, Aoyagi H. W350—The roadmap of super high-rise timber building. International Journal of High-Rise Buildings. 2020; **9**(3):255-260. DOI: 10.21022/IJHRB.2020.9.3.255

[46] Abdulwahid MY, Galobardes I, Radoine H. Understanding the use of timber in semi-arid regions: Kurdistan region of Iraq, A case study. Sustainability. 2021;**13**(21):11845. DOI: 10.3390/su132111845

[47] Iqbal A. Developments in tall wood and hybrid buildings and environmental impacts. Sustainability. 2021;**13**(21): 11881. DOI: 10.3390/su132111881

[48] Almusaed A, Almssad A. Introductory chapter: Overview of sustainable cities, theory and practices. In: Sustainable Cities—Authenticity, Ambition and Dream. London, United Kingdom: IntechOpen; 2018. DOI: 10.5772/intechopen.82632

[49] Sanner J, Fernandez A, Foster R. River beech tower: A tall timber experiment. CTBUH Journal. 2017: 40-46. ISSN 1946-1186

Section 2

Wood Processing and Products

Chapter 4

The Past, Present and Future Outlook of the Wood Industry in Nigeria

Abel O. Olorunnisola

Abstract

Nigeria's vegetational diversity ranging from mangrove swamp along the southern coast through freshwater swamp, lowland rainforest and savanna, progressively into the interior of the country makes possible the growth of over 560 indigenous species of tropical hardwoods, many of which grow to merchantable dimensions. Hence, wood processing for domestic consumption and exportation played a vital role in the Nigerian economy from the late 1700s up till early 1970s, with the 1960s often referred to as the golden age of Nigerian forestry. However, due to forest resources mismanagement, infrastructural deficiencies, economic recession and other factors, the industry fell on hard times beginning from the mid-1970s. While primary wood processing establishments including timber logging, sawmilling and charcoal making managed to survive, virtually all the secondary wood processing factories, excluding those involved in furniture production, became defunct by the year 2000. Although a set of newer medium-sized plywood and match production factories have emerged in recent years, massive importation of secondary wood products has become inevitable in the face of rapid population growth, urbanization, deforestation and desertification. This chapter discusses the past, the present and the future of the wood industry in Nigeria.

Keywords: timber, wood preservation, charcoal, panel products, paper products

1. Introduction

Wood usually forms the stem of a tree though it is not all plants that possess woody stems. It is also not all woody stems that produce timber suitable for use as industrial material. According to current estimates, the earth contains about one trillion tonnes of wood, which grows at a rate of 10 billion tonnes per year [1]. Woody plants that produce merchantable timber are divided into two broad groups, i.e. softwoods and hardwoods. Softwoods (also known as conifers or gymnosperms) are cone-bearing trees which tend to have needle-like or scale-like evergreen leaves. Hardwood trees (deciduous trees or angiosperms), on the other hand, usually have broad leaves that are shed annually.

The vegetation of Nigeria can be broadly classified into two types, i.e. forests and savanna. The forests can be further subdivided into mangrove, freshwater swamps and tropical rainforest, while the savanna can be subdivided into Sahel, Sudan, Northern Guinea, Southern Guinea, and derived savannas. The diversity in vegetation makes possible the growth of different species of tropical hardwood species, many of which grow to merchantable dimensions, i.e. up to 12 m height and 0.6 m girth. The lowland rainforest which occupies the southern one-quarter of the country has carried the burden of supply of timbers for domestic consumption and export for ages, while the savannas supply fuelwood and a variety of minor forest products used for food, medicines and industrial raw materials. Species such as *Milicia excelsa*, *Khaya ivorensis* and *Triplochiton scleroxylon* were very common in cocoa farms all over Western Nigeria, *Khaya senegalensis* trees were very common in the savanna areas, while *Terminalia superba*, *Antiaris africana* and other lesser-used species were commonly found in the secondary forests in times past [2, 3].

Timber exploitation predates the amalgamation of the Southern and Northern Protectorates in 1900 and the creation of Nigeria as a single entity and British colony in 1914. For example, a forestry department was established for the protectorate of Southern Nigeria in 1899, while a forestry proclamation was passed in 1901 to control concessions and regulate timber exploitation; two forest ordinances were also promulgated in 1908 and 1916, respectively, that contained further regulations for the control of timber exploitation. Plantation forestry commenced in the country in the early 1930s and forest reserves established in different agro-ecological zones across the country were licensed for timber exploitation [3, 4]. The notable indigenous plantation species include *Terminalia species*, *Triplochiton scleroxylon*, *Lovoa trichilioides*, *Nauclea diderrichii* and *Cedrela odorata*, while the four major exotic plantation species are *Tectona grandis*, *Eucalyptus spp.*, *Gmelina arborea* and *Pinus spp.* [5].

Wood products have, from time immemorial, played a significant role in satisfying the basic human needs for energy, shelter, transportation, durable and non-durable goods of all blends. In the early parts of the eighteenth century, timber for the construction of ships became essential for nations that controlled the seas for trade and/or territorial expansion. Prior to the invention of modern plywood, the ancient Mesopotamians had produced plywood as far back as around 3400 B.C. Paper, the first prepared composite wood fibre, was invented by Egyptians more than 3000 years ago, while fuelwood from the forests of continental Europe provided source of energy that powered the Industrial Revolution during the early stages of its development [6].

Primary and secondary wood products have also always played a vital role in the Nigerian economy. In the 1960s up until the mid-70s, wood-based forest industries earned substantial foreign exchange and ranked the highest among local industries in terms of employment generation [3, 4, 7]. The major products included are as follows:

- Posts used principally for fencing, scaffolding, rafting and as columns and wall plates for farm houses, sheds, livestock buildings, storage structures, beams for drying platforms, and generally for fencing.

- Poles used principally to support telephone, electrical transmission lines, pit props, piles, studs, columns, beams, wall plates, rafters, and purlins, and for scaffolding in building construction.

- Logs used for lumber manufacture.

- Firewood and charcoal used for cooking, heating and power production.
- Lumber used for building construction, furniture making, etc.
- Plywood, particleboard and fibreboard utilised in diverse forms in building construction, furniture making, packaging, etc.
- Paper and paper products including newsprint, stationery paper for writing, drawing, printing, photocopying, etc., and cardboards or paperboards for packaging.
- Various wooden items such as tool handles, sport goods, weaving equipment, and wooden toys.

Engineered wood products such as Laminated Veneer Lumber (LVL), Parallel Strand Lumber (PSL), Laminated Strand Lumber (LSL) and Cross-Laminated Timber (CLT) are not yet available in the country [1].

The building industry alone consumes about 80% of Nigeria's total annual timber production. Also, the sawmilling and furniture production constitute over 70% of the wood industry in terms of wood consumption, employment generation and business volume. This is not unexpected since Nigeria currently has the largest population in Africa (estimated at around 200 million, approximately 16.8% of whom are youths aged between 15 and 35 years), as well as a relatively high population growth rate (2.53%) and urbanisation growth rate of 2.8–3% per annum. By 2050, the population would have doubled to over 400 million people. These statistics do not only explain the reasons behind large consumption but also have significant implications for future demand for wood products. However, Nigeria has witnessed a progressive deterioration in wood supply for over five decades. The two decades spanning 1950–1970 that witnessed massive exploitation of timber resources laid the foundation for the subsequent deficits in timber supply in the country [4]. Once noted as a major exporter, by 1970, Nigeria could no longer sustain wood exports and by 1972, one of the country's richer forest areas had been degraded down to an average of three merchantable trees per acre [8]. This led to the prohibition of exportation of round logs and sawnwood in 1979. To worsen the situation, Nigeria lost 6,145,000 hectares (approximately 35.7%) of its forest cover between 1990 and 2005 due to over-exploitation and other factors [9]. Many of the large-scale secondary wood processing establishments closed down within this period resulting in Nigeria becoming a major importer of plywood, particleboard, fibreboard, matches, paper and paper products. It was only in the last few years that a new set of wood processing establishments have started to emerge, some of which rely on bamboo as the substitute raw material.

This chapter provides an insight into the past (1782–1999), present (2000 to date) and future outlook of the wood industry in Nigeria.

2. The past (1782–1999)

Nigerian forests of old contained over 560 indigenous species and have supported commercial timber logging for many decades. However, only about four of the merchantable species (*Khaya spp.*, *Manilkara lacera*, *Ochrocarpus spp.* and wild rubber) were heavily exploited in commercial quantities beginning from around 1890. Between 1925 and 1940, successful outcomes of laboratory tests conducted on samples of Nigerian timbers in the United Kingdom and other parts of Europe led to an increase in the number of accepted species in overseas markets from approximately 4 in 1910 to 40 in 1940 and about 100 in 1960 [4, 8, 10]. The other species were grossly under-exploited until the country began to experience timber famine beginning from the late 1970s. Some of the uncommercialised species posed formidable exploitation challenges – offensive sap odour, high buttresses and deep fluted or thorny boles, unmanageable dimensions too difficult and/or too dangerous to fell with the available logging equipment or too small to handle with the available log conversion machines, etc. [8].

The 1960s, often described as the golden age of Nigerian forestry, was also the beginning of its doom. The period was characterised by mismanagement and misuse of forest resources, with only the choicest portions of the most valuable timber species extracted for export markets. It was reported that only about 10% of the volume of trees felled was extracted, the remaining 90% being left to rot in the forest [4].

Sawmilling industry came into existence in 1782 with the establishment of a pit-sawing station in the then Lagos colony. Pit-sawing is a two-man operation involving the use of long handsaw. The log being sawn is supported on a long trestle about 2.5 m off the ground. One man stands inside the pit, while the other man stands on the log. Sawing is done with successive up and down movement of the handsaw. By 1887, pit-sawing (**Figure 1**) had become a small but thriving industry consisting of scattered groups of pit-sawyers supplying scantlings and boards to meet local requirements for lumber and railway sleepers. The first mechanised sawmill was established by the colonial government in 1907, the same year extensive private participation in sawmilling commenced, leading to rapid numerical growth of the industry [10].

The wide latitude in production capacities ranging from $3m^3$ of lumber per day achievable in mobile and semi-mobile installations to over $50m^3$ achievable by big mills made sawmilling an attractive investment for small- and big-time investors.

Figure 1.
Pit-sawing operation.

Period	Average capital investment requirement (Naira)	Average capital investment requirement (US $)	Percentage increase over 1969–1974 cost (%)
1969–1974	25,000.00	250.00	—
1975–1979	70,000.00	700.00	180
1980–1984	125,000.00	1250.00	4900
1985–1989	Not available	Not Available	—
1990–1994	1.5 million	15,000.00	5900
1995–1999	2 million	20,000.00	7900

*Source: *These estimates, based on prevailing exchange rates for each period, exclude costs of logging equipment since these are generally absent in the mills [11, 22, 23].*

Table 1.
Trends in capital investment requirements in small-scale sawmills in Nigeria: 1969 to 1999.*

(**Table 1** shows trend in capital investment requirements in small-scale sawmills between 1969 and 1999). The small-scale mills operated a single shift of 10 hours per day, 6 days a week and 35 weeks per annum. Mobile horizontal bandmills (**Figure 2**) were generally used for primary conversion of logs. The log-handling capacities of these machines ranged from 1.2 to 1.9 m in terms of log girth, while the sawing speed ranged between 180 and 240 revolutions per minute. Circular saws were commonly used for resawing operations such as crosscutting, edging and trimming of lumber. The rate of return on investment in a mobile horizontal bandmill operated one shift daily ranged from about 31% if the mill sawed on contract to 70% if the mill had forest concessions and undertook its own logging operations [11–14].

There were about 16 sawmills in Nigeria by 1939. This number had more than doubled by 1952, risen to 80 in 1964 and over 1,300 by 1999, majority being small-scale mills. The very first large-scale sawmill in the country, the United African Company (UAC) sawmill, was established in Sapele (now located in Delta State) in 1925. As shown in **Table 2**, the tremendous numerical growth experienced in the 1970s and 1980s when there was an upsurge in the demand for lumber created by the post-Nigerian Civil War reconstruction activities and the oil boom, however, declined in the 1990s due to economic recession [5, 11, 15].

The principal agencies that cause deterioration or destruction of timber are weather, fire, fungi, insects and marine borers. Adequate protection from the influence of these agents may indefinitely prolong the life of timber. Wood preservation can therefore be broadly defined as the protection of wood from fire, chemical agents (e.g. strong acids and alkalis), mechanical wear weathering and biological attack by agents such as fungi and insects. Most preservative treatments are, however, performed to protect timber products against attacks from fungi, insects (mainly beetles and termites) and fire. Wooden poles for power transmission, railway sleepers, lumber, plywood, furniture parts, wood carvings, particleboards, joinery materials, etc., are usually treated with preservatives against biodegradation. Many Nigerian timber species traded in commercial quantities were naturally durable, while others were perishable. By 1964, demand for treated wooden poles exceeded 10,000 units. As of 1977, there were about 20 well-established wood treatment plants handling electric/telegraphic poles and lumber. The number of the treatment plants had decreased to 16 by 1988 by which time the total production output was about 55,000 m^3 per annum [2, 5, 16].

Figure 2.
A Horizontal Bandmill. Source: [14].

Year	Estimated number of sawmills
1939	16
1949	21
1959	35
1969	80
1979	1000
1989	1500
1999	1700

Sources: Mackay (1946), Okigbo (1964), Anonymous (1993), Akande (1993), Ogunwusi (2012).

Table 2.
Numerical growth in the sawmilling establishments in Nigeria: 1939–1999.

Timber preservation processes were targeted at the moderately permeable perishable timbers. The choice of preservative and treatment processes depended largely on the ability of the timbers to absorb preservatives. Some were practically impermeable even under pressure treatment. Others were resistant to penetration and only limited protection could be given by treatment, impregnation being either superficial or patchy. At the other end of the scale were timbers that absorbed preservatives readily which were adequately treated by steeping in cold preservatives. Permeability classification as specified in the Nigerian code of Practice for Timber Design published in 1973 involved grouping timbers into five classes according to the degree of penetration obtainable by hot and cold open tank treatment and by cold steeping. These were as follows:

Class I – Extremely resistant.

These were timbers that were extremely resistant to penetration for which impregnation by prolonged open tank treatment was insignificant and treatment using this method was therefore impracticable, e.g. *Afrormosia elata*, *Albizia spp.*, and *Lophira alata*.

Class II – Very resistant.

These were timbers that were very resistant to penetration – lateral penetration being about 3 mm to 15 mm, and end penetration about 1.5 to 13 mm. Such timbers, e.g. *Gossweilerodendron balsamiferum*, *Khaya grandifoliola* and *Khaya senegalensis*, could be given moderate protection by short-term open tank treatment.

Class III – Resistant.

These were timbers that allowed reasonably good penetration by the open tank process. Lateral penetration was over 1.5 mm and could be considerably more, but absorption was not very heavy. End penetration of such timbers, e.g. *Anogeissus leiocarpus*, *Cordia millennii* and *Distemonanthus benthamianus*, was usually deep.

Class IV – Moderately resistant.

These were timbers that allowed good penetration, heavy absorption and deep penetration with the open tank process. Most of these timbers, e.g. *Holoptelea grandis*, *Triplochiton scleroxylon*, etc., were given moderately good protection by prolonged cold steeping.

Class V – Permeable.

These were timbers that absorbed very large quantities of preservatives and could generally be given almost complete impregnation either by open tank treatment or cold steeping. No elaborate impregnation plant was required for treating them. Examples include *Alstonia boonei* and *Antiaris Africana*,

In general, the wood preservation sector was not fully developed, and preservation against fire in particular was virtually completely neglected.

Drying, also commonly referred to as seasoning, is an essential process in lumber manufacture. Seasoning improves strength. It may prevent warping and splitting, thus ensuring product stability in service. It also prevents rot and decay and facilitates preservative penetration and acceptance of paints and polishes when required. Air-drying is the oldest method of wood seasoning. Modern lumber seasoning methods involve forced-air-drying in either electrically or solar-powered kilns. Regrettably, the wood seasoning sector of the wood industry was also not fully developed. In 1983, there were only about five timber drying kilns in the country [8]. Much of the timber was piled out-of-door to be air-dried without any protection beyond the use of some primitive form of roof in some instances. Timber products air-dried in this manner included railway sleepers, poles and planks. It was possible to dry timber down to about 12% in the dry season in the South and still further in the North, but 18% was a more usual figure in the rainy season in the South.

The origin of furniture making is rooted in carpentry and joinery which were carried out in the timber-producing areas of the country from time immemorial. Wood products (i.e. lumber, particleboard and plywood) and rattan were the two major raw materials employed. By the late1990s, about 200 large-scale wooden furniture establishments were in operation in the country. There were, also, numerous (unquantified) small-scale furniture makers operating from modestly equipped workshops largely operated by craftsmen [17–19].

Traditional charcoal making also has a long history in the savanna areas of Nigeria where the locally available wood species were dense, slow-growing and highly lignified, thus giving a good charcoal yield when carbonised. The relatively short wet season and correspondingly long dry season experienced in savanna areas facilitate fuelwood drying with minimum loss through insect attack and fungi decay. It also prolongs the charcoal production period, making it an almost all-year-round operation. To meet domestic energy requirements, fuelwood plantations were established near several towns and villages, including Ibadan, Ejigbo, Ede, Ogbomoso, Jos, Kano and Ilorin in the 1950s [20]. Virtually, all the charcoal supply in the country was made by small business enterprises with low capital investment. The two methods widely used for charcoal production and which involved the use of earth as a barrier in the charring process were the open pit and the earth mound methods. The use of earth to keep out oxygen and to insulate the carbonising wood against excessive heat loss goes back to the dawn of history. Both methods are still commonly employed for charcoal production across sub-Saharan Africa. The open pit method involves digging out a pit, putting in firewood and covering the hole with excavated earth to seal and insulate the chamber. This method is often used where the soil is well drained, deep and loamy. Bolts of wood cut into length of 1–2.4 m are prepared and closely stacked in rectangular pits with a capacity of about 4 to 5 m^3 of fuelwood charge per burn (a typical small pit may measure 3 m long by 1.2 m wide and 1.2 m deep). After stacking, the bolts are covered with leaves and grasses, usually about 20 cm thick. Sand is spread evenly over the leaves to the same thickness. Carbonisation may last for 20 to 30 days resulting in marked reduction of the wood charge to between 50 and 70% of its initial volume [20]. The earth mound method involves covering a pile of wood on the ground with earth, sand and leaves. The cover usually consists of a lower layer usually made with leaves, straw or grass, and an upper layer of sandy soil or loam, applied approximately 20 to 25 cm thick. This cover forms the necessary gas-tight layer behind which charcoaling can take place. This method is commonly used where the soil is rocky, hard or shallow, or the water table is close to the surface.

Secondary wood processing commenced in Nigeria with the transformation of the UAC sawmill, Sapele, into the first integrated facility engaged in sawmilling, veneer and plywood production in 1948. The company was later renamed African Timber and Plywood, Sapele. It was reputed to be the first plywood mill in West Africa [11]. About 20 years later, the first paper mill, Nigerian Paper Mill in Jebba, Niger State, was established in 1967, while commercial particleboard production started in 1977. By the mid-1980s, there were six plywood and veneers mills in operation with an estimated log input capacity of 270,000 m^3 per annum, two particleboard mills with combined log input capacity of 55,000 m^3 per annum, seven match factories with estimated log input capacity of 75,000 m^3 per annum, and three paper mills. The Nigerian Paper Mill, Jebba, had two paper-making machines, each with a capacity of about 33,000 tonnes/annum and a complete 32,000 tonnes/annum pulping plant. The pulping plant was utilising mixed tropical hardwood, bamboo, Gmelina, and Pinewoods. The second mill, the Nigerian Newsprint Manufacturing Company, Oku-Iboku, Itu, Cross River State, was established in 1975 and started operation in 1986 with two paper machines each having a rated at capacity of 50,000 tonnes per annum but has remained shut since 1994. The third mill, the Nigerian National Paper Manufacturing Company Limited, Iwopin, Ogun State (formerly Iwopin Pulp and Paper Company), with a rated production capacity of 100,000 tonnes per annum commenced paper production in February 1995 but was never fully operational. By end of the 1990s, there were 10 plywood mills, 4 particleboard mills, 8 match factories, 3 pulp and paper mills, and 8 wood treatment plants in the country [8, 10, 16, 21].

3. The present (2000 to date)

The current main sources of log supply for the wood industry in Nigeria are natural forests consisting of secondary forests, farmlands and derived savanna, forest reserves, forest plantations, and Taungya farms. Taungya system as practised in the humid rainforest zone in Southern Nigeria is a method of joint production of food and forest tree crops using free farmer labour input [4]. In many cases, semi-manual logging method, involving combined use of power chain saws and axes, is employed in tree felling. Two means of log transportation are generally employed. These are water transportation in the riverine (swampy) areas which will not support heavy logging equipment and road transportation with timber lorries. However, harvesting of at least 26 Nigerian-grown hardwood tree species was banned in different states across the country as far back as 1999 (**Table 3**) due to their endangered status [1]. The other major challenges facing timber loggers in the country include as follows:

- The very rapid rate of deforestation and desertification in many parts of the country leading to log supply crisis.

- Lack of appropriate logging equipment and facilities. Full-scale logging season is just about 5 months, i.e. November to early March. Only minimal logging is possible during the rainy season between April and October.

The sawmilling industry is still predominated by small-scale privately owned enterprises located in clusters within and outside the towns and cities in the wood-producing areas and constituting the largest wood processing industry in the country in terms of numerical strength, geographical spread, wood consumption and employment generation. There is a preponderance of semi-illiterates in the workforce of these mills in view of the fact that manual input into sawmilling operations is considerable. Conversion planning decisions involving the determination of appropriate opening face and optimum sawing method are left to the judgements of the sawyer, who, in turn, relies solely on intuition and past experiences. It is therefore often difficult to predict with sufficient accuracy log conversion efficiency [14]. A reversal of this trend requires the introduction of some form of mechanisation such as the use of cranes and gantries to replace human labour in log-handling operations and proper staff education.

The prevalence of sole proprietorship in sawmilling enterprises delimits owners' access to investment funds. Raising capital for modernising production facilities could be challenging. A recent positive development is that quite a vast number of log conversion machines, e.g. band saws, circular saws, frame saws, thicknessers, mortising and tenoning machines, and saw doctoring equipment, are now manufactured locally which make them relatively cheaper than imported ones and also promote local knowledge and skills development. Setting up small-scale sawmills without importation of machinery is therefore becoming increasingly popular. However, in general, the sawing technology and type of machinery employed in Nigerian sawmills are less sophisticated than what obtains in the developed countries where, by the 1970s, there had emerged large-sized sawmills with full automation and extensive computerisation of log-processing activities [11, 22, 23].

The wood preservation sector experienced a brief period of awakening in the early 2000s when numerous small-scale treated pole retail outlets sprang up in many parts of the country. This was due to the move by different State Governments to electrify the rural areas and the simultaneous move by the Federal Government to extend telephone lines to all Local Governments Headquarters. Wood seasoning has remained largely based on traditional air-drying. Wooden furniture production has also remained dominated by small-scale enterprises with much fewer number of medium- and large-scale factories. These furniture workshops generally turn out a

S/No	Species	Local trade name	State(s) where harvesting has been banned
1	*Afzelia africana*	Apa	Imo
2	*Afrormosia elata*	Afrormosia	Cross River
3	*Canarium schweinfurthii*	Origbo	Plateau
4	*Diospyros mespiliformis*	Kanran	Ondo, Imo
5	*Erythrophleum ivorense*	Erun	Rivers
6	*Erythrophleum spp.*	Erun obo	Ekiti
7	*Funtumia spp.*	Ako Ire or Ire Benin	Cross River
8	*Gossweilerodendron balsamiferum*	Agba	Ekiti
9	*Guarea spp.*	Olofun	Ogun
10	*Holoptelea grandis*	Inajoko	Ekiti
11	*Irvingia spp.*	Oro	Cross River
12	*Isoberlinia doka*	Isoberlinia,	Niger
13	*Khaya grandifoliola*	Benin Mahogany	Enugu, Kaduna, Kwara
14	*Khaya ivorensis*	Lagos Mahogany	Rivers
15	*Khaya senegalensis*	Dry Zone Mahogany	Kaduna, Kebbi, Kwara, Plateau
16	*Lophira alata*	Ekki	Ondo, Imo
17	*Mansonia altissima*	Mansonia	Ekiti, Imo, Ogun, Osu
18	*Milicia excelsa*	Iroko	Abia, Osun, Akwa-Ibom, Anambra, Benue, Ebonyi, Ekiti, Enugu, Kwara, Niger, Ogun, Plateau, Rivers
19	*Mitragyna stipulosa*	Abura	Ekiti, Ogun
20	*Nauclea diderrichii*	Opepe	Ekiti, Enugu
21	*Nauclea latifolia*	Opepe	Niger
22	*Nesogordonia papaverifera*	Otutu	Ekiti
23	*Pterocarpus erinaceus*	Apepe	Kano
24	*Pterocarpus osun*	Osun	Kaduna
25	*Triplochiton scleroxylon*	Obeche (Arere)	Abia
26	*Uapaca spp.*	Akin	Ebonyi, Imo

Source: [1].

Table 3.
Tree species banned from harvest in different states in Nigeria since 1999.

wide range of products, including assorted household, school and office furniture, produced in different styles and qualities. The current challenges facing the furniture production include are as follows:

- inadequate supply of mature logs is attributable to the dwindling availability of woods of choice species in the forests and the rising cost of logging.
- rapidly escalating cost of wood raw material.
- dearth of wood seasoning kilns resulting in the scarcity of well-seasoned lumber particularly during the rainy season.
- low level of literacy among the workers coupled with lack of appropriate educational facilities for employee training/retraining which is hindering modernisation and productivity.
- frequent electricity outages and voltage fluctuation which often halt production, damage equipment and affect product quality [7, 17, 19, 22].

Apprenticeship remains the major form of pre-employment training available for a vast majority of new entrants into sawmilling, furniture and other sectors of the wood industry, with no clearly specified training duration [1, 15, 17, 18, 23]. While there is nothing patently wrong with apprenticeship as a form of training, the unstructured format is deficient in terms of performance monitoring and evaluation of apprentices. Two of the consequential effects of this situation are the unsustainable use of wood raw materials and poor product quality.

Charcoal production still thrives in the savanna regions of the country. The notable charcoal depots are located in Oyo, Iseyin, Saki, Igbo-Ora and Ogbomoso in the south-western region; Jebba, Omu Aran, Egbe and Kabba in the Central region; and Minna, Jos and Kaduna in the north-western region. **Table 4** shows a list of the species of wood commonly used for charcoal production. However, the primitive pit and the earth mound techniques are still used for charcoal production in the country. Both methods could produce reasonably good charcoal acceptable in the local market if properly carried out. These methods have survived largely because of their simplicity and cheapness.

The locally produced charcoal usually reaches its ultimate domestic user by a simple route involving wholesalers and retailers. The fewness of the links in the supply chain ensures economy of distribution. Retail points include markets sand makeshift stands along major roads. Retailing is done using the volume approach, i.e. selling in bags, baskets and other simple containers. This method renders invalid the addition of water and other adulterants and discourages mixing in fines to increase weight. It also reduces the chances of mishandling the charcoal in such a way that more fines are produced, which would reduce the bulk volume. However, the charcoal cannot compete effectively in international markets due to gross variation in quality [20, 24]. Forest certification and chain-of-custody certification which are now used to track wood from the forest through harvesting and manufacturing to the point of sale have led to quantitative restrictions on imports of such unsustainably produced charcoal. Some charcoal producers' associations have, however, established tree plantations for sustainable charcoal production in recent years. Efforts are also being made to create awareness and promote adoption modern kilns for charcoal production with wood, bamboo and agricultural residues. Specifically, brick and metal kilns which are more effective and give good quality and yields of charcoal are being promoted.

The seven match factories in existence in 1988 had reduced to six in 1996 and three by 2002. The number of particleboard factories remained constant at 4 from 1992

S/No.	Wood species
1	*Afzelia africana*
2	*Anogeissus leiocarpus*
3	*Burkea Africana*
4	*Cassia siamea*
5	*Casuarina equisetifolia*
6	*A. africana*
7	*Anogeissus leiocarpus*
8	*Burkea Africana*
9	*C. siamea*
10	*C. equisetifolia*
11	*Gliricidia sepium*
12	*Gmelina arborea*
13	*Isoberlinia doka*
14	*Khaya senegalensis*
15	*Parkia biglobosa*
16	*Pericopsis laxiflora*
17	*Prosopis africana*
18	*Pterocarpus erinaceus*
19	*Tectona grandis*
20	*Terminalia catappa*
21	*Leucaena leucocephala*
22	*Spondias mombin*
23	*Vitellaria paradoxa*

Sources: Dada (1990), Adeniji et al. (2015).

Table 4.
Wood species used for charcoal production in Nigeria.

to 2010 [16, 21]. Virtually all the large-scale paper, match production, plywood and particleboard mills in Nigeria went out of operation before 2015 due to the unabated economic recession of the previous two decades, electricity insecurity, and other factors. With the closure of the paper mills, the bulk of paper manufacturers in the country are engaged in mere paper conversion. Nigeria has been constrained to import large quantities of paper and paper products, plywood and particleboard. According to the United Nations COMTRADE database on international trade, Nigeria imports of paper and paperboard, articles of pulp, paper and board was US$696.51 million in 2020. A positive development is the springing up of new secondary wood processing factories in recent years. For example, a pencil and toothpick factory, located at Ekom Iman in Etinan Local Government Area, Akwa Ibom State, was commissioned in the second quarter of 2017. The factory produces toothpicks from bamboo. Running 8 hours a day, three major production machines combine to give a daily output of 30,000–60,000 pencils. Also, a medium-scale plywood factory (**Figure 3**) located

Figure 3.
A medium-scale plywood mill in Akwa Ibom state, Nigeria.

in Awa, Onna Local Government Area, Akwa Ibom State, was commissioned on September 21, 2019. A number of other factories are producing toilet rolls and allied products on large scale from bamboo in the country. It is not surprising that there is no significant development in the particleboard production sector, since particleboards are not so well accepted in the Nigerian market [16].

4. The future outlook

In terms of dominant financial structure, small- and medium-scale enterprises are likely to dominate the primary and secondary wood processing sectors of the wood industry in Nigeria in the foreseeable future. One reason for this projection is the fact that for many wood processing enterprises, smallness has an advantage, access to raw materials and markets are largely unobstructed and minimal technical skills for production are required. The size and structure allow them the flexibility to endure adverse economic conditions. Also, these enterprises are usually more labour-intensive than larger firms, they have lower capital costs associated with job creation and they improve the efficiency of domestic markets by making productive and flexible use of scarce and/or underutilised resources. For example, small plants with production capacities of around 10 to 12 m^3 of plywood per 8-hour shift, i.e. 13.5–16.2 m^3 of green veneer, can be established to meet local demands [25]. However, there are challenges that must be tackled.

Research and Development efforts are required to produce effective and affordable log and lumber handling devices that can reduce the drudgery in timber logging and sawmilling [26]. The very high level of illiteracy among the workforce in the industry also has to be addressed. Establishing training centres and/or certification programmes for intending and current workers in the various sectors of the industry will go a long way in addressing the training needs. It is also important for the government to formulate policies and develop strategies that address the crosscutting issues of vocational education, i.e. quality and relevance of training, employability, collaboration between training institutions and employers, accreditation of training providers (in the formal, non-formal and informal sectors), assessment, certification, internal and external quality assurance of training programmes, funding, and instructor training.

In terms of markets, the future of the wood industry in Nigeria looks bright. This is because construction activities, in particular, gross fixed capital formation in dwellings, which has the most direct influence on the level of consumption of lumber and other wood products, is booming in the country, and the trend is most likely to continue into the foreseeable future in view of the demographic projections and the upsurge in the activities of private developers working with financial institutions to build large serviced estates in different parts of the country. This is notwithstanding the fact that the level of construction activities depends on other factors such as government policies on housing, the state of the existing housing stock, construction and land costs, disposable income, and interest rates.

In terms of raw material supply, the future of the wood industry in Nigeria will depend on how forest resources are managed, henceforth. In order to expand the raw material base for the different sectors of the industry in Nigeria, there is a need for the establishment of large-scale timber, bamboo and ratan plantations, utilisation of more of the lesser-used but proven timber species as well as partial substitution of wood with bamboo and rattans in building construction, furniture and charcoal production. Bamboos and rattans mature faster than wood; they are easier to harvest, transport and process; they are lightweight, durable and flexible; they accept paints and stains like wood; they possess structural properties sufficient for the demands of diverse handicraft and furniture products; and they can be worked into many styles. Besides, bamboo plantations in particular can be used for reforestation and restoration of degraded lands, thus utilising marginal lands that would otherwise be unproductive. Bamboo takes about 3 years to get established. Once established, the new shoots will continue to get bigger and more numerous from year to year as the colony grows towards maturity. Furthermore, the overall yield and profitability of bamboo plantations can be increased by means of intercropping with timber (e.g. *Tectona grandis*). A number of studies have been conducted on enhancing the utility of bamboo as a structural material in the country leading to generation and documentation of baseline information on the density, strength and other material properties of *Bambusa vulgaris* required for engineering design and the development of processes and equipment for bamboo furniture production [27–30].

5. Conclusion

The wood industry in Nigeria has witnessed growth and decline in successions since its beginning over three centuries ago. It all started with timber logging from time immemorial followed by pit-sawing in 1782, sawmilling by 1907 and plywood manufacturing in 1948. A missing link was the full development of the wood preservative and seasoning sectors. The primary wood processing sectors did not witness any significant development in terms of mechanisation and/or automation of production process over the period reviewed. The timber logging and sawmilling sectors in particular witnessed major deficits in log supply. Excluding the furniture sector, all the other secondary wood processing sectors experienced a rise from a humble beginning to a decline in the early 2000s, with the collapse of virtually all the plywood, particleboard, match, pulp and paper production factories in the country. Fortunately, new plywood and match production factories are emerging. In conclusion, the future of the industry in Nigeria in terms of growth in consumer demand for wood products, is quite bright. However, raw material availability in sufficient quantities required to meet the demands; and the possibility of upscaling production and productivity are uncertain unless the highlighted sustainable intervention strategies are adopted.

Conflict of interest

The author declares no conflict of interest.

Author details

Abel O. Olorunnisola
Dominion University, Ibadan, Nigeria

*Address all correspondence to: abelolorunnisola@yahoo.com

IntechOpen

© 2022 The Author(s). Licensee IntechOpen. This chapter is distributed under the terms of the Creative Commons Attribution License (http://creativecommons.org/licenses/by/3.0), which permits unrestricted use, distribution, and reproduction in any medium, provided the original work is properly cited.

References

[1] Olorunnisola AO. Harnessing the forester's Harvest for Sustainable Development. Ibadan, Nigeria: University of Ibadan Publishing House; 2013. p. 102

[2] Adekunle AO. A conversion system for the management of coppiced teak plantations. In: Proceedings of the First Nigerian Forestry Conference; 3-7 February 1964. Kaduna, Nigeria: Forestry Association of Nigeria; 1964. pp. 9-11

[3] Jaiyesimi AK. The role of savanna woodland in the economic development of western Nigeria. In: Proceedings of the First Nigerian Forestry Conference; 3-7 February 1964. Kaduna, Nigeria: Forestry Association of Nigeria; 1964. pp. 88-92

[4] Enabor EE. Deforestation and Desertification in Nigeria: The Challenge of National Survival. Ibadan, Nigeria: University of Ibadan Publishing House; 1992. p. 24

[5] Akande JA. Potential for growth and development of the Nigerian sawmilling industry. Nigerian Journal of Forestry. 1993;**2**:85-90

[6] Bodig J, Jayne BA. Mechanics of Wood and Wood Composites. Malabar, Florida, USA: Krieger Publishing Company; 1993. p. 736

[7] Lucas EB, Olorunnisola AO. Wood processing and utilization in Nigeria: The present situation and future prospects. In: Ajav EA, Raji AO, Ewemoje TA, editors. Agricultural Engineering in Nigeria: 30 Years of University of Ibadan Experience. Nigeria: University of Ibadan; 2002. pp. 98-109

[8] Lucas EB. Factors preventing wider commercialization of Nigerian trees. Forest Products Journal. 1983;**33**(5):64-68

[9] Anonymous. Climate Change and Biological Diversity. Convention on Biological Diversity [Internet]. 2009. Available from: http://www.cbd.int/climate

[10] Mackay JH. On the Utilization of Forest Products in Nigeria [Thesis]. Edinburgh, United Kingdom: University of Edinburgh; 1946

[11] Olorunnisola AO. The Structure, Practices and Modelling of the Sawmilling Industry in Ebute-Metta, Lagos State[Thesis]. Nigeria: University of Ibadan; 1997

[12] FAO. High Forest Development in Nigeria: Nigeria's Development Alternatives for Forest Resources. UNDP/FAO Doc. For.NIR/71/1546, Technical Report 2. Rome: FAO; 1979. p. 25

[13] Swiderski J, Heilborn G. Mechanical wood-processing industries in developing countries- problems, causes and search for solutions. UNDP/FAO doc. In: On First Consultation on the Wood and Wood Products Industry, 19-23 September, 1983. Rome: FAO; 1983

[14] Olorunnisola AO. Monte Carlo simulation of hardwood log conversion operations in small-scale sawmills in Nigeria. In: Proceedings of the 40th Annual Conference of Forestry Association of Nigeria. Lagos, Nigeria: Forestry Association of Nigeria; 2018. pp. 880-890

[15] Olorunnisola AO, Oyelami DO. An appraisal of the sawdoctoring personnel and facilities in selected sawmills in

Ibadan. Oyo State. Nigerian Journal of Forestry. 1997;**27**(1):28-31

[16] Dada SA. Wood and wood products as alternative source of revenue for economic development of Nigeria. In: Proceedings of Workshop on Export Potentials of Value-Added Wood and Wood Products; 5-6 May 1999. Lagos, Nigeria: African Network for Wood Research and Development; 1996. pp. 1-20

[17] Olorunnisola AO. Workshop structure in the small-scale furniture industry in Ibadan metropolis. Journal of Tropical Forest Resources. 2000;**16**(1):46-57

[18] Olorunnisola AO. An investigation on the small-scale wooden furniture production practices in Osogbo, Osun state. Journal of Forestry Research and Management. 2005;**2**:42-51

[19] Olorunnisola AO, Adewole NA. Small-scale wooden and rattan furniture production in Nigeria. In: Olorunnisola AO, editor. Renewable Natural Resources Engineering: Essays in Honour of Canon Prof. Ibadan, Nigeria: E. Babajide Lucas. Zenith BookHouse; 2016. pp. 123-138

[20] Awoyemi TT, Amao AO, Fatogun O. Household expenditure pattern on energy consumption in Ibadan, Oyo state Nigeria. Journal of Economics and Rural Development. 2006;**15**(1):79-87

[21] Ogunwusi AA. The forest products industry in Nigeria. African Research Review. 2012;**6**(4):191-204

[22] Olorunnisola AO, Omoniyi TE. Wood conversion and processing in Nigeria: A status report. In: Olorunnisola AO, editor. Renewable Natural Resources Engineering: Essays in Honour of Canon Prof. Ibadan, Nigeria: E. Babajide Lucas. Zenith BookHouse; 2016. pp. 101-121

[23] Olorunnisola AO, Lucas EB. Sustainability of forest industries in Nigeria: A case study of Ebute-Metta sawmills, Lagos state. In: Proceedings of the 30th Annual Conference of Forestry Association of Nigeria. Kaduna, Nigeria: Forestry Association of Nigeria; 2005. pp. 304-312

[24] Adeniji OA, Zaccheaus OS, Ojo BS, Adedeji AS. Charcoal production and producers' tree species preference in Borgu local government area of Niger state, Nigeria. Journal of Energy Technologies and Policy. 2015;**5**(11):1-8

[25] Albin RH. Economic Criteria in Planning and Projecting Secondary Wood Processing Industries. Vienna, Austria: United Nations Industrial Development Organization Industrial Development Working Document, UNIDO ID/ WG338/6; 1981

[26] Olorunnisola AO. Research and capacity building for the transformation of the forest industry in Nigeria. In: Proceedings of 6th Federal University of Technology, Akure (FUTA)-AGRIC Conference, November 7-9, 2012. Akure, Nigeria: Federal University of Technology; 2012. pp. 1-7

[27] Ogunsanwo OY, Terziev N. Mechanical properties of glue-laminated boards of bamboo, *Bambusa vulgaris* from Nigeria. In: Proceedings of 6th International Symposium on Wood Structure and Properties. Zvolen, Slovakia: Arbora; 2010. pp. 183-186

[28] Aina KS, Areghan SE, Adeniyi IM, Alao OJ, Osuntuyi EO. Variability studies on strength and fibre properties

of *Bambusa vulgaris* Schrad. For panel products. Pro Ligno International Journal of Wood Engineering. 2012;**8**(1):3-14

[29] Ogunsanwo OY, Terziev N, Panov D, Daniel G. Bamboo (*Bambusa vulgaris* Schrad.) from moist forest and derived savanna locations in south West Nigeria – properties and gluability. BioResources. 2015;**10**(2):2823-2835

[30] Olorunnisola AO, Omotayo R. Development of a composite bookshelf with bamboo (*Bambusa vulgaris*) strips, lumber and plywood. 2020. Pro Ligno, International Journal of Wood Engineering. 2020;**16**(1):11-16

Chapter 5

A Review of Traceability Systems in the Timber Industry

Maryam Shirmohammadi

Abstract

The Australian timber industry generated $23.1b in revenue in 2019–2020, contributing $7.2b to Australia's gross domestic product. Total Australian timber export in 2019–2020 was estimated at over $3b, with log exports of approximately $650 m. Major export destinations are China, Japan, and New Zealand, with China importing over $1.6b of Australian timber products. An effective two-way tracing system will help secure product export to these major trading partners by eliminating product rejections due to a lack of certification, treatment, and pest management traceability, and enhancing the certification of product performance and compliance of imported structural and non-structural products. An opportunity exists to promote the development of proposed tracing systems to major import trading partners as a means of proving product integrity and maintaining market share as Australia continues to eliminate practices that facilitate illegal logging processes. This review aims to highlight the need for a national product tracing system in place for the Australian timber industry. This review aims to present information about current and potential future technologies that the timber industry can use across the supply chain to trace and monitor product quality and origin.

Keywords: timber products, traceability systems, illegal logging, non-certified timber

1. Introduction

The Australian timber industry generated $23.1b in revenue in 2019–2020, contributing $7.2b to Australia's gross domestic product [1]. Total Australian timber export in 2019–2020 was estimated at over $3b, with log exports of approximately $650 m. Major export destinations are China, Japan, and New Zealand, with China importing over $1.6b of Australian timber products. An effective two-way tracing system will help secure product export to these major trading partners by eliminating product rejections due to a lack of certification, treatment, and pest management traceability, and enhancing the certification of product performance and compliance of imported structural and non-structural products. This review aims to present information about current and potential future technologies that the timber industry can use across the supply chain to trace and monitor product quality and origin.

The development of an effective tracing system will enhance the reputation of Australia's timber products as legal, traceable, clean, and sustainable commodities.

Additionally, Australia currently imports timber products worth approximately $4.4b annually. Reportedly, $400 m of this total import value is considered to be illegally logged timber, resulting in an estimated $23 m per year in social and environmental costs (including negative impact on Australian businesses) to the Australian economy [2]. An opportunity exists to promote the development of proposed tracing systems to major import trading partners as a means of proving product integrity and maintaining market share as Australia continues to eliminate practices that facilitate illegal logging processes. This will lead to a value-added process that will be beneficial to both Australian timber exports and imports and position Australian timber products as a reputable and legally manufactured commodity through all supply chain stages.

2. Importance to industry

This section of the report aims to represent the industry skeleton by reviewing the main stakeholders and their role in the supply chain from the resource type point of view. Once the major industry stakeholders were identified, the benefits arising from an advanced traceability system and a standardized chain of custody were analyzed. The areas of importance to the industry comprise; Consumers, Illegal Logging, Accountability, Certification and Legislations/Regulations, Economics, Information Accessibility, and Independent Verification.

Table 1 shows that privately-owned plantations constitute 75.5% (1,459,900 hectares) of Australia's forest plantation estate. Publicly owned plantations comprise 20.8%, with the remaining 3.7% jointly owned. Jointly owned plantations are partnerships between private companies and state forest agencies.

Table 2 shows a steady increase in plantation ownership by institutional investors and private owners and a steady decrease in ownership by the government, MIS (managed investment scheme), and timber industry companies over the last decade. However, when looking at the two most recent figures, the ownership percentages have remained essentially unchanged.

State/Territory	Unit	Private	Public	Joint	Total
New South Wales	'000 ha	123.6	261.8	7.9	393.2
Victoria	'000 ha	415.9	2.5	0.1	418.5
Queensland	'000 ha	230.4	0.1	0.0	230.5
South Australia	'000 ha	150.6	16.2	0.0	166.8
Western Australia	'000 ha	233.5	79.5	46.9	359.9
Tasmania	'000 ha	258.4	35.1	16.2	309.7
Northern Territory	'000 ha	47.4	0.00	0.0	47.4
Australian Capital Territory	'000 ha	0.00	7.4	0.0	7.4
Total	'000 ha	1459.9	402.6	71.0	1933.4
Proportion of ownership	%	75.5	20.8	3.7	100

Table 1.
Plantation area, by state/territory and ownership, 2018–2019 [3].

Plantation owner.	2008–2009	2013–2014	2017–2018	2018–2019
Unit	(%)	(%)	(%)	(%)
Institutional investors	13	40	49	49
Governments	34	19	21	21
Farm foresters and other private owners	10	8	21	21
Managed investment scheme	36	20	5	5
Timber industry companies	7	13	4	4

Table 2.
Plantation ownership, selected years [3].

The tables provide an insight into the current ownership of timber plantations within Australia in terms of size and proportion and identify which industry groups would benefit most from the incorporation of a traceability system.

2.1 Forest ownership

2.1.1 Forest managers

Operating an efficient and profitable forest as well as maintaining a sustainable and legal forest is the major focus of forest managers and forest owners. However, illegal logging can threaten any sustainable forest management system and affect the environment, wildlife, and ecosystem [4, 5]. One of the major benefits of having an effective tracing system in place is the possibility of providing timely and accurate feedback to various sections of the industry, including the forest managers allowing them to adjust harvest, planting, and other goals and activities in the long and short term. The tracing system will enable access to data about the variation in quantities, grading, dimensions, the scale of products for specific market supply, and species removed from each specific site within the forest. This data can be then used as a practical map for any internal or external R&D and predictive efficiency models by providing an accurate comparison between anticipated and actual results during growth and at the harvest. This research and model creation can be then used to adjust the harvesting plans based on market demand, location, density, and quality, providing pathways to increase the revenue from the forest.

2.1.2 Government agencies

State Governments own approximately 21% of the total forest plantation area within Australia, making them a major stakeholder in the industry (**Table 2**). Throughout most states and territories, the plantation land is predominantly owned by private companies and investors. However, in New South Wales and the Australian Capital Territory, 60–100% of the forest plantations are publicly owned. Although private plantations exceed those owned by the government can be considered the top sole organization in terms of plantation area within Australia. Given this majority ownership by governments, they have a responsibility to the public and taxpayers to ensure that plantations under their control and ownership are being utilized to their maximum potential with regard to growth and revenue. As well, the government agencies also have to enforce laws and regulations within each publicly owned forest estate. A two-way tracing system that gathers information about timber products produced in Australia and imported timber products can address any issues with regard to illegal logging at various stages along the supply chain. This means ensuring any log brought into this country is sourced from sustainable forests and any log exported is taxed/regulated appropriately. Some countries such as PNG and Russia apply taxes and tariffs to the export of timber grown on private plantations on a per ton basis in an attempt to promote local manufacturing [6]. Empowering local manufacturing by ensuring resource availability, and eliminating non-compliant and low-quality products from the market is another advantage for an efficient tracing system in the longer term. It should also be noted that in some developing countries, a poor or complete lack of any chain-of-custody or traceability system and failure in compliance and capturing of tax has led to potential export revenue going into the pockets of illegal loggers or corrupt officials as opposed to the government reserves [7]. An example of this is seen in Section 7.1.1 in which PNG was struggling with this exact issue and employed the services of SGS Ltd. to implement a forestry and export management system. Russia also applies tariffs and export duties to unprocessed softwood logs in an attempt to reduce the amount of product exported and improve the prospects of the local timber industry [8].

2.1.3 Timber product developers

The timber industry worldwide continues to advance and innovate through research and product development undertaken by the companies themselves and by external R&D facilities. Product developers and researchers rely heavily on consistent and correct information about the products available in the marketplace [9]. This information is also a key part of any potential design of new products or building systems as the specifications need to account for all possible variations in quality, size, and physical properties to decide if a particular timber product is suitable for a specific application. A traceability system that records and details comprehensive and significant amounts of data will allow these research, design, and manufacturing facilities to produce new products and processes based on real-time and accurate data about the origin of a product, variations, and types of resources available from both domestic and international markets. The timber industry will benefit significantly by increasing both efficiency and output of new products.

2.1.4 Timber suppliers, Mills, and companies

An inefficient product inventory and transport system can have major impacts on the companies selling the timber resource and all other sections of the supply chain. Australian timber companies and timber mills must adhere to Australian and International standards for the quality and sustainability of their products. A linked traceability system protects them from any penalties and provides a great market opportunity for their product as opposed to imported products with potential issues regarding quality compliance and origin. Timber companies could be liable for recovering costs/fines if they sell any illegally logged/sourced products from imported or domestic supplies. Having a tracing system in place (funded through increased transport, production, and inventory costs, or litigation) will enable the timber suppliers to protect their rights [9].

2.1.5 Timber importers and exporters

Timber importers must follow the laws of their country that have been put in place to benefit both the environment and other industries along the supply chain. In Australia, this means they must be certain that the timber they import has been sourced legally based on the criteria provided in the Illegal Logging Prohibition Regulation 2012. The full extent of this regulation is outlined in Section 7 Standards and Legislations [10]. All timber exported from Australia is subject to the Export Control Act 2020 and Export Control (Wood and Woodchips) Rules 2021. Failure to comply with any of these rules and regulations could result in significant financial and licensing penalties and legal consequences. Importers and exporters have several options to ensure they are acting legally. These include: conducting their own internal audits, purchasing only from certified forests, and purchasing only from companies with a certified chain of custody. However, certified forests at present only comprise a small portion of the international forestry market. Another option is to purchase timber from organizations that have been certified either by the appropriate government body within their jurisdiction or as is becoming more popular a third-party auditing organization such as Program for the Endorsement of Forest Certification (PEFC), Engineered Wood Product of Australasia (EWPAA), etc.

2.1.6 Consumers

Consumers of structural and non-structural timber products are vital for the continued growth of any timber industry. The average consumer has become more aware of the detrimental effect that illegal logging has on the environment. An ever-increasing number of consumers want to know the origin of products they are purchasing to ensure they have been sustainably sourced [11]. End product costs can increase dramatically if parts of the supply chain are inefficient. Currently, manufacturers have two options to prove to a customer that the product they are supplying is certified sustainable. One is to attach a certificate from a trusted verification body/organization such as PEFC, EWPAA, or operate an entire store that only distributes sustainably sourced products, reducing the need for labels or certificates.

Structural timber products are required to be compliant with specific structural standard requirements. This is another element of traceability for those products. The issue of compliance was recently highlighted in the EWPAA's submission [12] to parliament regarding non-conforming structural timber products. The alarming statistic from this report was that 28% of imported timber products were found not to meet Australian standards. This could have serious implications for end-users such as builders responsible for ensuring the materials they are using as fit for purpose. Changes in sustainability and compliance laws internationally could affect the sale of products that are not sourced from sustainable forests or do not comply with the relevant standard. An example of this is that product compliance requirements in the EU and USA could impact Australian products in the future.

2.1.7 Product failures and insurance

Insurance companies play a key role in determining who is at fault when products fail through internal investigations linked with the governing body of that industry, for example, National Construction Code (NCC), etc. An improved and transparent traceability system would provide significant benefits for end-users and property owners and product manufacturers, and importers by reducing the time and cost of insurance claims and providing indisputable evidence of the origin of materials and their suitability for a particular building application.

2.1.8 Illegal logging

Illegal logging results in social, economic, and environmental challenges in different parts of the world [13]. The cost of illegal logging, fishing, and wildlife to global natural resources is estimated at $1–2 trillion annually [14]. In Australia, up to 10% or $800 million of imported products comes from high-risk resources with evidence of high rates of illegal logging [15, 16].

In Victoria, it was reported that 1 in every 20 trees logged was harvested from areas that were not allowed access for harvesting in 2004. Illegal logging in Australia can risk vulnerable native species and ecosystems [5]. The news reported by ABC in 2018 listed areas of East Gippsland that were illegally harvested affected the population of a range of native animal species causing some deaths [5]. Images shown in **Figure 1** are satellite images showing the areas where illegal harvesting was undertaken in Victoria in 2004 [5].

2.2 Accountability

When a consignment of timber products is found to be not fit for purpose, there needs to be a means of tracing back to the original supplier or manufacturer, whether it be pre-construction or at any point in the product's service life. Unsuitable or faulty materials can seriously affect construction timelines and financial outcomes for major projects. Being able to quickly identify the origin of faulty products will assist in reducing undesirable outcomes. This will also ensure that the supplier of the product does not avoid responsibility as a genuine product supplier. Another complication with major projects is that material is sourced from multiple companies, often over long periods of time, and tracing each piece of timber back through the supply chain requires a highly efficient traceability system. Such a system could rapidly identify other products that may be related to a failed member and avoid future issues postconstruction.

Under the Building Services Act 2011, there is a 6-year structural guarantee on building elements [17]; however, when it comes to structural timber elements, depending on product condition and environmental factors, any changes in performance or failure can occur long after the product is installed in a building. Timber

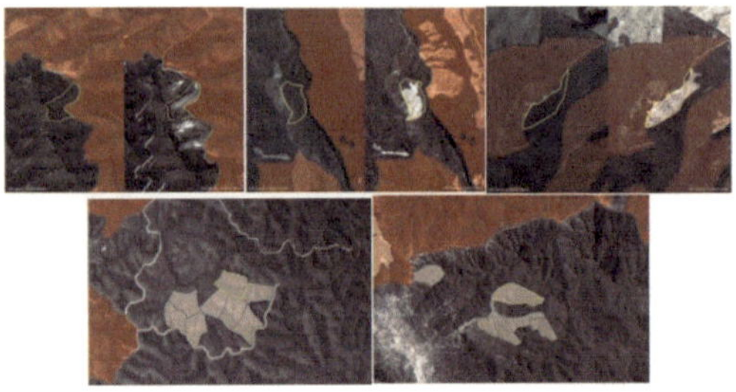

Figure 1.
Images of sections illegally logged in Victoria (red section shown is where harvesting was allowed and yellow lined sections were harvested illegally) [5].

failure can occur for various reasons, including design issues, environmental conditions, natural changes in timber dimension, lack of effective treatment and maintenance protocols, etc. [18–20]. A two-way tracing system that encompasses both domestic and imported product information could provide better clarity on the service requirements of the product in short and long time frames.

2.3 Certification, legislation, and regulation

Currently, In Australia, there are no mandatory standards or regulations in place for traceability or chain of custody specifically. However, with illegal logging still of major concern in other countries, it may become a mandatory system (at present many are voluntary). So, it is best for timber companies to design and implement a chain of custody based on current voluntary practices to future-proof their business. Also of consideration are importation laws that other countries have in place to ensure they are meeting their desired standard. Despite there being no mandatory chain of custody standards in Australia, the Illegal Logging Act 2012 places restrictions on what timber products can be imported.

Australia could be the preferred destination for importing timber products from other parts of the world due to our export certification processes being reliable, robust, and able to meet any import standard set out by a specific country. For example, China and Australia have entered much free trades and other trade agreements since 1970, and this relationship would not have continued if Australia were producing sub-standard products [21]. A tracing system that can provide detailed information about Australian products' practices, processes, and performance specifications could provide better market access and future pathways for our products compared with countries with a high rate of illegally logged and non-compliant products.

2.4 Economic

Table 3 details the economic value of Australia's timber exports. As discussed in Section 2.4, even though a high percentage of Australian forest and timber products are sustainably sourced and are compliant with Australian and International standards, a lack of an effective national tracing system could cause issues with exported [22] and imported products.

Product	Exported Value ($m)
Woodchips	1300
Aper/paperboard	963
Roundwood (logs)	644
Miscellaneous	137
Secondary Wood Products	456
Total	3500

Source: ABARES [16].

Table 3.
Value of timber products exported from Australia in 2019.

2.5 Information accessibility

When referring to an effective tracing system, it is important to highlight the significance of information accessibility by different users at every stage of the supply chain. Various tracing processes (mainly paper-based and internal documents used within companies) at different stages of the supply chain (through the chain of custody) limit the ability to retrieve information quickly and efficiently. With improved accessibility, critical pieces of information can be located and relayed to the relevant body in a timely and effective way. Organizations and companies have different permissions and security levels for their internal systems. By compiling this into a single nationwide and standardized system, all supply chain members will have better access to the information. The ability to update and add relevant product information to the system is also enhanced. This will provide information on product recalls, illegal logging, warranty/accountability issues, and certification. The transparency and standardization of the system will reinforce Australia's ability to track and guarantee the quality of its products to international importers.

2.6 Independent verification

Currently, the origin of a piece of timber can be determined through communication with the supplier of the product. However, this process can be time-consuming, information may be inaccurate and the process costly depending on the age of the product. With a more standardized traceability system, there will be independent audits of organizations to verify the information provided by each level of the supply chain linked to the previous levels/operations. This system also clarifies each stage of production and fills the gaps in the potential information flow, reducing any chance of fraud or misinformation. As reported from the Australian chain of custody certifying companies e.g. EWPAA, PEFC), conducting regular audits within the companies and certification authorities by themselves and by third parties is crucial to maintaining a high level of trust in the certification provided [23].

3. Standards, legislations and compliance

3.1 Australian standards

The Australian Standard (AS 4707:2014 Amd. 2:2018)determines the chain of custody for forest products [24]. The sustainability of timber resources is encapsulated in this standard. This standard ensures that timber products are compliant with the sustainable forestry management standard (AS4708:2013) [25] from forest grower to the end-user. Although these are the only standards provided by Standards Australia, other organizations such as the Australian Forestry Standard Ltd. (AFS) have formulated similar standards and schemes. The chain of custody for forest products standard was developed and based on the PEFC (Program for Endorsement of Forest Certification) standard (PEFC ST 2002:2020) [26] and then modified to suit Australian procedures and processes.

Currently, the standard is not compulsory for any organization within the chain of custody, however, implementing the standard in the business will ensure customers are buying a certified and legal product. It is also possible that in the future and based on national and international requirements, Australia will introduce a similar compulsory standard therefore future-proofing the system. The chain of custody standard is reviewed every 5 years which allows for any changes to operational and technical knowledge and national and international community expectations to be implemented.

In addition, from the standards above which are not formulated by government organizations, the Australian government introduced an illegal-logging due-diligence test as of November 2014. This test was developed from AS and PEFC standards and as a result, any product certified under either AS 4707:2014 or PEFC ST 2002:2013 has passed the due diligence test. The test acts as a basic level of liability for businesses to verify that their products come from legally logged forests.

Any business that is responsible for manufacturing, processing, converting, or repackaging wood can be certified under the Australian Standard for chain of custody [27]. This enables all companies along the supply chain to be completely transparent in demonstrating their use of only sustainable timber. This enables Australia to continue to be a preferred supplier for international importers as they can assure their own government that the timber is legally sourced.

Although most Australian timber manufacturing facilities use only local timbers some will use imported species if they need to suit a certain application (e.g., Indian rosewood for musical instruments). These imported materials require close consideration of the Illegal Logging Prohibition Regulation 2012 which was procured under the Illegal Logging Prohibition Act 2012. This act has proven to be extremely successful and should stand as the basis for future acts, rules and laws in the timber industry. As mentioned above in Section 3.1.5 *Export Control Act 2020, Export Control (Wood and Woodchips) Rules 2021* also introduces some considerations [28].

3.2 Compliance

Currently, the laws and compliance standards surrounding imported and domestically produced engineered wood products (EWPs) are outlined under documents such as the National Construction Code (NCC), The National Building Code (NBC), and The Competition and Consumer Act (2010) within Australia. However, a submission to the *Inquiry into Non-Conforming Building Products* in the 44th parliament by the EWPAA highlighted some key issues and flaws with the relevant government bodies policing and enforcement of these codes and acts [12]. In 2018–2019 64% of the EWPs imported to Australia came from Asia, followed by Europe and Oceania with 20% and 5%, respectively (EWPAA reported [1]).

Between January 2013 and August 2015, the EWPAA conducted almost 25,000 tests on both certified and non-certified engineered wood products. The tests found that 28% of engineered wood products imported to Australia did not meet Australian standards, whereas only 1.5% of locally manufactured EWPs did not meet the standards. A majority of this 28% of non-compliant product was claimed to meet Australian standards by the overseas exporter. Australia imported $210 million of plywood, $2.1 billion in paper, and $468.5 million of sawn wood in 2013–2014 [29]. In 2015, Australia imported timber products from China, Indonesia, Malaysia, the US, the UK and New Zealand [30], and in 2016–2017, 60% of the imported products came from China [31]. **Table 4** represents the reported ratio of non-certified timber products manufactured by various countries in 2002 [7].

This further highlights the need for a quality control point either conducted by the importer or by a government body. With the volume of imported building products increasing rapidly throughout Australia this is becoming a major source of concern. The

Manufacturing country	Product type	% Non-certified
Indonesia	Plywood	55
	Lumber	65
	Roundwood	58
Malaysia	Plywood	11.8
	Lumber	11.8
	Roundwood	11.8
Russia	Plywood	15
	Lumber	20
	Roundwood	17
China	Plywood	30.6
	Lumber	30.6
	Roundwood	30.6

Table 4.
Percentage of non-certified timber products from the different international manufacturers [7].

report by EWPAA indicated that any further delay in Australia could mean a significant failure event such as the Dockland Cladding Fire [12, 32] to improve its enforcement of building compliance and regulations on imported engineered wood products.

The reason for the increase in use of imported engineered wood products is a cost factor. Australian companies simply cannot compete with the imported non-compliant products being produced internationally. Wood products manufactured in Australia must meet the requirements outlined by the following codes, all of which increase production costs:

- Building Code of Australia (BCA) & Australian Standards
    - Meet strength and durability properties required to ensure safe construction and acceptable structural integrity of buildings in major high load events such as storms, cyclones, fires and occupant activities.
- National Construction Code (NCC)
    - Air quality (with respect to carcinogen off-gassing).
- Department of Health National Industrial Chemicals Notification and Assessment Scheme (NICNAS).
    - Maximum emission class of E1 to ensure worker safety during manufacture of cabinetry and furnishings.

For example, the Australian standard for compliance testing for plywood can be either a 72-h boil test at 100°C or a 6-h boil test at 200Kpa of steam pressure which simulates 50 years of full weather exposure. These tests are mandatory which results in a manufacturing cost increase for Australian manufacturers. Currently, international manufacturers are not held to these standards, and they can sell their products cheaper than in Australia.

Currently, the Competition and Consumer Act 2010 does address brands and manufacturers using misleading product information and falsely presenting the quality of a product. However, as seen by the alarming rate of non-compliance in imported EWPs, it is required to establish a more clear and more effective tracing system that could provide details of product origin and compliance with Australian standards. Importers are willing to take the risk of supplying non-compliant products in Australia as the benefits far outweigh the penalties.

The major problems brought forward by the EWPAA in their submission were related to lack of surveillance and prosecution. Identifying non-compliant wood products is not possible given the lack of inspection. Importers are predominantly small companies. These companies have limited resources in terms of assets and capital which means if a significant failure of their products did occur the legal fees and penalties could be substantial. This means customers and creditors could be left with very little, if any, compensation.

Environments where non-compliance is common, are often generated by circumstances such as poor surveillance, lack of enforcement, and low disincentives and penalties for failing to comply with the governing laws. This can put public safety at risk.

3.2.1 Challenges and solutions

The major challenge with non-compliant timber products is the potential structural failures which could lead to serious injury or even death and flow on costs of failure [33]. As a direct solution to avoid the performance issues outlined above the EWPAA proposed establishing an organization that undertakes surveillance, enforces policies, and applies significant penalties in the case of non-compliance. A two-way traceability system that is managed and monitored by that organization provides the details of products manufactured nationally and imported by international suppliers. It details the testing completed on them, chemical treatments and standards they comply with that will enforce the required structural and durability specifications.

3.2.1.1 Identification of non-compliant products

When identifying non-compliant products, the process must be clear, stage by stage defined and non-discriminate meaning it will apply to all engineered wood products manufactured both domestically and internationally. The proposed Independent Compliance Body (ICB) [12] must investigate all complaints of non-compliance using independent testing facilities that are National Association of Testing Authorities (NATA) certified to ensure impartiality.

3.2.1.2 Enforcing penalties for use of non-compliant product

As has been seen in the plumbing and electrical sectors mandatory certification is not always effective in reducing the amount of non-compliant product [34]. This can be due to the international manufacturers supplying fraudulent certification and documentation even though they sometimes do not even possess the equipment required to carry out the testing. This means we are not able to verify if the testing has actually taken place. Therefore, a product can have the appropriate certification documentation and label but not actually be compliant.

This is a serious problem as quite often due diligence tests that construction site managers are required to perform only include inspecting product for documentation and labeling meaning the products will pass this test and therefore endanger the health and safety of everyone on the site. A mandatory government and third-party testing and investigations into all EWPs that are imported into Australia were proposed by an EWPAA submission [12]. Along with mandatory testing, a significant increase in penalties is also required which will directly influence both categories below:

a. *"Sell non-compliant or misrepresented product"*

b. *"Use non-compliant or misrepresented product where it is directly imported by the first user."*

Some major building supplies companies only refer to their sustainable resource policy for timber products which is a general short-length document. There is no clearly defined policy for compliance with structural EWPs. This issue was also highlighted by the EWPAA in their submission regarding compliance [12, 34].

Australia has the 'S' marking which is very similar to the European 'CE' marking (see **Figure 2**) [35] and given this system is already in place it should present very few problems if compliance is to be added into the chain of custody certification standard in Australia.

As of July 1, 2013, all structural engineered wood products that are to be permanently incorporated into constructions in Europe must have the CE marking stamped on them which means they have been identified as fit for purpose by a 'notified body' [12, 35]. In addition to the CE marking any manufacturer of structural timber components must supply a Declaration of Performance (DoP) which contains additional information that is not displayed on the individual products. This DoP is to be made available throughout the supply chain to all users via a printed document and also a digital copy. The DoP is also matched to a unique identification code that is labeled on the product and this code can be used to obtain the DoP through the original supplier if the physical copy of the DoP is lost [36]. This requirement only applies to importing 'finished components' (LVL etc.) not raw material but if this raw material is used in a 'component' then it will be certified anyway by the manufacturer in Europe. If a product being supplied by a manufacturer or seller fails to produce the CE Marking and all supporting documents the product can be withdrawn from the market and the trader can be prosecuted. The CE marking does not require samples of the product to be tested at specific intervals (one product from every batch or one product every hour etc.) because it assumes serial production. Serial production means that every product is manufactured using the same process and materials and therefore any product from that process is compliant if one is. Details of this system can be found in CE marking/certification section of CSTB webpage (https://evaluation.cstb.fr/en/ce-marking/) [12].

Figure 2.
CE marking introduced in Europe compulsory from 2013.

4. Chain of custody

This section includes information about the Chain of Custody (CoC) and its application in the timber industry as well as its standing as a reliable certification method.

4.1 What is the chain of custody?

A chain of custody ensures each stage of the manufacturing and distribution life cycle of timber as both a resource and a product are documented and recorded by the certified parties. This system ideally is composed of a central database that gives access to information for all users via a simple login or similar system. Within this system, the information stored should be clear and extensive with respect to both sustainability and compliance. Compliance is not currently integrated into any chain of custody standard or certification within Australia. This compliance aspect added to the CoC will be solely for structural wood products. The addition of compliance to the CoC will increase accountability and ease of information checking which will result in decreased response time when critical information is needed (giving open access to information at any stage of the timber supply chain). At any stage of the supply chain, prospective consumers of the product should be able to view relevant information about a specific sample/batch of timber in relation to both sustainability and compliance. Other countries such as Europe are beginning to introduce or have introduced mandatory legislation for traceability and that could potentially limit Australia's access to export markets. The impacts of a voluntary CoC restrict companies that intend on being certified by the Australian standard but do not have parties in their supply chain certified (supplier of raw products etc.) This may result in a loss of revenue or business for the company if the buyer prefers to purchase from only certified producers.

4.2 Critical control points in CoC

4.2.1 Identification

Identify the product using a physical brand e.g. paint, hammer brand, or plastic. The label needs to be able to withstand all processes the timber may be subjected to e.g. chemical treatment. If one type of label is not suitable, then multiple types need to be used throughout the timbers manufacturing process. Labels can be fraudulent when systems are not cross-checked with documentation at all stages of the supply chain.

4.2.2 Quantities

Quantity is a very rudimentary form of tracking and controlling inventory within an industry. Quantities can be in terms of weight, cost, total pieces, volume, or value. Using quantities ensures the predicted amount of product is removed or retained at each individual stage in the CoC. For example, if 100 logs were felled on a certain day and you receive 120 logs from transport there has been an error made or there has been an attempt to launder logs. Given the digitalisation of most modern inventory systems, this is something that should be able to be tracked with relative ease.

4.2.3 Segregation

The next key critical control point is the segregation of the certified timber from the non-certified timber. Quite often in mill and log yards timber and logs are separated by characteristics such as size, shape, quality, and species. Systems like this can remain in place but need to be done within groups of certified and non-certified timber to avoid any accidental mixing of the two. The other option for timber facilities is to reject any non-certified products which will remove the need for segregation.

4.2.4 Personnel

As much as the systems and technologies of a CoC play a significant role in its success, the personnel responsible for applying these systems play a critical role. Personnel can influence the performance of a CoC system through errors and fraudulent behavior. Training and upskilling personnel are required as the CoC is applied especially to new products or suppliers.

4.2.5 Errors

Often personnel makes errors due to a lack of training or application to the job. [37]. It is important to provide adequate training as the new CoC may be far more advanced than the previous system. This training is key to ensuring the employee can successfully implement the CoC.

4.2.6 Fraudulent behavior

Fraud is not considered a particular problem within the Australian domestic timber industry; however, some countries that Australia imports products from are known for fraudulent and corrupt practices. Fraudulent activity is conducted to directly benefit the individual employee or the organization. The most effective way to reduce fraud within a CoC is to develop a system that makes fraud difficult to conduct without detection. Another step is to increase remuneration because quite often in developing countries the salary of workers is way below a basic wage. This makes employees more susceptible to bribery and fraud, given the increased financial incentive. As well as increasing the incentives authorities can increase the severity and frequency of penalties for fraud and corruption as this will likely act as a deterrent. Conducting random audits is another efficient way to expose fraud and corruption within a CoC.

4.3 Design and implementation

A CoC must consider the following key criteria:

1. Stage Specific Needs—Multiple technologies can be used within the CoC as long as they can all carry the same set of information and be easily transferred at each stage.

2. Standards—The CoC must conform to Australian standards such as AS4707:2014 and AS4708:2013 and acts/regulations such as the Illegal Logging Act 2012.

3. Cost—The cost of the technology must be proportionate to the value of the timber species it is being applied to. The cost of implementation (training, equipment, etc.) must also be considered as some small manufacturers may not be able to meet this cost.

4. Feasibility/applicability—The technology and systems must be applicable to the stage in which it is being implemented. Some technology/equipment is not suitable for use within a forest or mill due to the high sensitivity of equipment to environmental factors (dust, temperature, and humidity changes) or other requirements (such as regular updates and calibrations).

5. Species—Some species are generally not the target of illegal logging due to their low market value and may not require a CoC.

Implementation of a CoC is just as important as the design because key aspects and steps of the system can be missed or performed incorrectly when not implemented properly. To reduce this each stage of the CoC should be analyzed to identify which systems need to be incorporated. Certifiers such as the EWPAA and PEFC outline how they certify a CoC within a timber company. A summary of the key steps is detailed below:

1. Applicants are required to identify and address any deficiencies found when comparing their current CoC with the standard CoC. Once this is completed, the mill must implement these procedures across all sites. As certification is not free, ensuring the business is ready for certification before the audit will reduce costs.

2. Identify, brief, and provide training to all staff with CoC duties.

3. Implement Due Diligence Systems for all suppliers to ensure sourced material is certified.

4. Implement physical separation or inventory control systems to monitor the certification status of timber.

A short time after the CoC is considered implemented; the certifying organization will perform an audit and issue a certificate if satisfied. Audits will be performed annually. Internal and third-party audits should also be conducted frequently to avoid loss of certification.

4.4 Key stages in supply chain

There are several key stages to the supply chain of wood products, both structural and non-structural, and each of these stages has its requirements when it comes to the systems being put in place. These systems include traceability technology, CoC documentation, and compliance. As a result of this, the overall CoC developed will have multiple technologies and systems within it depending on the applicability of each system.

4.4.1 Forest

The forest is the first of the critical points in the supply chain and is susceptible to illegal logging. Logs are laundered by mixing illegally and legally harvested logs at a stage where they may be indistinguishable. Labeling technology should be applied immediately to both the logs and the stumps after the trees are felled. Quantities and other data (size, species, diameter distributions) must be inventoried and tracked at this stage i.e. If 100 were harvested from a section and 150 logs were transported to a mill, then illegal logging may be a consequence. This should be rectified immediately through clear communication between the forest manager and the next stage in the supply chain. Given the remoteness of many forests and logging camps, this can be the most problematic stage of the CoC as complex/bulky/sensitive technology may not be accessible directly in the field. The lack of access to information at the forest level re-enforces the need for a traceability system that has been developed to suit all stages of the CoC. Complex tracing technologies may not be able to be implemented until the next stage in the CoC, which is perfectly acceptable, providing the level and quantity of information are maintained.

4.4.2 Forest to mill

Transporting the felled logs from the forest to the mill is the next critical point in the chain of custody. This is usually the stage where the timber, depending on the region, travels long distances through remote areas less regulated by government officials. Most trucking companies and national authorities require the weight of a truck to be recorded at the beginning of a journey to ensure they are within the vehicle limits [38]. Depending on the laws and regulations of the area, trucks are also required to be inspected at any weighbridges/points along major highways and transport routes. This information should vary little from leaving the forest to arriving at the mill and therefore is a good system to verify no logs have been switched or added. When timber arrives at the mill, all the initial data collected such as quantities, species and size should all be recorded and cross-checked/verified with the information from the forest. A labeling technology and data recording system are required to be efficient as any lengthy time delays caused by this process will impact the reputation of the industry supply chain.

4.4.3 Shipping between countries (importing/exporting)

Most illegal logging occurs in developing countries which tend to have less regulation and enforcement, making it easier for timber to be laundered or rebranded as legal. Once the timber moves between countries, it is difficult to prove if something that has been labeled legal was illegally sourced if the systems are not linked. This is where due diligence tests are crucial. Due diligence tests involve using the previous chain of custody documentation (from forest and mill) included in shipping documentation from the exporting country to decide if the timber is legal. Independent auditing and inspection at ports were adapted by countries like Papua New Guinea (PNG) to ensure revenue was not being lost from State-owned forests as well as to halt the illegal logging trade.

As noted in Section 3.2, the non-compliance of imported EWPs in Australia was high. Because of this, compliance needs to be added to the CoC with regard to imported products. Importers of EWPs must comply with Australian requirements and international standards for different product types, considering the potential level of fraudulent certification within products manufactured overseas.

4.4.4 Processing Facility

Timber from both local and overseas sustainable forests can arrive at the processing facility, meaning the mill will need to be familiar with CoC procedures from multiple countries. The easiest way for a processing facility to reduce time and cost for their part of the chain of custody is only to purchase already verified, sustainably sourced timber. Timber that has been certified from a sustainable and legal source must be kept separate from any timber that is in question or awaiting verification. Therefore, a segregation system needs to be in place to ensure they are not mixed together, which could see a product lose its certification or be incorrectly certified.

The processing facility is the first stage within the supply chain where compliance will need to be integrated as this is the stage when structural products will be manufactured. As outlined in Section 7.2, the compliance of EWPs is very closely linked to sustainable sourcing and illegal logging issues and as such, it is recommended that compliance become part of the CoC system. This has been implemented in other regions such as Europe, and this process was also outlined in Section 7.2. The compliance aspect of the CoC will only need to be mandatory for structural timber and wood products, and all relevant information with regard to compliance must be accessible by the builder and/or consumer.

4.4.5 Transport

The next stage involves moving products/materials between primary and secondary manufacturing processors. Secondary processors often have the least onus on them in terms of checking multiple levels of the CoC to verify the timber is legally sourced. Secondary manufacturers often rely on information solely from the primary processor, including transport documents, customs declarations, and sales documents. If an item has been verified as certified at all CoC points before the secondary processor, it is highly unlikely that any error will be picked up at this point.

Secondary processors manufacture things like furniture and small wood products that are usually non-structural, and as a result of this, it is not likely compliance will be a part of the chain of custody design for this stage. However, the biosecurity and pest and disease issues that could arise from this category need to be considered.

5. Current technologies/systems

5.1 Information systems

Traceability information systems consist of processes to maintain records that expose the trace of a particular input from suppliers to final customers. Traceability means the capability to track any product throughout all phases of production, processing, and distribution. Some of the important aspects of a traceability system include protocols to identify the batch or item, details of product processing stages such as dates, records of steps etc. the step-by-step movement of products throughout the supply chain and also a global managing system that link all data available for each batch or product [39].

The key to an effective tracing system is an information system capable of reading and compiling all the information and data collected about the product. This system should be accessible at any stage of the CoC to verify the origin of a product. The tracing technology is irrelevant if the data stored is not able to be gathered and easily accessible. Some mandatory functions of the information system are:

- Central database
- Accessibility
- All critical data stored—sample name, region, dimensions, quantities, quality, species, batch number, plantation, transport documentation, etc.
- Ease of use

An example of this data storing system is the Russian program "Uniform State Automated Information System (EGAIS)". EGAIS and its many variants are used not only in the timber industry but also in alcohol and prescription drug industries in Russia. This software system is designed as a national database for storing all data and documentation relating to a product. It can be used on any computer with an internet connection and has the ability to be operated with ordinary barcode readers which gives retailer ease of use. The consumer can then also verify the information of the product via a QR code on the label of the final product. The type of national database designed provides a reliable access way to ensure complete transparency and reliability for the traceability of products at any stage of the chain.

5.2 Traceability technologies

Traceability means the ability to track any product throughout all stages of harvest, production, processing and distribution. This tracking system can refer to recording information through various means such as barcodes, radio frequency identification (RFID) tags, and other tracking methods. Timber resources can be imported as round wood and exported as different product types, including structural (beams, etc.) and non-structural (paper, etc.). The relevant information about the source of the raw product, where the wood was grown, what processing operation was used to produce any of the products and any chemical treatment applied needs to be clearly defined and recorded for the product to be certified sustainable and compliant with required standards and regulations. An effective traceability system is required to record and manage different types of information collected at each stage of the supply chain and provide accessible data to the users, product developers, and end-users interested in sustainability aspects and performance compliance of products. Various technologies are available for tracking and identifying products such as timber; however, a continuously managed system from forest to the consumer is yet to be developed in Australia. This section aims to summarize potential technologies available and their advantages and limitations to be used in the timber industry.

5.3 Forensic technologies

5.3.1 Wood anatomy

The wood's cellular arrangement including macroscopic and microscopic formation can be used in identification and tracing of species and products [40–42]. The larger specifications depending on species and product type could include the timber color, cell arrangement, and growth rings. The smaller scale cellular combinations including the cell type, ray shape and size, and frequency can be checked under microscope. Some of these properties can be used in developing tracing systems and protocols. These characteristics could be used as a unique image/logo to record specifications and information about the product/resource. However, the detailed smart software system needs to be then designed to relate the images and information to the product. This could be limited to stages that have clear images and large enough faces to allow an image to be taken. In plywood manufacturing, for example, currently, smart systems are used to take images of each veneer face and the image collected from face could potentially be used in a trial program to turn into a fingerprint for tracing that piece of product further in the supply chain [43–45]. Similarly in other stages of the supply chain, there is information collected for quality, the pattern of cut, grading/sorting, and storing of products. This information could be used in a traceability trial.

5.3.2 Mass spectrometry

The wood chemistry and composition can be identified and used to trace the product back to its origin and growing environment/habitat. The wood species genetics and geological origin can be used to determine species specifications and types.

Mass spectroscopy uses the application of a stream of helium ions heated to 350°C to the surface of the timber. The ionized chemicals in a mass spectrometer that are used to generate a chemical profile for the sample and used to compare with known reference profiles. The data generated can be used to develop potential chemical fingerprints for species and products.

More recently, ambient atmospheric ionization techniques have been developed that minimize sample preparation steps and provide very fast results; specifically the "Direct Analysis in Real Time, Time of Flight Mass Spectrometer" (DART TOFMS) [46, 47] has shown great promise when used for timber identification [48].

The chemical fingerprints developed for species can be developed for unknown samples and species by comparing them to reference groups.. However, it is important to note that models used for clasifiying samples are only valid for taxa included in the reference dataset. The suitability of these systems could be influenced by the cost, training requirements, and maintenance and upgrades, making them less suitable for earlier stages of the supply chain.

5.3.3 Staple isotopes

Stable isotopes are variants of the same atomic element that are stable and have the same amount of protons but with different numbers of neutrons.

Materials such as water, air and soil are characterized by stable isotope ratios (made from known elements) are affected by the climate and origin of their geology. Considering these known parameters a tree grown in specific area and sourced from water, minerals, and carbon dioxide in the same location will have similar compositional effects on the wood generated.

By investigating the chemcial element compositions and ratios at each origin the isotopic "fingerprint" for that site can be developed. The combination of the multiple stable isotope analyses, including elements such as sulfur and strontium, an improved spatial granularity of the identified isotope can be developed into a signature. On this basis, it is possible to use stable isotopes to identify or rule out particular regions of timber provenance. The detection method is suitable to be used for identifying the geographic origin of the products however a detailed reference data set is required. This method however does not have the ability to determine the genus, species of individuals products [49–51]. The application of stable isotope in combination with analyses of trace elements can improve the prediction accuracy [13, 52]. Trace elements and stable isotopes together can be considered "Geochemistry". Although it has not been tested, it is likely that trace element analyses could also augment other methodologies that seek to determine timber provenance, such as DNA analyses.

5.3.4 DNA analyses

Small changes in the genetic code accumulate over generations, resulting in greater differences between the DNA sequences of distantly related compared with closely related individuals. By reading the DNA sequence at particular parts of the genome, individuals can be assigned to a particular group (i.e., species, population) on the basis of similarities and differences in their DNA compared with reference data. Success can be limited by the technical challenges inherent in extracting and amplifying sufficient DNA from timber.

Genetic DNA is extracted from the wood cells by first pulverizing the wood and then using several chemicals to isolate the DNA from other cell content. Specific parts of the DNA are then read and compared with reference data to identify the species or geographic origin of the wood sample.

5.3.5 Radiocarbon

Carbon occurs naturally as the radioactive isotope 14C ("radiocarbon") and the stable isotopes 12C and 13C. Radiocarbon decays naturally to nitrogen (14 N) [43]. By measuring the ratio of radiocarbon to the stable carbon isotopes, it is possible to calculate a "radiocarbon age" of timber. During the early 1960s, levels of 14C in the upper atmosphere were augmented through nuclear-bomb testing producing a spike in calibrations (the "bomb curve"), which can be used to date recent material. The accurate calculation requires two samples of different ages (such as different tree rings within a piece of timber). The results reveal the age of the individual tree rings tested, but this may not equate to the felling date if the outermost tree rings were not present in the sample.

5.3.6 Near-infrared spectroscopy

Near-infrared spectroscopy (NIRS) identified elements by exposing the samples to near infrared electromagnetic energy to capture the materials' spectra absorption. The process records the information from product' chemistry and physical structure. The collected data will be analyzed using appropriate multivariate modeling methods in order to produce useful information about the product's chemistry and physical variations. The NIRs analysis has the capability of identifying genera, species within the same genus, and between species from various regions.

One appropriate analysis and mdoeling are completed, NIRs technology can accurately test and detect product specifications with minimum operator skills required. Current research is working on developing models and data sets to optimize the NIRs systems' accuracy of output in predicting product properties when various variables including humidity, moisture level, and cutting direction are introduced.

Results from current existing research results in the field have shown that families and species of products can be identified using NIRs.. NIRs have been successfully used in differentiating Brazilian mahogany wood from Mexico, Honduras, Peru, and Venezuela. However the technology still requires further research and is not currently widely available to industry. There are also various limitations such as access to accurate data sets, and variabilities between species and product types that slows the development of predictive models. The required large data sets of information to develop a reliable model and variability of timber species could be some of the possible disadvantages in using the NIRs technology in timber production supply chains.

5.4 Labelling technologies

5.4.1 Conventional paint and chisel labels

The oldest methods of log labeling involve the painting or chiseling of company information and log identification information, usually on one or both ends of each log. Such labels are commonly used in conjunction with documentation to provide more detailed information about log origin, species, dimensions, and volume. A chisel also called an inscribing tool or scribe, is a specialized knife used to engrave the information into the end of the log. Although both painting and chiseling require more time than hammer branding, considerably more information can be included in the labels produced with these methods. The labels produced by painting and chiseling also are generally more legible than hammer brands.

5.4.2 Stamped codes

Coding methods have been developed in which patterns of dots or circles are stamped in the ends of the logs. These stamped codes can be applied automatically by harvesting machines [53] or by using special stamping devices [54]. They can subsequently be interpreted by handheld or machine-mounted readers. The codes can contain a significant amount of information and may also refer to additional documentation.

5.4.3 Branding hammers

A branding hammer has been used as a traditional labeling method in log processing and has a simple mechanism. The hammer used creates a unique pattern on the surface of the log that is used to identify the origin of the log. Other documentation and details can be used alongside the branding hammer to provide clearer information about the log origin than the hammer branding only.

5.4.4 Conventional labels

Conventional labels are used widely in timber industry which can be as simple as a treated paper tag or plastic label. Metal or hardened plastic staples, nails, and adhesives are usually used to attach the labels on the product surface. For more specific products such as pulpwood that are processed or "digested" during product development these lebels are not as effective. The levels can provide details of company name or log number, however, further details can be included if a barcode is added to the label. The addition of barcode will require barcode scanner throughout the product life and supply chain.

5.4.5 Nail-based labels

Nail-based labels are usually installed on the wood products or logs using hammer. These labels are generally made from metal or hardened plastic. There are nail-based labels will imprinted barcodes that increase their security and capacity to include more information however a scanner or reader is then required to read the product information throughout the supply chain.

5.4.6 Magnetic stripe cards

Paper or plastic based magnetic stripe cards contain a black magnetic strip and has capacity to store productinformation. However, the use of these cards require reader and special scanning devices to read and modify the product information. These cards are used widely in various industries such as airport transit tickets and bank cards that can provide ubiquitous technology in the financial and security sectors. The new technologies such as smart cards and two-dimensional barcodes are becoming more commonly used and easier to access. Potential advantage of these cards could be the possibility of proprietary encoding and programmability of the and there already is a specific International Organization for Standardization (ISO) standard for encoding stripe cards.

5.4.7 Smart cards

Smart cards are basically credit-card-sized plastic cards that could contain large amounts of product details and production specifications in a microchip. These cards are also called "Chip card," "integrated circuit card," and "smart card". There are two types of smart cards:

- Dumb smart card that only has memory to store product details. An example of these types of cards is the cards that are used forstoring details of a shipping manifest. Its memory a shipping manifest.

- True smart card actually has an embedded microprocessor in addition to the storage memory. The true smart card provides the possibility of storing and making changes in the data recorded. The security of information in these cards can bemaintained in various ways. This security has been touted as the main reason that smart cards will eventually replace other card technologies.

The reader requirement for the smart cards can be a potential disadvantage of them considering the supply chain type and environment. The "contactless" cards however can provide a more effective solution for timber tracing. Short-range cards operate by electrical inductive or capacitive coupling when the reader and card are brought within a millimeter or so of each other; longer-range cards communicate by radio signals.

5.4.8 Radiofrequency identification

The basis of Radio Frequency Identification (RFID) is to place tags with a micro radio transponder that allows a read and write capacity whereby small amounts of information about the product can be sent from the tag to a reader unit. The tags are actually transponders in technical terms and include a minute computer chip with an inbuilt antenna. The data transmit between tags and RFID units using radio waves, which commonly involves a time and date stamp reading at specific locations in a defined process. This identifies where the object is at a given point in time [55]. There are two types of RFID tags, passive and active. Passive tags are powered by the incoming electromagnetic waves generated by the RFID readers, with a signal captured by the tag's antenna. This allows passive tags to be simplified and small, but with limited capabilities of signal propagation, data storage and processing. Active tags contain their own internal power source (a battery). This enables the tags to emit a signal to the RFID reader with an increased propagation range. A range of sensors and modules (e.g. sensors and/or GPS) can also be supported by the tag with the increased power.

Table 5 provides a comparison of the two tag technologies.

Passive RFID technology is more suitable for supply chain tracking applications. This technology is compatible with the forestry industry, especially with product certification. The placement of these tags at the cutting and loading time ensures that the origin of the timber is from well-managed forests and not from illegal harvesting. RFID systems in the shape of a nail are more resistant to shocks, vibrations, and humidity, which could be suitable for earlier stages of the timber industry while cost needs to be always considered. In the industry's product manufacturing and treatment section, the technology could have less applicability due to its sensitivity and time consumption for installation.

RFID tags were used in a pilot project for tracking the process of cutting down trees and transporting logs to a processing plant in Germany in 2006 [56]. About 500 tags were used in the test in a forest near Munich. None of the tags were damaged during the process of felling and stacking logs, while approximately 5% were lost during transportation from forest to processing plant. The application cost was estimated to be approximately $6 per cubic meter of harvested wood at the time.

5.4.9 Microtaggants

Microtaggants are microscopic, color-coded plastic particles that are specifically designed to positively identify a wide variety of substances or objects. These unique

Characteristics	Active	Passive
Power	Battery	No internal power
Required signal strength	Low	High
Communication range	30–100 + metres	Near contact—25 metres
Data storage range	128 kb	128b
Per tag cost	US$25–US$50	US$0.09–US$20
Tag size	Varies depending on application	Sticker to credit card size
Fixed infrastructure costs	Lower—cheaper interrogators	Higher—particularly fixed readers
Beat area of use	High volume assets moving within designated areas in random and dynamic systems	High volume assets moving through fixed choke points in definable, uniform systems

Table 5.
Comparison of the active and passive RFID technologies.

identification particles are composed of distinct layers whose colors and sequences can be changed, making several million codes available. Layers of fluorescent or magnetic material can be added to the particles so they can be found easily. Fluorescent layers are detected by viewing under long-wave ultraviolet light, and particles with magnetic layers can be recovered from loose-flowing or bulk materials by using a magnet. The color codes can be read using a pocket microscope of at least 100× magnification.

Another type of microtaggants is NanoTags, which can be made from various materials such as nickel, octagon-shaped, 6–10 microns thin and 0.3–0.5 mm wide. The Security Identification Code (SIC) is etched physically through the body of the nickel tag. NanoTags can be mixed with adhesives or embedded into the body of plastics. Once the mixture of tags and adhesives (or plastics) becomes dry and solid, the encased NanoTags become resistant to water, most chemicals, and environments.

The microtaggants with plastic substrates are vulnerable to rapid deterioration at high temperatures, which starts at temperatures above 150°C, and then leads to gradual loss of all information and completely burning at 350°C, while the NanoTags remain intact. This technology could have potential applications for various stages of the timber industry; however, its suitability needs to be checked against the conditions before and after product manufacturing, storage, and in-use life of products. The accessibility of reading/detecting particles and their variations also need to be investigated to provide a robust and secure system for the industry to use.

5.4.10 Nanotechnology

Optical markers at the nanoparticle level are used to mark timber at various processing points. The markers can be embedded in a clear or color spray and applied to live trees or cut logs and other timber products. A hand detector can help to detect the presence of nanoparticles. This technology is currently under development and not available for wide application.

5.5 Other technologies

5.5.1 Automated macroscopic wood anatomical identification

Recent development in the field of wood anatomy is the automated recognition of species (machine vision) and biometric log traceability, making use of image reference collections. “Machine vision” technology is currently being developed for automated macroscopic wood anatomical identification and has potential for use as a handheld timber identification device. The system captures images under conditions of strict light control through its camera, and it uses signal processing approaches to extract information and then analyze it in a way that establishes a classification scheme. A prototype device has been developed, which has been utilized in two field situations to test multiple specimens in real-time. The potential accuracy of this method is excellent—as good, if not sometimes better than that which can be achieved by a trained expert, due in part to the increased sensitivity to light of the optical receptors employed in the system when compared to the human eye. The skill level required to operate a functional system at the front line to obtain an identification is minimal and comparable to that required to take macroscopic photographs suitable for off-site expert identification. However, the technology is at the prototype stage and has been tested on a limited number of species, so it is not widely available at present.

5.5.2 Blockchain technology

Blockchain connects multiple time-stamped records—or 'blocks'—together using cryptography to form a linked, linear chain; these blocks cannot be altered retroactively, making such systems highly secure and resistant to manipulation. Each block is connected to the preceding block, validates the transactions, and distributes information throughout a network of users in the form of a decentralized ledger system.

The application of blockchain technology in timber traceability is at the development stage. In the preliminary studies, blockchain technology has been introduced to electronically trace timber as it travels from the forest to the final product, using an information tracing system based on open source and Radio Frequency Identification (RFID) technology [57].

PEFC International has funded the "Wood-chain project", which will test and stimulate the application of blockchain technology as an innovative IT solution for forestry and wood applications. Blockchain technology may allow transparent and complete supervision of wood and timber products traceability, fully compatible with PEFC Chain of Custody certification.

6. Comparison of technologies

Details of technologies compared, and their advantages and disadvantages are listed in the following parts of this section in a tabulated format. Details of each technology including type, strength, and weaknesses are presented in **Tables 6** and 7.

6.1 Advantages and disadvantages of forensic technologies and labelling technologies

List of advantages and disadvantages of technologies used for tracing products is presented in **Tables 6** and 7.

6.2 Suitability of labelling technologies at different stages of supply chain

This section reviews the applicability and effectiveness of the techniques from application, security, labor required, accuracy, and effectiveness point of view. Further comparison and discussion are required if any of the techniques were selected for any of the production stages, including the scale, price, and number used for the product batch. **Table 8** represents a list of labeling types and briefly details their suitability for the timber industry.

6.3 Security characteristics of labelling technologies

A list of security characteristics of labelling technologies is presented in **Table 9**.

6.4 Costs and lead times

The summary of cost estimates and required time for each type of technology is listed in **Table 10**.

Technology type	Strengths	Weaknesses
Microscopic wood anatomy	Microscopic analyses are relatively quick and inexpensive to conduct and can provide an indication of the species group involved. It could potentially be designed based on images already being taken in industry operations for grading and sorting products.	It can rarely provide confirmation of an exact species and is not an indication of the geographic region of origin beyond the species group's natural range. It's also more suitable for raw materials than later stages in the supply chain. The development of a smart system to detect specific species or products can be time-consuming and costly.
Automated machine vision	Faster than traditional microscopy technique and if abundant reference images exist, can be more accurate.	Limited reference image database for species at present can be costly to set up and would require upgrades and further modifications. Requires further calibration and modification for adding species and product types.
Mass spectrometry (e.g. Direct Analysis in Real Time, Time of Flight Mass Spectrometer (DART TOFMS)	This method requires nearly no sample preparation, is non-destructive (a sliver of wood is sufficient) and is fast. Promising for its ease of use and once developed fully can be low cost.	The application of DART-TOF Mass Spectrometry in wood forensics is currently at an early stage of development. Faces the same constraints as other technologies in regard to reference data. Potentially require training, calibration and maintenance, could be too sensitive to be used in all supply chain stages.
Stable isotopes	It has the potential to possibly identify origin and species (depending on how unique species take up chemicals differently and reference database) down to the concession level.	Cannot identify species. The widespread application requires the collection of great numbers of geo-referenced samples to provide reference data.
DNA barcoding	It can be used to identify both species and origin with great accuracy and precision. It can tie an individual log (or the products derived from it) to the stump it came from (genetic fingerprinting).	The success rate for the extraction of usable DNA sequences from wood products is currently low. DNA techniques are also limited by the number of reliable DNA barcodes sequenced for different species, the number of reliable genetic reference maps available; and their spatial resolution.
Near-infrared spectroscopy	This method is non-destructive and fast. Closely related species can be differentiated, and the technique has the capacity to discriminate between geographic provenances. An integrated approach with analysis of isotopes and trace elements can yield high levels of accuracy.	NIRS reference data are still limited. As a stand-alone method, the identification accuracy is variable. Initial large data set is required to develop a validated and reliable model. The requirement to update and calibrate the model could cause extra costs.

Table 6.
Advantages and disadvantages of technologies used for tracing various products.

Technology type	Strengths	Weaknesses
Conventional paint and chisel labels	Paint and chisel marks are easy to apply, low-cost, and require no special training. These labels can be very robust and survive road and water transport very well. They can also be integrated with forest management, logistics, and stock inventory functions.	Hand-printed labels are used in various stages of supply chain and can be used on large-size logs as well as other products. They are not as secure as some other labeling options and can be lost or damaged easily. The other disadvantage of using these labels is the amount of paperwork required to record and manage the information.
Branding hammers	The hammer branding is a cost-effective and easy-to-use method, does not require any training and can be applied on any size log. The hammer branding can be used in combination with coded serial numbers and can be used as an option in both forest management system as well as transport and stock inventory in the log yard.	Hammers can be easily replicated and widely distributed to unauthorized personnel. Hammer marks are not easily keyed to associated documentation, and thus, they cannot easily be used as part of a comprehensive chain of custody system. It can be labor intensive and not easy to follow if any part of the data is missing. Also, could be difficult to refer to imported products.
Conventional labels	Attaching the label is relatively quick. Conventional labels are inexpensive and are easier to read than other marking technologies. Large amount of data related to product location, and ownership. Size and scale and any other production specifications can be stored using this labelling option. Barcoded labels can also provide better security and possibility of including more information about the product.	Conventional labels can be easy to duplicate or counterfeit unless suitable security mechanisms are integrated into the design of the labels. Barcoded labels can easily be removed or fall off. Experience shows that 1–5% of labels fall off before the product reaches its destination. Conventional labels cannot usually be manufactured in the forest and therefore have to be pre-printed for log tracking purposes. Can be replicated and accessed by other parties throughout the chain.
Nail-based labels	The nail-based labels are more durable than paper or plastic-based labels. Their installation process is similar to the hammer brands and large amount of information can be included in them. The addition of barcode to nail-based label could provide possibility of adding more product information and the nature of these labels (difficult to reprint or change) provide better security of information throughout the supply chain.	The nail-based labels are not easy to replace, and any modification requires re-printing and needs to be done prior to their installation. The limitation associated with any change in the details and need for reprinting makes them less flexible to be used throughout the supply chain.
Magnetic stripe cards	Magnetic stripe cards are useful for attaching information to documentation rather than for labeling individual products. The information stored on these devices is relatively secure and difficult (but not impossible) to alter or counterfeit. These devices can facilitate data processing and security audits of documents. It is possible to manufacture labels at processing plants and at many storage facilities, allowing more data to be inserted into the documents.	Magnetic cards are not as effective to be used for log labelling as some other labelling options. The card readers can be expensive and not easily used in various stages of supply chain. The data recorded on the cards also has limited size and is not as flexible as information that can be stored on other options such as smart cards.

Technology type	Strengths	Weaknesses
Smart cards	The large amount of data that can be stored on smart cards with high level of security is their main advantage. They are also good replacements for paper-based labels and the large amount of paperwork required for some of the other labelling options. They provide the security of information that cannot be easily replicated or modified by non-authorized parties. These devices can significantly facilitate data capture, data processing, and security audits. It is possible to capture data at processing plants and at many storage facilities allowing more data to be inserted into the documents. These labels can enhance logistics and stock inventory functions.	The potential disadvantage would be the cost associated with their use, reading, and maintaining their information system. The cost can make them less effective for individual log purposes. Their need for readers/ scanners makes them less mobile and flexible throughout the supply chain.2
RFID labels	The RFID labels are easily and rapidly readable in various environments and remote conditions including underwater. They can store large amounts of product information and are highly secure and difficult to tamper with or modified by non-authorized parties. They provide flexible system for data management, processing, and make data reviews and audits easier. They also can be used in various stages of supply chain to enhance logistics, raw, and processed product data recording, and inventory functions.	The cost can be one of their disadvantages in comparison with other labelling options. The scanners used to read the data also can be expensive and can require a high level of technical experience to program and maintenance.
Microtaggant tracer	Microtaggants are very secure and provide an accurate level of product information. They can nt be replaced or counterfeited easily while they are inexpensive labelling options and simple to use. They can be used in various stages of supply chain and are comparable to other current labelling options used by industry (such as conventional and printed labels). They are durable and can be used on products during processing stages of supply chain.	They are not a full tracing system and are only effective when used in labelling batch products. Their application for individual products is not economically viable. They are read manually and do not provide electronic reading options. Although the microtaggants are low cost the cost of setting up the system for them is still high.
Chemical tracer paint	The tracer paint is an accurate system with high level of security that cannot be easily tampered. It is a low-cost labelling solution that can be utilized easily. The tracer paint option can provide flexibility of use throughout the supply chain. The oil-based options are more durable than the normal options and could be used during the timber processing lines.	Solvents used with oil-based tracer paints may induce allergies in some people. Requires proper accountability and secure storage facilities to prevent theft (and misuse) of the paint. Laboratory identification of the painting signature is time-consuming and expensive. More investigation into their applicability at different stages of product development (treatment, cutting, gluing, etc.) needs to be done.
Nanotechnology	Nanoparticles can be easily sprayed onto wood and detected by a hand-held device. It has the potential to be applied to timber and pulp, and paper products as a cheaper alternative to	The application can be cheap, but the technology is proprietary. The range of distinct and identifiable nanoparticles is not infinite to prevent complete

Technology type	Strengths	Weaknesses
	barcodes, radio-frequency identification (RFID), and other tracking technologies. Products marked with nanoparticles can be authenticated at any time, instantly, non-destructively, an unlimited number of times, and without cumbersome lab testing or slowing the flow of goods.	exclusivity in identification and traceability use. Further testing and large-scale trials are needed to develop practical protocols and solutions for their applications in each stage of the supply chain.

Table 7.
Advantages and disadvantages of technologies used for labeling products.

Label type	Tree label	Log labels	Processed wood labels	Transport documentation
Conventional paint and chisel labels	Suitable	Suitable	Not suitable	Not suitable
Branding hammers	Not suitable	Not suitable	Not suitable	Not suitable
Conventional labels	Suitable	Suitable	Suitable	Not suitable
Nail-based labels	Suitable	Suitable	Not suitable	Not suitable
Magnetic stripe cards	Not suitable	Not suitable	Not suitable	Suitable
Smart cards	Not suitable	Not suitable	Not suitable	Suitable
RFID labels	Suitable	Suitable	Suitable	Suitable
Microtaggant tracer	Suitable	Suitable for adding security to other labels for tracking batches of logs	Suitable for adding security to other labels for tracking batches of logs	Not suitable
Chemical tracer paint	Suitable	Suitable for adding security to other labels for tracking batches of logs	Suitable for adding security to other labels for tracking batches of logs	Not suitable
Nanotechnology	Suitable	Suitable	Suitable	Suitable

Table 8.
List of potential labelling technologies for tracing timber products.

It should be noted that the above-listed cost does not include the cost for maintenance, upgrades, and calibration.

6.5 Technology currently available/used

This section includes information about the existing and some potential technologies that can be used in tracing timber throughout the supply chain (**Table 11**). The main focus of this section has been on the specific information about each technology, their potential advantages and limitation that could have for each stage of the supply chain.

Label type	Security characteristics
Conventional paint and chisel labels; Hammer brands	These labels do not provide any advanced level of security and only represent the data included in the paper-based product management system they link to. Their accuracy and security are checked by in-field audits and cross-examining their information with the potential data management system in place. The accuracy and security of these systems is highly dependent on the data recording system developed for them and any issues and mistake in the system could cause in-accuracy and uncertainty about the product information [58] For painted labels, the security can be enhanced if the paint is used in combination with a microtaggant or some type of chemical marker.
Conventional labels	The conventional labels are more secure than the paint, chisel, or branding hammers however still can be tampered and replaced. To improve the security of these labels they can be printed on different materials such as watermarked paper or hologram-embedded plastics. The labels can also be used with microtaggant and marker chemicals. Addition of barcodes to these labels can provide higher level of security. The design of these labels to destructible can provide some level of security by deforming or disintegrating in case of any attempt of tampering, however, this can also make them less durable throughout the supply chain. The security and accuracy of information on these labels are checked by audits and filed checks. And the quality of the referenced documentation and up-to-date details affect the effectiveness of these labels [58].
Nail-based labels	• These labels are more difficult to be replaced due to their materials and the information printed on them in comparison with paper or plastic-based labels. To improve their security, they can be used in combination with microtaggants and marker chemicals. The use of encrypted barcodes on nail-based labels can also enhance accuracy and security. It is usually costly and difficult to remake the nail-based labels on-site or in-field and the change or modification of product information on the label is difficult. They provide information according to the referenced documentation and to check their accuracy audits are required. The comprehensiveness, up-to-date and accuracy of referenced documentation reflect the nail-based labels' quality and accuracy [58].
Magnetic stripe cards	• The stripe cards are secure and can be encoded to enhance the security of information they provide. Their readers can be programmed to provide better accuracy and security of information. The use of these cards with watermarked paper or hologram-embedded plastics can enhance their security. Use of marker chemicals and microtaggants is also possible to improve the level of security. And the information included on the stripe cards can be encrypted to reduce the possibility of tampering. The supporting documentation can be used with the stripe cards and auditing and field checking of source material needed to cross-check the accuracy of the referenced information.
Smart cards	• The smart cards are very secure and possibility of encoding the stored information enhances their security in comparison to other labelling systems. If they are designed properly, they automatically stop operating when they are outside the designed voltage and frequency ranges providing additional anti-tampering characteristics. The design of them can be modified to become inoperable once the programming the cards is completed so they can't be altered or modified by non-authorized parties.
RFID labels	• RFID systems are secure and can be used to process large volume of information in a short timeframe, remotely and in real-time. Their

Label type	Security characteristics
	security is as high as the smart cards with potential for encrypting information. RFID labels are covertly used due to their hidden mechanism within the product or product batch and also can be used on other labels. The existence of RFID labels can be examined easily, rapidly, remotely, and in real-time.
Microtaggant Tracer	Microtaggants are tamper-proof labelling options and can be used in combination with other labels. They are a cost-effective system to identify potential tampering and replacement of labels. However, they are only effective if they are used with a thorough surveillance operation system that is well designed and programmed.
Nanoparticles	Nanoparticles are secure as they are not easily tampered with or replaced. They provide possibility of tracing raw and processed products in various stages of the supply chain. They require a management system and referenced information if they are used on large scale however the appropriately designed management system also provides the possibility of modifying and adding information as product is processed throughout the supply chain.

Table 9.
Comparison of security characteristics of labelling systems for application in the timber industry.

Traceability techniques	The approximate cost (USD)	Minimum time required for the process
Wood anatomy (including machine vision/ dendrochronology)	<$100*	Minutes–days
Mass spectrometry	<$1–$100*	Minutes–days*
Near-infrared spectroscopy	<$1–$100*	Minutes–days*
Stable isotopes	$100–$400*	Several days*
Radio-carbon	$300–$400*	Several days*
Genetics	$100–$300*	Several days*
RFID	$0.09–$20**	N/A
Microtaggant	$145***	N/A
Nanotag	Can vary depending on types and material used/has been successfully used for food industry previously.	N/A
Nanoparticles (Stardust****)	Under development****	N/A

**It should be noted that these are the approximate cost range for a trained expert to complete the laboratory test of one sample and minimum lead times based on the time required to complete the laboratory test.*
***Cost range of one passive RFID tag. RFID readers can vary from around $400 to up to $3000 or more.*
****The cost of 236.6-milliliters bottle of Microtaggants (easily marking at least 1000 logs).*
*****Stardust is being developed and has the potential to replace barcodes, RFID, and other technologies as a cheaper alternative.*

Table 10.
Summary of technology costs and their required processing time.

Technology type	System	Supply chain stage	Product details	Advantages and limitations
Nanotechnology	Covert marking and tracing of raw materials with dust-like nanoparticles in various applications, including timber.	From forest to the consumer	Stardust www.stardustus.com Stardust has developed solutions enabling covert marking and tracing of raw materials in a range of applications, including timber, responsibly sourced goose down and leather, organic fibers, and coral.	Pros: Easy to apply, tamper-proof and cheap. It can be scanned and identified by a handheld device. Cons: Under development and proprietary.
DNA analysis	A chemical profiling technology that verifies the provenance of the product, including food and non-food.	Provenance verification	Source certain www.sourcecertain.com	Pros: Accurate and precise with identifying species and origin. Cons: Dependent on the number of reliable genetic reference maps.
Microtaggant	Metal microdot which provides the option to customize branding, for identification purpose.	From forest to the consumer	NanoTag www.nanotag.com	Pros: Easy to apply, tamper-proof, applicable to the whole supply chain. Cons: Needs to be manually read. Sometimes not easy to find and read.
Microtaggant	Microtaggant particles contain multiple color layers, which translate to a numeric code. Other materials can also be added to the Microtaggant to aid in location and authentication.	From forest to the consumer	Microtrace www.microtrace solutions.com	As previous
Information system/ Nanotechnology	An information system that promotes transparency and accountability along the supply chain ensures regulatory compliance and improves supply chain integrity.	From forest to the consumer	Ivo42 https://iov42.com/ The system provides blockchain digital identities to each of the stakeholders that are part of the supply chain (be it an individual or an organization) and represents timber as digital assets.	Pros: Accurate and can handle a large amount of information entered into the system. Cons: Can be expensive; the setup can be time-consuming and requires a holistic, systematic action.
GPS system	A GPS system unique in the European timber industry for transparent tracing of log deliveries in Romania. It	From forest to mill	TimFlow www.timflow.com	Pros: Can be used along with other GPS operating systems and is easy to use. Cons: Requires connectivity of

Technology type	System	Supply chain stage	Product details	Advantages and limitations
	seamlessly monitors the transport route from the loading place to the factory gate. The information collected includes GPS data and photos of the consignments.			information, and the scale of data requires filtering and further analysis.
Durable tags and labels	Dura-ID Solutions specializes in labels and tags which survive hostile procedures and conditions.	For timber treatment	Dura-id solutions dura-id.com	Pros; Can survive hostile procedures and conditions during timber treatment. Cons: Requires a purpose-built system to use the data; however, the data needs to be added to a system separately to be accessed and used in future.
Information system/DNA and isotope testing, and blockchain	A timber traceability platform that combines traceability, verification, and visualization.	From forest to the consumer	Nature's barcode timber traceability platform www.naturesbarcode.com The platform makes critical supply chain information from forest to consumer available to different stakeholders.	Pros: Enables compliance and procurement officers to organize huge volumes of supply chain data and due diligence evidence. Cons: On-the-ground experts are needed to check supply chain practices; DNA analysis and isotope testing are needed to verify data.
Information system/GPS, branding hammer, image analysis, and blockchain	Hammer branding combined with database and image processing. *"The OtmetkaID marking system stamps a globally unique code at the root end of each log, automatically creating the first link in a blockchain."*	From forest to mill	Otmetka otmetka.com OtmetkaID© allows verification of the geographical origin for each marked log. Currently developing automated tagging and tag reading technologies for New Zealand harvesting equipment and New Zealand supply chains.	Pros: Can be easily accessed, and information is up to date and in stage by stage. Cons: Set up is costly and time-consuming and requires regular data entry and updates.
Information system/Paper tag	A centralized repository of information about transactions between wood owners, its customers, carriers,	From forest to mill	Skogsbrukets Datacentral (SDC) in Sweden http://www.sdc.se/default.asp?id=1007&ptid An independent IT company set up by 50	Pros: Easy to access the information. Cons: Cost of setting up and keeping the information up to date.

Technology type	System	Supply chain stage	Product details	Advantages and limitations
	sawmill factories, and independent organizations that carry out measurement and determination of wood quality.		timber companies in Sweden that ensure record-keeping of agreements on timber, its measurement, and transportation.	

Table 11.
Summary of labelling technologies and their product details and advantages and limitations.

7. Case studies (Australia and International)

7.1 Illegal logging

7.1.1 Papua New Guinea (PNG)

7.1.1.1 Issue

Illegal logging in PNG was recorded as high as 70% of the total logged timber in 2006 causing major concerns for the PNG authorities [59].

7.1.1.2 System introduced

The PNG government has used a full-time third-party auditor to check the product information throughout the supply chain for many years. The product details audited include species, volume, and quality of raw products harvested and exported. The auditing system and process are outsourced to SGS PNG Limited are present in the country's exporting docks and actively track products leaving the port. The auditor uses barcode labels and portable data terminals to enhance the accuracy of data checked. The system also is designed with a backup offline and manual system in case there are issues with the labeling technology. The system in place has provided various benefits in identifying illegal logs and reducing the associated issues by:

Providing accurate information about the details and scale of products being exported from PNG. The increased profits have compensated for the cost associated with third-party auditing.

Providing better understanding of the industry stages and the influential factors in production and export stages. This has led to better communication between the PNG government agencies and forest industry.

Created historical accurate information about the country's production rate and exported log.

Transparency and clarity of supply chain and providing a verifiable audit history that can be used by industry stockholders.

Providing better information for training program development for forest industry and future industry planning.

7.1.2 Russia

7.1.2.1 Issue

Mass illegal and unregulated logging of Russian forests pushed the Amur tiger to the brink of extinction. Most of Russia's exported timber goes to China to supply its furniture and flooring industry.

7.1.2.2 System Introduced

In 2013, the Russian Federation introduced "The Development of Forestry 2013–2020", an 8-year plan to reduce illegal logging and increase profits from the timber sector which was underutilized. To ensure the plan was immediately implemented the criminal code was also updated in 2014 to include stricter penalties for illegal logging, transport, and sale.

Timber labeling, traceability, and monitoring system requirements were updated in the "Federal Law on Amendments to the Forest Code of the Russian Federation 2013" as part of The Development of Forestry 2013–2020. In 2015 the Russian government launched a new electronic system for recording timber-related information i.e. the Uniform State Automated Information System (EGAIS). All forest and timber organizations are required to submit information on the volume of logs harvested, labels used, and timber sold. Although all forests in Russia are State-owned, they are operated by private companies and organizations that are licensed. Valuable forest species are determined by the Russian Federation and the list is updated regularly. Below is a summary of the amendments made in 2013 tEWPs original document from 2006:

- The wood of valuable forest species, for example, oak, beech, and ash, is subject to mandatory marking and labeling by legal entities with procedure/specifics of markings yet to be developed.

- The information must be submitted to Uniform State Automated Information System (EGAIS) no later than one day before export. Similar systems for alcohol, chemicals, and medicines exist.

- Documentation accompanying the logs during transport should include the following information: exporter, consignee, carrier, species, volume, and assortment.

- All exported logs should also be accompanied by a transaction declaration that can be found within the EGAIS. The form should contain the following information: exporter, volume, species, assortment (such as sawn log grade, pulpwood grade, or firewood grade), information on the lease agreement, and information on the log purchase contract.

7.1.2.3 Benefits

Illegal logging of valuable forest species decreased by 37% during 2017–2018. However, species that are not labeled as valuable are not covered under EGAIS, which means illegal logging still exists. A proposal to introduce electronic tagging of all logs may not be economically feasible depending on the cost of the log chip. Chips are estimated to cost between USD 0.5–5 each and the least valuable logs come in at around USD10.37.

7.1.3 Austria (Schweighofer)

7.1.3.1 Issue

Austrian company Holzindustrie Schweighofer and 32 others were accused and prosecuted for running an illegal logging operation in Romania. The companies ignored laws relating to the amount of timber able to be harvested legally.

7.1.3.2 System introduced

After legal action was taken against Schweighofer they rebranded to HS Group (Holzindustrie Schweighofer Group) and worked on developing and employing an internally designed timber/log tracking system. The system developed was Timflow and allowed complete transparency and tracking of all log shipments from forest to mill. The system consisted of GPS trackers fitted to trucks and hand-held terminals (smartphones/tablets) given to the drivers. After a load of logs is placed onto the truck, the drivers use the handheld terminals to take photos from all sides of the trailer as well as a photo of the registration plates. The drivers then also register the transport data and any additional information into the software along with the photos. Once the truck begins its journey to the mill, the photos and information is uploaded to the GPS tracking route. The GPS software allows detection of even slight deviations from the approved route. Once the truck arrives at the mill, it is not allowed entry until the HS Group has verified the paperwork and information gathered by the GPS and handheld terminal. The photos taken when the truck was loaded, are then compared with the physical load on arrival to ensure the load has not been altered or disturbed in any way. HS group also verify the approved route with the GPS data from the truck to ensure no deviation has taken place. If any of these comparisons are flagged by the HS Grouptaken immediately taken aside, and further investigations take place. To ensure the driver's privacy is maintained the information is uploaded to a publicly accessible database to view 24 h later.

7.1.3.3 Benefits

The main benefit of a system like this is that the company is able to prove beyond doubt that the timber they are processing and manufacturing is sourced from a legal and sustainable forest. This is particularly important for a company like HS Group which has previously been prosecuted for illegal logging and may be under close scrutiny by authorities. Another advantage is the increased public knowledge of the efforts the company is taking to source only legally harvested logs.

7.1.4 Tokyo

7.1.4.1 Issue

The construction of several of Tokyo's Olympic stadiums used plywood boards as form wood for concrete, 87% of which were sourced from South-East Asian rainforests. It is well known that there are significant illegal logging operations in Asia but despite this, Japan's protocol for sustainability is not strict or clear. The policy has an inherent lack of due diligence by having no obligation for full traceability. As seen with inquiries in Australia, there is a probability the quality and strength of the plywood could be in question.

7.1.4.2 System introduced

In January 2019, a few months after the original report was released highlighting the use of timber that was not sustainably sourced, the Tokyo 2020 Olympic organizing committee reviewed the Wood Procurement Standards (WPS). They made two changes to the WPS, the first is that any timber products sourced from that point onward not be sourced from natural forests converted to plantations. Secondly, Japan is to collect more data on manufacturers before procuring from them and add recommendations for additional measures to reduce sustainability risk. However, because the construction of the majority of buildings had been completed before the changes to the WPS, the impact of using non-sustainable plywood may not be reversible. There was also a question about the implementation and enforcement of the new changes.

7.1.4.3 Benefits

Given the construction of the Olympic buildings was still underway when this review was conducted, no reports of the success of these changes to WPS have been reported. However, the lack of a solid sustainable timber sourcing policy has resulted in a severe critique of the Olympic organizing committee from environmental and forestry organizations worldwide. This has the potential to have a detrimental effect on public opinion and acceptance of the construction aspect of the Olympic games.

7.2 Compliance

7.2.1 Docklands Melbourne cladding fire

7.2.1.1 Issue

Noncompliant with Australian cladding combustibility regulations, cladding materials used in external of the Lacrosse Tower which was damaged severely by fire in 2014 which caused up to $40 million in damage.

7.2.1.2 Process followed

In 2017, the building owners received 5.7 million dollars in compensation for fire damage due to non-compliant fire design by the architect, failure in building permit by the certifying group, and failure of fire engineer to assess, recognize, and warn the construction company about the non-compliant cladding [32].

8. Conclusions and recommendations

The report investigates the need for a traceability system at various stages of the timber supply chain, issues related to illegal logging globally and in Australia, and compliance requirements for domestic timber products and imported products. This review focuses on potential challenges that illegal logging and non-compliant timber products could have on domestic, export, and import markets. A list of technologies and systems that have been used previously for tracing timber throughout the supply chain has been presented. Other technologies available and their potential to be used in tracing timber products were also discussed. Advantages and limitations of these technologies at different stages of the timber supply chain, including cost, was listed and compared.

Some case studies and examples of current systems used to trace timber from plantation through to the end-user around the world were also included. A list of failures and the scale of damage in cases where timber was illegally logged and non-compliant products used in the building was discussed.

Overall, from the review conducted, it can be concluded that depending on the supply, for example, stage, operation, and cost of material, different types of tracing technologies need to be implemented. This can include the use of cheaper and easier-to-implement options at the beginning of the supply chain. As the value of the product increases, the flexibility to use more advanced technologies will increase. However, a detailed and systematic global data management system is required to link all data collected through different means at each stage of the timber supply chain.

In Australia, considering that the majority of the forests operate under a sustainable protocol and follow a certifiable procedure to comply with the chain of custody, illegal logging may not be a major issue. However, the potential detrimental effects on wildlife and the environment due to illegal logging need to be investigated and considered on a case-by-case basis from both resource loss and economic points of view. The illegal logging issue will be a major challenge for imports to Australia from parts of the world where logging is not legally certified. This can be addressed by having a two-way traceability system with specific information and documentation for each category of timber product.

The compliance with national and international standards and traceability requirements for domestic products as well as imported products are additional issues and challenges that the timber industry faces. The traceability system will address this aspect by requiring details for each product at every stage of the supply chain provided by the producer, manufacturer, or supplier.

Author details

Maryam Shirmohammadi
Queensland Department of Agriculture and Fisheries, Brisbane, Australia

*Address all correspondence to: maryam.shirmohammadi@daf.qld.gov.au

IntechOpen

© 2022 The Author(s). Licensee IntechOpen. This chapter is distributed under the terms of the Creative Commons Attribution License (http://creativecommons.org/licenses/by/3.0), which permits unrestricted use, distribution, and reproduction in any medium, provided the original work is properly cited. (cc) BY

References

[1] Forest and Wood Products in Industries 2021, Australian Industry and Skills Committee

[2] Munro T. Tracking timber in the supply chain—Is it possible? In: Matthews Intelligent Identification. 2014

[3] Downham R, Gavran M. Australian Plantation Statistics 2020 Update. Canberra: W.a.E.-A. Department of Agriculture; 2020

[4] Slezak M, VicForests' logging that kills gliders done so intensively 'it may have breached law', in ABC. 2018, National Environment, Science and Technology. https://www.abc.net.au/news/2018-07-31/vicforests-greater-glider-logging-may-have-breached-law-claim/10052612

[5] Timms, M.S.A.P., Australia's endangered forests are being 'stolen' and sold in hardware and office stores, in ABC. 2018, ABC NEWS: https://www.abc.net.au/news/2018-11-21/victorian-forests-appear-to-have-been-logged-illegally/10496424

[6] Service P.C. Papua New Guinea Import & Export Customs Tariff Schedule. P.C. Service; 2017

[7] Schloenhardt A, Schloenhardt A. The Illegal Trade in Timber and Timber Products in the Asia-Pacific Region. Canberra: Australian Institute of Criminology; 2008

[8] Apthorp B. Update on Russian Log Export Tax. Friday Offcuts 2011 [cited 2021 25-06]; Available from: https://fridayoffcuts.com/dsp_article.cfm?id=412&aid=4024. [Accessed: June 25, 2021]

[9] Arts B, Heukels B, Turnhout E. Tracing timber legality in practice: The case of Ghana and the EU. Forest Policy and Economics. 2021;**130**:102532

[10] Australia's Forest Policies—Importers W.a.t.E. Australian Government—Department of Agriculture. Australia's endangered forests are being 'stolen' and sold in hardware and office stores - ABC News. 2019. Available from: https://www.agriculture.gov.au/forestry/policies/illegal-logging/importers#:~:text=It%20is%20a%20criminal%20offence,penalties%20and%20even%20prison%20time

[11] Tzoulis I, Andreopoulou Z. Emerging traceability technologies as a tool for quality wood trade. Procedia Technology. 2013;**8**:606-611

[12] (EWPAA), E.W.P.A.o.A., EWPAA Submission to 44th parliament inquiry into non-conforming building products. Engineered Wood Products Association of Australasia (EWPAA). 2015. Available from: https://ewp.asn.au/ewpaa-says-substandard-imports-non-conforming-products-risk-australian-lives/

[13] Bontempo L et al. Traceability along the production chain of Italian tomato products on the basis of stable isotopes and mineral composition. Rapid Communications in Mass Spectrometry. 2011;**25**(7):899-909 %@ 0951-4198

[14] Blarel B. The real costs of illegal logging, fishing and wildlife trade: $1 trillion–$2 trillion per year, in World Bank Blogs. 2019, Voices. Available from: https://blogs.worldbank.org/voices/real-costs-illegal-logging-fishing-and-wildlife-trade-1-trillion-2-trillion-year

[15] Illegal logging in Australia—Are you buying into it? In: Wilderness Society | Illegal logging in Australia - are you

buying. 2020. Available from: https://www.wilderness.org.au/news-events/are-you-printing-on-illegally-produced-paper

[16] ABARES. Australian Forest and Wood Products Statistics, September and December Quarters 2018. Canberra: A.B.o.A.a.R.E.a. Sciences; 2019. pp. 15-18

[17] Government of Western Australia, DoJ. Building Services (Complaint Resolution and Administration) Act. Western Australian Legislation Department of Mines, Industry Regulation and Safety. 2016

[18] Palaia L. Structural failure analysis of timber floors and roofs in ancient buildings at Valencia (Spain). In: International Conference on Mechanical Behaviour and Failures of the Timber Structures. Florence Venice: Citeseer; 2007

[19] Jiri Brozovsky, Jiri Brozovsky, Jr., Jiri Zach. An assessment of the condition of timber structures. In: 9th International Conference on NDT of Art. 2008. Jerusalem, Israel. Available from: https://www.ndt.net/search/docs.php3?MainSource=65

[20] Shirmohammadi M, Leggate W, Redman A. Effects of moisture ingress and egress on the performance and service life of mass timber products in buildings: A review. Construction and Building Materials. 2021;**290**: 123176

[21] China's Import and Exports. 2019 [cited 2021 06/07]; Available from: https://asialinkbusiness.com.au/china/getting-started-in-china/chinas-imports-and-exports?doNothing=1https://asialinkbusiness.com.au/china/getting-started-in-china/chinas-imports-and-exports?doNothing=1. [Accessed: July 6, 2021]

[22] Sullivan K. Victorian timber log exports blocked from entering China due to bark beetle. In: ABC. ABC NEWS; 2020

[23] About EWPAA - Who We Are. [cited 2021 24/06]; Available from: https://ewp.asn.au/about-ewpaa/who-we-are/

[24] Australia, S. Chain of Custody for Forest Products. Australia: Australian Forestry Standard Limited; 2018

[25] Australia S. Chain of Custody for Forest Products. Australia: Australian Forestry Standard Limited; 2014

[26] PEFC. Chain of Custody of Forest and Tree Based Products—Requirements. Geneva: PEFC; 2020

[27] Standard AF. Revised Australian Standard Chain of Custody for forest products published. Architecture and Design: Architecture and Design. 2014. Available from: https://www.architectureanddesign.com.au/suppliers/australian-forestry-standard/revised-australian-standard-chain-of-custody-for-f. [Accessed: June 2, 2021]

[28] Export Control Act 2020—Export Control (Wood and Woodchips) Rules 2021 [F2021L00318]—Replacement explanatory statement, W.a.t.E. Department of Agriculture, Editor. 2020, Australian Government. Available from: https://parlinfo.aph.gov.au/parlInfo/search/display/display.w3p;query=Id%3A%22publications%2Ftabledpapers%2Fdbc6b239-d17f-4028-acc1-e39fe5f57383%22;src1=sm1

[29] Smith DA, Stratton JE. Food preservation, safety and shelf life extension. Food Processing Entrepreneurs Series. In: Food & Nutrition Preservation. NebGuide: University of Nebraska-Lincoln

Extension. 2007. Available from: http://ianrpubs.unl.edu/live/g181, 2007. 6.

[30] Austraia 2015 import partner share. 2015: world integrated trade solutions

[31] R.b.t.A.B.o.A.a.R.E.a. Sciences. Australian Forest and Wood Products Statistics September and December Quarters 2017. Australian Government, Department of Agriculture, Fisheries and Forestry; 2018

[32] Dunstan J. Lacrosse apartment owners awarded $5.7 million in damages after flammable cladding blaze, in ABC. 2019, ABC News. Available from: https://www.abc.net.au/news/2019-02-28/lacrosse-apartment-owners-win-5.7-million-cladding-fire-damages/10857060

[33] Power J. Combustible cladding—A tale of regulatory failure. Australian Hardware Journal. 2014

[34] Pailhoriès H et al. Oak in hospitals, the worst enemy of *Staphylococcus aureus*? Infection Control & Hospital Epidemiology. 2017;**38**(3):382-384

[35] Negro F, Cremonini C, Zanuttini R. CE marking of structural timber: the European standardization framework and its effects on Italian manufacturers. Drvna Industrija. 2013;**64**(1):55-62

[36] Netherlands, G.o.t. What is a Declaration of Performance for construction products? [cited 2021 06/7]; Available from: https://www.government.nl/topics/construction-products/question-and-answer/what-is-a-declaration-of-performance-for-construction-products#:~:text=A%20Declaration%20of%20Performance%20(DoP,required%20to%20have%20a%20DoP

[37] Dykstra DP et al. Technologies for Wood Tracking: Verifying and Monitoring the Chain of Custody and Legal Compliance in the Timber Industry. Washington, DC: World Bank; 2002

[38] Weighbridges N. All About Weighbridges in Australia. [cited 2021, 18/06]. Available from: https://nationalweighbridges.com.au/all-about-weighbridges-in-australia/.

[39] Business TGLo. GS1 Global Traceability Standard. GS1 AISBL. 2017. p. 58

[40] Ng CH et al. A geographical traceability system for Merbau (Intsia palembanica Miq.), an important timber species from peninsular Malaysia. Forensic Science International: Genetics. 2020;**44**:102188

[41] Gurau L et al. Image processing method as a supporting tool for wood species identification. Wood and fiber Science. 2013;**45**(3):303-313

[42] Hwang S-W, Sugiyama J. Computer vision-based wood identification and its expansion and contribution potentials in wood science: A review. Plant Methods. 2021;**17**(1):1-21

[43] Dormontt EE et al. Forensic timber identification: It's time to integrate disciplines to combat illegal logging. Biological Conservation. 2015;**191**:790-798

[44] Schmitz N et al. The Timber Tracking Tool Infogram. Overview of Wood Identification Methods' Capacity. Vol. 10. Joensuu, Finland: Global Timber Tracking Network, GTTN Secretariat, European Forest Institute and Thünen Institute; 2019

[45] Lowe AJ et al. Opportunities for improved transparency in the timber

trade through scientific verification. BioScience. 2016;**66**(11):990-998

[46] Cody RB, John Dane A. Direct analysis in real-time ion source. Encyclopedia of Analytical Chemistry: Applications, Theory and Instrumentation. 2006;**81**(3): 1101-1107

[47] Cody RB, Laramée JA, Durst HD. Versatile new ion source for the analysis of materials in open air under ambient conditions. Analytical Chemistry. 2005; **77**(8):2297-2302 %@ 0003-2700

[48] Musah RA et al. A high throughput ambient mass spectrometric approach to species identification and classification from chemical fingerprint signatures. Scientific Reports. 2015;**5**(1):1-16 %@ 2045-2322

[49] Kagawa A, Leavitt SW. Stable carbon isotopes of tree rings as a tool to pinpoint the geographic origin of timber. Journal of Wood Science. 2010;**56**(3): 175-183 %@ 1611-4663

[50] Förstel H et al. Fighting illegal logging through the introduction of a combination of the isotope method for identifying the origins of timber and DNA analysis for differentiation of tree species. In: Deutsche Bundesstiftung Umwelt: Universitat Hamburg. 2011. p. 102

[51] Horacek M, Jakusch M, Krehan H. Control of origin of larch wood: discrimination between European (Austrian) and Siberian origin by stable isotope analysis. Rapid Communications in Mass Spectrometry: An International Journal Devoted to the Rapid Dissemination of Up-to-the-Minute Research in Mass Spectrometry. 2009;**23**(23):3688-3692 %@ 0951-4198

[52] Camin F et al. Characterisation of authentic Italian extra-virgin olive oils by stable isotope ratios of C, O and H and mineral composition. Food Chemistry. 2010;**118**(4):901-909 %@ 0308-8146

[53] Sorvik B. The Woodpecker system for coded log stamping in mechanized harvesting systems. Phnom Penh, Cambodia. 2002

[54] Uusijärvi R. European Lineset Project—Combining Log Stamping with Trasponders for Wood Product Tracing. Stockholm, Sweden: Swedish Institute for Wood Technology Research. 2002

[55] Forsythe P, Carey B. Application of RFID in the prefabricated timber industry. In: Australasian Universities Building Education Association Conference 2017. EPiC Education Science. 2017

[56] Wessel R. University in Munich Develops RFID-Enabled Log Harvesting-An RFID-enabled Harvester Staples Tags into Logs Automatically to Help Track Timber Moving Through the Processing Line. RFID Journal. 2006. Available from: https://www.rfidjournal.com/university-in-munich-develops-rfid-enabled-log-harvesting

[57] Figorilli S et al. A blockchain implementation prototype for the electronic open source traceability of wood along the whole supply chain. Sensors. 2018;**18**(9):3133

[58] Dykstra DP et al. Technologies for wood tracking: verifying and monitoring the chain of custody and legal compliance in the timber industry. R.G.o.C. Department of Forestry and Wildlife; 2002

[59] Milling A et al. Survival of bacteria on wood and plastic particles: Dependence on wood species and environmental conditions. Holzforschung. 2005;**59**(1):72-81

Chapter 6

Potential, Challenges, and Application for Wood–Plastic Composite Fabricated with Several Additives

Amit Prem Khare, Nidhi Dwivedi and Shamsul Haq

Abstract

The expeditious transformation of the atmosphere and economy is pushing researchers from various fields to do more by using a lesser amount of resources. Especially, in the field of forest-based resources, such as the utilization of wood resources for different utility purposes in wood industries. It is meant to say that, the wood estate should be used as an efficient means or expedient. It is also the necessity of world atmosphere, according to the point of view ecosystem or global warming condition. Thus, we will need to sustainably use forest-based resources as major sources of wood materials and reuse the underutilized woods and waste wood in any form. Further, it will require the reuse of the underutilized wood material and present wood waste material in an environment with the assistance of the latest and newer growing technology. In general, for improving the performance of wood-based materials, additives may be used for performing different functions, such as lubricants, pigments, colorants, anti-microbial agents, antioxidants, UV stabilizers, fire retardants agents, coupling agents, or stabilizers, in the wood industry.

Keywords: WPC (wood–plastic composites), MOE (modulus of elasticity), MOR (modulus of rupture), MAPP (maleic anhydride poly-propylene), NFC (natural fiber composites), RPP (recycled polypropylene), LDPE (low-density polyethylene)

1. Introduction

Most wood items incorporate added substances. They might be additives to safeguard the wood opposition natural debasement or opposition fire, coatings for insurance or to offer the wood a better stylish look, other than wood materials to work on the exhibition of the item and conquer shortcomings in the wood material, or plastics in blends with wood deposits to make new kinds of wood–plastic composites. The worldwide wood manufacturer is, for instance, the biggest client of adhesives; around 80% of all timber and timber-based items include some type of holding and 70% of the total quantity of adhesives created are consumed in the carpentry business. Wood can consequently be seen as a composite containing lumber-based materials got together with various materials to shape the complete material. A model is a compressed wood, in which facades are gotten together with glue to frame a level board. Different sorts of wood composites incorporate different board items, primary composite lumber, and furniture and joinery parts, all counting some type of holding with adhesives. This present circumstance clearly impacts the manner by which we ought to connect with wood items and their natural influences. This part gives a cutting edge and shows that various added substances are now being utilized in wood items. These data are fundamental for additional concentrates on the impact, that is, these added substances have on the assistance life and ecological viewpoints, and the constraints which they might force on the use again, updating of wood items.

Wood and wood-based composites are key designing materials that can be effectively planned and fabricated with foreordained double-dealing properties, making them reasonable for a wide scope of utilizations and end utilizes. Outstandingly, wood-based composites can be designed to meet explicit execution pre-requisites, which make them a practical answer for lessening the utilization of strong wood. The logical objective of this distribution is to give the peruse of new data on late practices in pressed wood research. Indeed, pressed wood is certainly back. Toward the finish of the twentieth hundred years and the start of the twenty-first hundred years, there was a reasonable decrease in pressed wood research. Be that as it may, its unforeseen expansion underway and the development of its application likewise caused an expansion in research work [1]. Ecological sources of info can work fair and square of development by interconnecting them with customary sources of info in regards to the properties of materials and processes as a vital eco-plan system. High-level designed polymer composites are expected to meet the different necessities of clients for elite execution auto, development, and items that all the while expanding the supportability of woodland assets. In the ongoing work, wood polymer composites (WPCs) are examined to advance long-haul asset manageability and to decline ecological effects compared with those of existing items. A progression of polypropylene wood–fiber composite materials having 20, 30, 40, and 50 wt% of wood filaments were arranged utilizing a twin-screw extruder and infusion shaping machine. Tractable and flexural properties the not entirely set in stone. Polypropylene (PP), as a lattice utilized in this study, is a thermoplastic material, which is recyclable. Reasonableness of the pre-arranged composites as an economical item is examined [2, 3] (**Figure 1**).

Wood–plastic composite (WPC) is emerging in the market. A portion of the great qualities of this material is biodegradability, recyclability, low assembling cost, high compound resistivity, high solidarity to weight extent, imperviousness to fire, and high firmness to weight extent. WPC is the better alternative for virgin wood and plastics, therefore, finds application in various fields, such as aircraft, automobile industry, electrical, sports, wrapping, and furniture. Wood–plastic composite is an eco-friendly material that also reduces the exhaustion of petroleum resources and also reduces the emission of CO_2 [4].

1.1 Challenges for improved or new innovations can be distinguished along the entire wood supply and cycle chain

1.1.1 Wood supply

Woodland material is being crushed between developing requirements (counting quickly, developing interest for timber as a power transporter) and natural limitations. This will open the unrefined substance distribution to semi-regular backwoods,

Figure 1.
Application of wood waste product [2].

timberland estates, agroforestry, and farming assets and new preparation ideas for wood assets. This new unrefined substance range, including the rising utilization of reused material, will immensely affect wood innovation and material plan also.

1.1.2 Timber manufacture

Wood is an exceptionally incorporated and streamlined unrefined substance from the earth with load-bearing capacities as one of the principal functionalities. Involving wood as lumber in development comes close to the normal highlights of wood; however, man actually can work on the technician execution of wood by legitimate evaluating and barring regular example and developing designed material designs. Material and building part models and recreation will turn into a significant device to comprehend and work on the materials and parts (**Figure 2**).

1.1.3 Material engineering

Designed wood composite materials and designs on every single progressive level (from nano to macrostructures) are as of now a fundamental area of innovation examination and will turn out to be significantly more significant to make wood materials more cutthroat. A solid spotlight on assets and environmentally friendly materials, including unrefined components from any sustainable sources, will lead us to "Green Composites" as visualized.

1.1.4 Wood attractiveness

Design and composition including the different extractives make an incomparable exterior of wood, particularly with the different hardwoods. Tragically the shade of

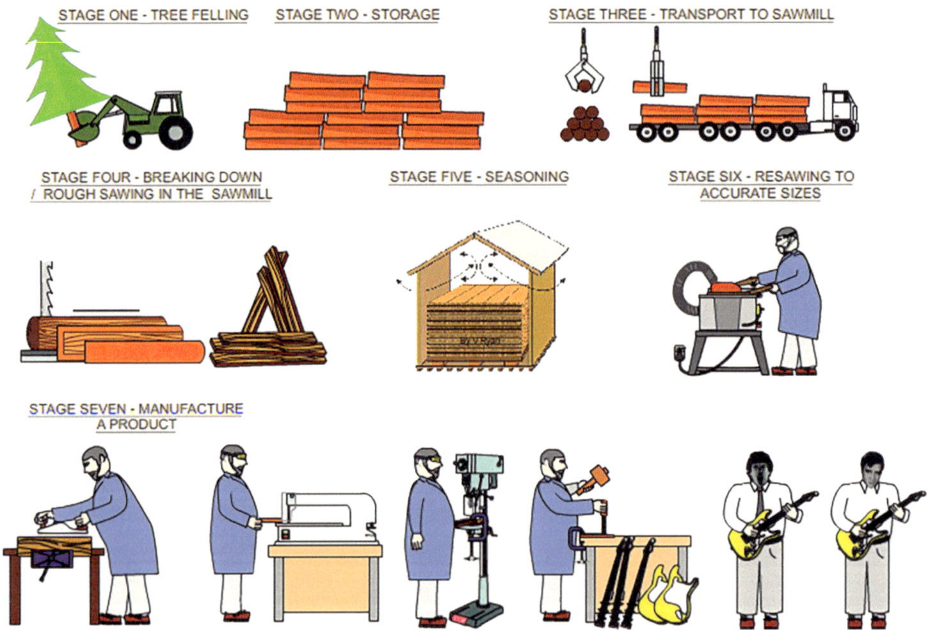

Figure 2.
Processing natural wood from logging to manufacturing a product [5].

wood is not ultraviolet is a fundamental test to forestall blurring and staining to a further effective and reasonable utilization of wood surface (facade and strong wood) in interior and exterior application in contest with specialized surface designs.

1.1.5 Wood adjustment

Much accentuation has been placed on wood change somewhat recently to make it more tough and steady and so on. Creating new processes in the wood surface will be important to make another wood execution, which is prepared to support brilliant materials.

1.1.6 Fractionizing wood

Different mechanical deterioration and compound decay processes are deeply grounded to separate and fractionize the natural substance of wood and to re-organize and yet again engineer it into stuck parts, wood boards, paper sheets, and so forth, nonetheless, improved and totally new cycles of crumbling must be conceived.

1.1.7 Making and processing

Wood handling has worked on a ton somewhat recently (e.g., high limit sawmills, consistent presses for wood boards, and superior execution wood machining), yet new cycle advances, fabricating ideas (mass customization, fitting of items, and so on) must be created. Asset and eco-proficient cycles must be conceived in wood enterprises through improved and new cycle examination and creating the executive frameworks, which thus are important for an idea of information-based creation.

1.1.8 Wood refinery

Thermo-synthetic cycles, and progressively, biotechnology are utilized to separate lignocellulosic raw material to their structure blocks being compound and power industry. The expressions "incorporated biomass innovations" and "wood biorefinery" turned into catchphrases inside the rise of another modern area of renewable-based advancements. Today we are in a maze of various; however, aggressive ways to deal with unfastening lignocelluloses to their structure impedes so they can be utilized for additional cycles. Despite the fact that pieces of that idea now exist, a broad monetary advancement is yet absent.

Figure 3.
Recycling of wood waste [6].

1.1.9 Recycling

Indeed, even as most timber items are considered as standard and big items, expanded utilization of wood develops a colossal optional feedstock to be utilized as a material as well as an energy transporter. The material, modern, and building plans must be coordinated to an upcoming obliterating of utilized structures and the recuperation of wood. Wood innovation turns into a significant job in the idea of a cascading utilization of wood (**Figure 3**).

1.1.10 Technology education

Wood innovation as a scholastic discipline must be additionally evolved (and examined inside the wood science and innovation local area) enveloped by thorough scholarly educational programs to give a significant innovation schooling to the understudies, which needs to make the scholarly spine of the upcoming timberland-based ventures and a knowledge-based society too [7].

2. Role of additives in the wood industry

2.1 Zinc Stearate

It was observed that the mechanical and physical properties were improved using lubricant (ZnSt) in the WPC composition. It was added in a ratio of 0–3% [8]. Structure TRO16 acts as a coupling agent, anti-microbial agent (1RGAGUARD F 3510) as a fungicide, ultraviolet filter casting (TINUVIN1235), blue pigment (irgalite) were used as an additive in the manufacturing of WPC panels. In this concentration, a portion of the significant properties is tentatively made WPC is not entirely set in stone. Example having 60 and 80% molecule and fiber of radiata pine (Pinus radiata) were blended in with polypropylene (plastic) and four various added substances, to be specific Structure TR 016 which is coupling agent, CIBA anti-microbial agent (IRGAGUARD F3510) as fungicide, UV filter coating (TINUVIN 123S), blue pigment (irgalite), and their blends. Given the underlying finding of this work, static twisting properties of the examples upgraded as above synthetics were added into both molecule- and fiber-based samples. Thickness swelling was likewise improved with having added substances on the boards. Micrographs taken on SEM uncovered that coupling agent and pigment brought about the same combination of wood and plastic together. Twin surface harshness boundaries average roughness (Ra) and maximum roughness (Rmax) used to assess surface qualities of the tests showed that molecule-based samples had more rough surface qualities than those of fiber-based ones. No critical impact of synthetics included the samples was found on surface roughness upsides of the samples made from molecule and fiber of radiate pine [9]. Two different additives were added, that is, glycerol acts as a plasticizer and MAPP acts as a compatibilizer to improve the mechanical and thermal properties of the composites [10]. The aim was to examine the impacts of material structures on the mechanical properties of WPC made by injection molding. Utilizing a proportion of wood floor, plastic, MAPP, zinc stearate of 47:47:3:3, the modulus of rupture (MOR), and tensile strength of WPC made with LDPE. Notwithstanding, differentiating discoveries were gotten when the polymer grid was ABS (acrylonitrile-butadiene-styrene). In contrast with the mechanical properties of recycled polypropylene itself, the modulus of rupture increased furthermore, the tensile strength decreased for WPCs produced with RPP [11]. Wood–plastic composite (WPC) is a naturally progressive approach to consolidate reused plastics and wood floors. The composite regularly comprises four significant components: wood flour, thermoplastics, coupling agents, and lubricant. The mechanical and physical properties of WPC exceptionally rely upon the material plane, and the ideal material structure is a fundamental subject of momentum research. This concentrate on exploring the impacts of changing material arrangements on the mechanical and physical properties of WPC. The concentration on WPC was expelled shaping WPC made utilizing recycled polypropylene (RPP) plastics and wood floor. The review assessed four boundaries: (a) wood floor particle size, (b) coupling agent dosage, (c) oil content, and (d) the mass proportion of wood and RPPs. The outcomes showed that utilizing better wood loor can work on the controlled and strength of WPC, and lessen the enlarging because of water adsorption. The ideal grouping of the lubricant and coupling agent in WPC were both 3%. Adding the legitimate measure of coupling agent can work on the mechanical properties and essentially diminish the swelling, however, over-dosing the oil fundamentally increases swelling and decreases all the mechanical properties of the WPCs. Keeping up with wood content at half or less delivered the best mechanical properties, what's more, wood content above around half brought about a decrease in all mechanical and physical properties of WPCs. The review exhibited the connection between water absorption to thickness swelling. Decrease in thickness swelling and water absorption was encountered (**Figure 4**) [9].

Figure 4.
Replacement of glass by wood [12].

2.2 Biocides

Wood impregnation is carried out in order to preserve WPC from biological decay like resistance to rot and dipping plants, protection against mold and blue stain fungi, and resistance toward destructive organisms. Some of the dipping agents used are water-soluble fluoride agents and phenolic agents, and copper sulfate solution also used in parts for impregnating railway sleeper coaches. Impregnation with creosote in the future will become a somewhat common impregnation method. Impregnation salt that contained some arsenic, zinc, and chromium was also used in open tank plants. In early 1970, oil soluble protective agent was used for the impregnation of window frames. Open container impregnation is utilized for the impregnation of telephone poles. The wood is lowered into a tub with a hermetically sealed cover. Steam is driven into the tub and after 8–12 hours, the wood is warmed. After this warming, a chilly impregnation arrangement is taken care of into the tub and the cooling prompts an under pressure, because of which the arrangement is sucked into the wood. This piece of cycle takes 30–35 hours. The boliden impregnation salt is typically utilized in this strategy. Different impregnation methods that were used for WPC are Fuel-cell/ Bethell method and the Lawry method. In pressure impregnation, creosote is used as the main agent.

2.3 Fire retardants

Inorganic salts are mainly used as a fire retardant to protect WPC products against fire so that they cannot catch fire easily. Fire retardants impact the scorching rate, ignitability, fire speed, smoke improvement, and mechanical properties. Some fire retardants affect the properties of the wood, such as mechanical strength, shade, and paint ability. Inorganic salts are used as fire retardants and they contain ammonium sulfate, zinc chloride, boric acid, mono ammonium phosphate, etc.

Flame retardants are classified as intumescent and non-intumescent substances. The Intumescent formulation includes a char former, blowing agent, and

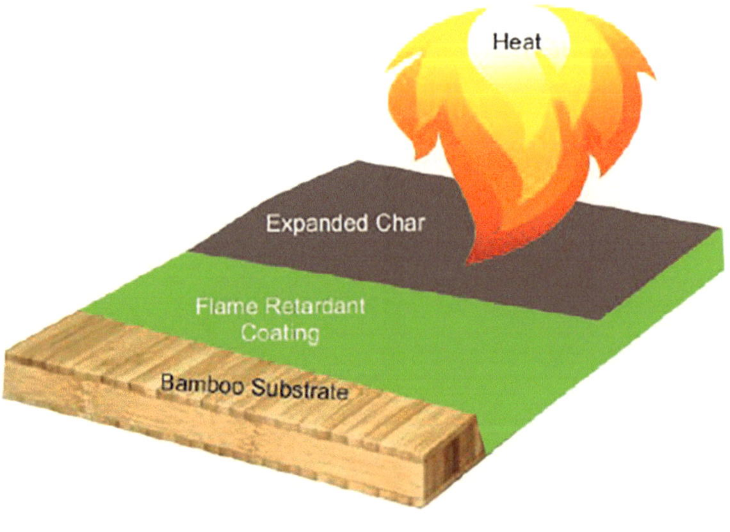

Figure 5.
Schematic diagram of fire protection by IFRC [14].

dehydrating agent. The Non-intumescent coating includes formulation of water-soluble salts, such as diammonium phosphate, ammonium, and borax [13]. The fire retardancy conduct of wood–polypropylene composites containing different fire retardants, such as ammonium polyphosphate (APP), zinc borate, and melamine, has been examined with the calorimetry procedure. The impact of ammonium polyphosphate (APP) in blend with graphite has been likewise examined with a calorimeter test. The fire properties estimated in the cone calorimeter are discussed, including the total heat release, heat release rate (HRR), ignition time, effective heat of combustion, smoke production, specific extinction area, and mass loss rate. The consequences of the review show that zinc borate decreases the heat release rate (HRR) productively. Based on the review, it is apparent that melamine has next to no impact on the combustibility of a wood–plastic composite, however, it lessens smoke formation. APP, utilized alone, has increased smoke creation altogether, whereas the development of smoke, as well as other fire properties, have been altogether improved when both ammonium polyphosphate (APP) and graphite have been added to the composite (**Figure 5**) [15].

2.4 Thermal modification

Thermally treated wood is used in order to improve resistance against fungi and insects, mechanical properties, dimensional stability, and also properties such as odor, color, coating performance, and gluability. Thermal treatment of wood is done in order to improve resistance to biological degradation and dimensional stability [13]. The effect of steam exploded (SE) wood floor added to wood–plastic composite was inspected utilizing wood such as Japanese cedar, red meranti, and beech, and three sorts of thermoplastic polymer: polyvinyl chloride, polymethyl methacrylate, and polystyrene. An increase of steam exploded wood floor increased the water resistance and fracture strength of the composite board to a degree subject to the polymer species and the structure of wood polymer composite. In any case, water resistance diminished with the rising extent of steam exploded wood when red meranti was added to the mixture. Effects of the steam-treated wood species on the properties of resulting board were small. An increased dampness content of steam exploded wood floor expanded the variety of board execution [16].

2.5 Surface treatment

Surface treatment of wood is carried out using paints and lacquers or varnishes in order to protect the surface and to look decorative. The main components of a coating include pigments, binders, fillers, solvents, and additives. The binder combines the pigment particles to each other and also to the wood as a protective shield. Typical binder includes alkyd resins, nitrocellulose, acrylates, amino resins, and polyester resins. With the addition of solvents, the coating has a viscosity so that it can be applied to the wood easily. Common solvents are white spirit, water, turpentine, and alcohol. Fillers are used to modify the gloss of the coating, the color strength, and the extent to which the coating covers the substance. Additives in the coating may include alcohols or glycerol, fungicides, in order to prevent mold growth, accelerate the drying process, make the color drip free, improve adhesion, and to regulate certain properties of the finish such as consistency, gloss, flow, wetting, sand ability, and blister prevention [13]. Additives, such as dolomite, lingo sulphonate, potato floor and peel, starches, and some motor and vegetable oil are used as additives for wood pallet production.

Additives used act as a lubricant and they decrease energy consumption and increase the production rate. Starch additives minimize the final moisture content more than lingo sulphonate additives. Additives such as corn starch, motor oil, urea, sodium carbonate, dolomite, and vegetable oil decrease the wood pallet particle density. All types of starch increase the mechanical durability of wood pallets. Ligno sulphonate increases SOx emission. Vegetable oil and motor oil when used as additives increase the calorific value of wood pallets. Dolomite additives increase ash formation. Corn starch and dolomite additive increase carbon emission [17].

2.6 Fillers

Natural fibers composites (NFCs) are an emerging material that proved to have good sustainability credentials. Following the principles of recent research in material and design field, it was suggested that an existing low-esteem image of NFCs can be greatly enhanced by modifying sensorial aspects, form, and associated processing [18]. Wood from two assortments of insect-killed trees was used to create wood–plastic composites. Lodgepole pine and loblolly pine creepy crawly killed trees were de-fibrated thermo-mechanically into fiber. Fiber also, sawdust delivered from the trees were altered with potassium methyl siliconate (PMS) and injection molded into plastic composites. Alteration of fiber and sawdust with PMS worked on the similarity between ethylene plastic and lignocellulosic materials in the composites, bringing about decreased water absorption, increased layered dependability, and increased resilience to morphological varieties in the fiber and sawdust. Fiber-to-sawdust proportion also, size of sawdust particles impacted the time expected for immersion with water, as well as dimensional stability [19].

2.7 Coupling agents

Wood fiber built-up plastic composites at fiber content half by weight have been prepared. Various sorts of timber strands (softwood fiber, hardwood fiber, wood chips, and long wood fiber) were treated with a coupling agent (MAH-PP) to build the interfacial grip with the framework to work on the scattering of the particles and to diminish the water absorption properties of the composite. The current review examined the flexural, tensile, impact, and Charpy properties of wood fiber built up polypropylene composites as a component of coupling agent and fiber. From the outcomes, it was seen that wood chips polypropylene composites showed better elastic and flexural properties relative to the other wood–PP composites with an increase of 5% of MAH-PP, which is around 65% by weight and half for elasticity and flexural strength individually. Hardwood fiber and polypropylene composites showed improved effect trademark values relative to other wood–plastic composites with an increase of 5% of MAH-PP and damping index decreased to 60%. Charpy impact strength likewise increased up to 60% with the increase of 5% of MAH-PP for long wood fiber. Water retention and scanning electron microscopy of the composites are more over-explored [20]. There are a number of organizations creating wood–plastic composite for underlying applications. In any case, wood–plastic composite (WPC) requires addressing two significant limitations: strategy and detailing before their plan esteem for a primary application not set in stone. The study focused on tackling the two significant imperatives by utilizing the injection molding method to create WPC and utilizing different business accessible coupling agents at various levels to create WPC. The impact of wood-to-plastic proportion was likewise assessed on WPC delivered, utilizing the coupling agents that gave the most noteworthy bending properties. Commercial polypropylene wood floor and coupling agents were premixed in a mixer for 30 minutes before the extrusion process at a temperature of 190°C utilizing a 110 mm co-rotating twin-screw extruder. The WPC sheets with a size of 150 × 150 × 3mm were then formed by a 40-ton press molding machine. From the outcome, WPC created from coupling agents Exxelor PO 1020 at 4% fundamentally performed better in bending. Further concentrate on the impact of Exxelor PO 1020 rate and the wood-to-plastic proportion shows that, WPC with 65% wood floor performed altogether preferable in modulus of rupture (MOR) and modulus of elasticity (MOE) over another sort of wood–plastic composites. WPC with 60% wood floor had fundamentally lower water absorption and thickness swelling contrasted with those 65 and 70% wood floor WPC. Decisively, WPC with 65% wood floor is the ideal substance to deliver from the injection molding technique. A higher amount of coupling agent utilized in WPC formation gave higher bending properties [21]. The present study focused on the surface nature of wood-based materials used to produce furniture in Singapore. Different sorts of monetarily delivered composite boards, including particleboard, medium thickness fiberboard (MDF), and pressed wood notwithstanding 10 unique strong wood species that are generally utilized in furniture creation, were considered for the analyses. A pointer-type profilometer and 3D picture analyzer were utilized to decide the surface roughness of the samples. Medium thickness fiberboard (MDF) tests came about in the smoothest surface with an across the average roughness (Ra) value of 5.07μm, while comparing an incentive for pressed wood samples was 8.09 μm among the composite board tests. On account of strong wood tests, estimations brought and across the sand mark from the outer layer of the samples estimated by the pointer type profile meter, balau had the roughest surface with an average roughness (Ra) value of 9.85 μm across the sand mark followed by beech and pecan. Pine specimens alongside cherry, ash, and nyatoh brought about moderately smooth surface qualities. The relationship between estimations taken by two unique techniques, to be stylus and 3D scanning, showed a decent concurrence with one another. Given the discoveries in this work apparently, both techniques can be effectively used to assess and to get objective mathematical qualities on the surface nature of these examples so that such introductory information can be utilized as a quality control instrument to have a more powerful further assembling steps in furniture creation [22]. The present study examined the impacts of wood fiber content, coupling agent content, and wood fiber type on the mechanical properties of wood–plastic composites (WPC). This study embraced a reaction surface procedure of a 20-run optimal design for these three elements. The composite's modulus of elasticity was essentially impacted by wood fiber content, wood fiber type and ductile pressure at break relied upon wood fiber content, wood fiber type, and coupling agent content, though resist break was essentially impacted by wood fiber content and coupling agent content, yet not essentially impacted by wood fiber type [23]. The impact of maleic anhydride joined styrene-ethylene-butylene-styrene block copolymer (SEBS-g-MAH), and *in situ* joining MAHon dynamic mechanical and mechanical properties of wood–plastic composites were examined. Reused plastic like high-density polyethylene (HDPE), polypropylene (PP), and polystyrene (PS), were blended in with wood floor in a high-speed blender and afterward expelled by a twin screw extruder framework to shape wood–plastic composites. Results showed that the impact properties of the composites were further developed all the more essentially by utilizing SEBS-g- MAH compatibilizer than by utilizing the combinations of MAH and DCP by means of responsive mixing *in situ*. Notwithstanding, opposite results were noticed on the flexural and tensile properties of the comparing composites. In general, the mechanical properties of composites produced using recycled plastic mixes were mediocre compared to those produced using virgin plastic mixes, particularly in elongation break. The morphological review confirmed that the interfacial attachment or the similarity of plastic mixes with wood floor was improved by adding SEBS-g-MAH or *in situ* joining MAH. A superior interfacial holding between HDPE, PP, PS, and wood floor was acquired by *in situ* joining MAH than the increase of SEBS-g-MAH. *In situ* joining MAH can be thought of as a potential approach to increase the interfacial similarity between plastic mixes and wood floor. The elastic modulus and damping factor of composites were additionally portrayed through dynamic mechanical analysis (DMA) [24]. The blend of manufactured thermoplastic polymers and wood is regularly risky on the grounds that wood surfaces are hydrophilic while normal thermoplastic polymers are hydrophobic. A potential arrangement is to utilize block copolymer coupling agents. In this work, it was shown that the utilization of a possibly valuable manufactured strategy for delivering hydrophobic–hydrophilic block copolymers as hydrophobic coatings and coupling agents in wood polystyrene composites. Specifically, wood façades have been covered with water-based emulsions of hydrophobic–hydrophilic block copolymers from methacrylic corrosive and styrene. Dried-covered surfaces are displayed to become hydrophobic through unique contact point estimations. At the point when a wood floor is covered with the hydrophobic–hydrophilic block copolymer in view of acrylic and styrene corrosive, critical improvement in an ultimate tensile strength of composites shaped from covered wood polystyrene combinations is understood. Since no volatile organic compounds (VOCs) are utilized in covering wood surfaces, what's more, resulting composite creation, improvement in mechanical properties of thermoplastic/wood floor composites are displayed to happen in ecologically capable plans [25].

2.8 Compatibilizer

Polypropylene (PP), a thermoplastic, enjoys a ton of benefits, for example, great handling properties, minimal expense, and so on. Nonetheless, PP has an unfortunate effect on opposition under high tests peed or low-temperature conditions. To further develop influence properties and low-temperature sturdiness of Polypropylene, the elastomer is frequently utilized in poly-propelene; elastomer adjustment of poly-propelene is known to cause a sensational decrease in both toughness and strength. The expansion of fortifications into poly-propelene can increase the strength and toughness, whereas it causes a decrease in fracture toughness. In this manner, to repay those downsides, an equilibrium in the durability and strength can be gotten by adding elastomer and support into PP. In this chapter, wood fiber as support was utilized to further develop firmness; furthermore, MA-SEBS was utilized as a compatibilizer and influence modifier (**Figure 6**) [27].

2.9 UV stabilizers

Four types of iron oxide pigments were added to wood floor/high-density-polyethylene composites (WF/HDPE) at three different concentrations. Then the effect of pigments on the color change and mechanical properties before and after UV accelerated weathering was determined. Wood fibers, HDPE, pigments, and other processing additives were dry-mixed in a high-speed mixer. The mixtures were extruded by a

Figure 6.
Wood-based material used in an exterior application [26].

S. No.	Additives used in wood based products	Efeect of additives on wood based products
1.	Coupling agent (MAPP) 3%	Increases mechanical properties like flexural and tensile strength,MOR, Storage modulus, decreases thickness swelling and damping peaks [8, 11]
2.	Lubricant ZINC STEARATE [ZnSt] 3%	Reduces physical and mechanical properties except MOR, increases thickness swelling [8]
3.	Additive STRUCTOR TR 016 CA	Promotes homogeneity, increases physical and chemical properties [9]
4.	CIBA anti-microbial agent	Protects against micro-organisms [9]
5.	UV filter coating CIBA (TINUVIN 1235)	Protect against UV radiations [9]
6.	Fungicides IRGAGUARD F3510	Protect against fungus [9]
7.	Pigment CIBA blue (Irgalite)	Avoids fading of structure [9]
8.	Plasticizer GLYCEROL	Increases thermal and mechanical properties, compatibility, and tensile strength [10]
9.	Fire retardant MELAMINE 30%	Reduces smoke formation, increases ignition time and total heat release [15]
10.	Fire retardant Zinc Borate 30%	Improves peak heat release rate[15]
11.	Fire retardant APP (Ammonium Polyphosphate) 20–30%	Increases smoke production by 20–30%, improves ignition time and total heat release, reduces peak heat release rate [15]
12.	Additive Lignosulphonate and starch	Improves mechanical durability, reduces the calorific value, increases SO_X emission [17]

S. No.	Additives used in wood based products	Efeect of additives on wood based products
13.	Additive Motor and vegetable oil	Increases the calorific value and CO emission, decreases the particle density [17]
14.	Additive Corn starch and Dolomite	Increases CO emission, reduces moisture content [17]
15.	Additive Wheat Starch	Reduces ash formation [17]
16.	PMS (Potassium Methyl Siliconate)	Improves compatibility, decreases water sorption, increases dimensional stability [19]
17.	Coupling agent MAH-PP 5%	Decreases water sorption, damping index and hygroscopicity, increases interfacial adhesion, charpy impact strength, tensile and flexural strength [20]
18.	EXXELOR PO 1020 4%	Improves bending properties, decreases water sorption [21]
19.	Compatibilizer SEBS-g-MAH	Improves impact strength, compatibility, tensile and flexural strength [24]
20.	MAH and DCP	Improves interfacial bonding and mechanical properties [24]
21.	Styrene-co-methacrylic acid	Improves ultimate tensile strength [25]
22.	Compatibilizer MA-SEBS 8%	Improves interfacial adhesion, impact strength, stiffness, toughness, and storage modulus [27]
23.	Pigment Iron Oxide 2.28%	Improves bending strength, avoid discoloration [28]

Table 1.
Effect of additives on wood-based products.

twin screw extruder. The color of the samples was determined according to CIE 1976 L*a*b* system by spectrophotometry. The bending properties were determined and the mechanical properties were evaluated before and after accelerated UV weathering. The result shows that the modulus of elasticity (MOE) of the composite did not change after incorporating the pigments, but the bending strength was improved. After accelerated aging for 2000 h, both mechanical properties and color were changed significantly. Red iron oxide and black iron oxide performed better than the other two pigments. It was also observed that the pigment dosage of 2.28% in the composites is favorable (**Table 1**) [28].

3. Conclusion

Wood-based products are an emerging material for wood industries nowadays. They have a number of applications, including window and doorframes, docks and railings, exterior and interior wall profiles, floors, stairs and hand rails, fencing, shelves, office furniture, garden furniture, soundproof cladding, and kitchen cabinet. Different types of additives are used to improve their efficiency and performance. Some of the additives are rheology control additives, lubricants, density reduction additives, UV stabilizers, product aesthetic additives, biocides, smoke suppressants, flame retardants, wax, colorant, foaming agent, blowing agent, fillers, etc. These additives are added to WPC according to the applications where they have to be used. Additives improve their efficiency, performance, durability, sustainability, and shelf life. Some of the benefits of using WPC instead of pure wood or pure plastic are high stiffness to weight ratio, high strength to weight ratio, more consistent, defects and distortion free, moisture resistant, highly durable, weather resistant, slip resistant, easy maintenance, recyclable and environment friendly, cost-effective, UV resistant, more shelf life, high insect and rot resistant, high MOR (Modulus of Rupture) and MOE (Modulus of elasticity). All the above-mentioned qualities of wood-based products encourage their manufacturing in wood industries rapidly nowadays. Wood-based product has almost replaced pure wood and pure plastic in a number of applications.

Author details

Amit Prem Khare[1], Nidhi Dwivedi[1] and Shamsul Haq[2]*

1 Mechanical Engineering Department, Madhyanchal Professional University, Bhopal, India

2 Mechanical Engineering Department, SAM Global University, Bhopal, India

*Address all correspondence to: shamsulhaq198615@gmail.com

IntechOpen

© 2022 The Author(s). Licensee IntechOpen. This chapter is distributed under the terms of the Creative Commons Attribution License (http://creativecommons.org/licenses/by/3.0), which permits unrestricted use, distribution, and reproduction in any medium, provided the original work is properly cited.

References

[1] Kristak L, Kubovský I, Réh R. New challenges in wood and wood-based materials. Polymers. 2021;**13**:2538

[2] Dreamstime. Available from: https://www.dreamstime.com/print-vector-set-wood-products-image152889873. [Accessed: March 7, 2022]

[3] Venkatesh GS, Deb A, Karmarkar A, Gurumoorthy B. Eco-friendly wood polymer composites for sustainable design applications. CIRP Design. 2012:399-408

[4] Dwivedi N, Khare AP, Haq S. Wood plastic composite: Emerging material for an environmental safety—A review. Advances in Clean Energy Technologies. 2021:85-99

[5] Ryan V. Natural wood- Raw materials and processing to product. 2011

[6] Ecplaza. New Material waterproof wood plastic composite WPC decking. Available from: https://www.ecplaza.net/products/new-material-waterproof-wood-plasticcomposite_4475462

[7] Teischinger A. The development of wood technology and technology developments in the wood industries—from history to future. European Journal of Wood Production. 2010;**68**:281-287

[8] Leu S-Y, Yang T-H, Lo S-F, Yang T-H. Optimized material composition to improve the physical and mechanical properties of extruded wood–plastic composites (WPCs). Construction and Building Materials. 2012;**29**:120-127

[9] Wechsler A, Hiziroglu S. Some of the properties of wood–plastic composites. Building and Environment. 2007;**42**:2637-2644

[10] Tajan M, Chaiwutthinan P, Leejarkpai T. Thermal and mechanical properties of wood-plastic composites from iron wood flour and recycled polypropylene foam. Journal of Metals, Materials and Minerals. 2008;**72**(2):165-176

[11] Kuo P-Y, Wang S-Y, Chen J-H, Hsueh H-C, Tsai M-J. Effects of material compositions on the mechanical properties of wood–plastic composites manufactured by injection molding. Materials and Design. 2009;**30**:3489-3496

[12] Greenhead. Available from: https://www.thegreenhead.com/2014/01/kami-wood-cups.php. [Accessed: March 7, 2022]

[13] Sandberg D. Additives in Wood Products—Today and Future Development. Environmental Impacts of Traditional and Innovative Forest-based Bioproducts. Environmental Footprints and Eco-design of Products and Processes. 2016

[14] Sharma NK, Verma CS. Vijayaraghavan M Chariar and Rajendra Prasad. Eco-friendly flame-retardant treatments for cellulosic green building materials. Indoor and. Built Environment. 2013;0(0):1-11

[15] Nikolaeva M, Timo K. Reaction-to-fire properties of wood– polypropylene composites containing different fire retardants. Fire Technology. 2013

[16] Takatani M, Kato O, Kitayama T, Okamoto T, MitsuhikoTanahashi. Effect of adding steam-exploded wood flour to thermoplastic polymer/wood composite. Journal of Wood Science. 2000;**46**:210-214

[17] Tarasov D, Shahi C, Leitch M. Effect of Additives on Wood Pellet Physical and Thermal Characteristics: A Review. ISRN Forestry; 2013

[18] Rognoli V, Karana E, Pedgley O. Natural fibre composites in product design: an investigation into material perception and acceptance. DPPI''11, Milano, IT. 2011

[19] Cheng P, Cai Z, Stark NM, Charles J. Monlezun Dimensional stability of wood–plastic composites reinforced with potassium methyl siliconate modified fiber and sawdust made from beetle-killed trees. European Journal of Wood Productions.

[20] Bhaskar J, Yadaw SB. Evaluation and testing of mechanical properties of wood plastic composite. Journal of Thermoplastic Composite Materials. 2012;**25**(4):391-401

[21] Haq S, Srivastava R. Investigations of wood thermoplastic composites for sustainable product applications. Discovery. 2015;**39**(176):8-14

[22] Haq S, Srivastava R. Wood polypropylene (PP) Composites Manufactured by Mango Wood Waste with Virgin or Recycled. Journal of Polymer Environmental. 2016. DOI: 10.1007/s10924-016-0845-9

[23] Haq S, Srivastava R. Measuring the influence of materials composition on nano scale roughness for wood plastic composites by AFM. Measurement. 2016;**91**:541-547

[24] Haq S. Effect of Materials Content on Dimensional Stability, Nano Roughness and Interfaced Morphology for Virgin or Recycled Polypropylene Based Wood Composites. IntechOpen; Engineered Wood Products for Construction; 2021

[25] Bledzki AK, Faruk O. Wood fibre reinforced polypropylene composites: Effect of fibre geometry and coupling agent on physico- mechanical properties. Applied Composite Materials. 2003;**10**:365-379

[26] Cedar decking: Prices, different types, maintenance & more. Available from: https://www.decks.com [Accessed: March 7, 2022]

[27] San HP, Nee LA, Meng HC. Physical and bending properties of injection moulded wood plastic composites boards. ARPN Journal of Engineering and Applied Sciences. 2008;**3**(5):13-19

[28] Zhong ZW, Hiziroglu S, Chan CTM. Measurement of the surface roughness of wood based materials used in furniture manufacture. Measurement. 2013;**46**:1482-1487

Chapter 7

Adhesion Promoters for Gluing-Selected Materials in Furniture Industry

Tomasz Krystofiak

Abstract

Surface treatment with plasma, corona, or air and the use of adhesion promoters (primers) are methods that can be used to improve the gluability of various materials. Adhesion promoters based on organosilicone compounds from the solventborne and waterborne catalyzed by isocyanates were used in the study. Dispersions and hot melt adhesives based on various thermoplastic polymers were used. Rheological properties and surface-free energy as well as dispersion and polar shares in substrate-adhesion promoter systems were evaluated. The strength and resistance of glue lines were determined. The tested primers and adhesives were classified as rheostable liquids, diluted in shear, not showing the flow limit. Covering of the surfaces of PVC foils and ABS, PS, PVC edges with primers caused increase in surface-free energy, especially polar share. Significant improvement of strength and resistance of glue-lines was observed (100% delamination in the substrate).

Keywords: adhesion promoter, HM adhesive, rheology, surface-free energy, strength, thermal resistance

1. Introduction

In the last 20 years, the production of different furniture has increased. With the continuous development of the furniture industry, research work on the various products and surfaces used in furniture is important and justified. They support the industry in its continuous development and aspiration of ever better quality and sales results.

In various areas of the furniture industry and interior design, various types of materials are increasingly being introduced, often representing surfaces with limited susceptibility to gluing. These include primarily plastics in edge tapes based on ABS (*acrylonitrile butadiene styrene*), PA (*polyamide*), PE (*polyethylene*), PMMA (*polymethyl methacrylate*), and PVC (*polyvinyl chloride*) [1].

They are used for wrapping narrow surfaces of panel elements in standard technology, soft forming, and machining centers [2, 3]. In particular, the problems with wrapping are caused by the edges used for office furniture, kitchen furniture, and interior design. They exhibit high rigidity and the resulting limited susceptibility to deformation, which is due to their relatively significant thickness reaching values up to 5 mm [4–9]. Materials with hard-to-glue surfaces include laminates produced in HPL (*high-pressure laminate*) or LPL (*low-pressure laminate*) versions, for example, are intended for postforming finishing of the surface of panel elements. The theoretical basis for possible adhesive interactions in adhesive-substrate systems in relation to plastics has been presented in numerous studies [10–12]. These publications do not take into account the specific surface properties of these materials, which can significantly affect the course of gluing processes, adhesion phenomena, and thus the strength and resistance of glue lines [13].

It is generally accepted that difficulties in gluing various polymeric materials are caused by their nonporous surface and relatively low surface-free energy, usually at the level of 30–40 mJ/m^2. The surfaces of many plastics have a nonpolar character, which is also considered one of the main reasons for limited gluability, especially since adhesives usually have a polar character. In these cases, the aim is to give polarity to nonpolar surfaces immediately before gluing through their special preparation. Duroplast-based plastics are characterized by a smooth, compact, low-porous surface, and high resistance to solvents, which practically eliminates the processes of penetration. In the case of these materials, serious difficulties can be observed during the curing of adhesives, associated with the evaporation of volatile components, which in turn may cause porosity of glue lines and reduce the quality of joints [14].

A significant influence on the bonding of plastics can be executed by a specific technique of their production, for example, extrusion, rolling, pressing, casting, extrusion, calendering, and vacuum forming. Individual processing methods affect both the macroscopic structure and the location of chemical groups on the surface of the material. It should also be noted that in many operations in the field of plastics production, various adhesion promoters are used to cover the surface of individual industrial equipment in given technologies to facilitate processes. The reason for inadequate gluing may be the content in plastics of various types of agents from the auxiliary group, for example, plasticizers. Plasticizers during the processing process may migrate to the glued surface and adversely affect the bonding processes, for example, by inhibiting the hardening processes of the adhesive [15].

Adhesives are then used in a properly selected set of solvents, which cause the effect of short-term plasticization of the surface of the varnish coatings [16].

From the practical point of view, an important criterion flowing from the adsorption theory of adhesion and allowing to determine the suitability of an adhesive for joining a given material is the appropriate contact angle and the surface tension of the adhesive and the surface-free energy of the surface to be glued [17]. According to literature data, the surface-free energy (γ_S) of the glued material should be higher by at least 10 mJ/m^2 than the γ_S of the used adhesives. This is required due to the need for proper wetting of the surface by adhesives and thus meeting the thermodynamic adhesion condition [18]. In order to increase the γ_S of plastics to the values appropriate for a given adhesive, their top layer can be modified, for example, by removing migrating auxiliary components from the surface and developing the geometric structure [19].

In particular, an interesting area of research turned out to be the issue of wettability, surface-free energy of glued materials and the search in the light of the assumptions of adsorption theory of adhesion, interdependence in the scope of specified characteristics and the strength of the obtained glue lines [20, 21].

The aim of this study was to determine the rheological properties of adhesion promoters, wettability properties, and the strength and thermoresistance of the obtained joints.

2. Materials and methods

2.1 Adhesion promoters

To carry out the experiments, adhesion promoters based on OSI were used in the version of one-component solvent products (from the aminosilane group) and in the form of two-component waterborne products (from the group catalyzed with isocyanates). In **Table 1** properties of solvent-borne and in **Table 2** waterborne adhesion promoters are given.

In the initial experimental phase, a total of 10 commercial products offered by Jowat AG in Detmold/Germany/were tested, including six solvents and four waterborne ones. Selected properties of these adhesion promoters on the basis of own tests and information obtained from the manufacturer are given respectively in **Tables 1–2**.

Taking into account the results of preliminary experiments, two adhesion promoters marked in the work as S-1 (solventborne) and W-1 (waterborne) were selected for the investigations.

2.2 Adhesives

For profile wrapping of edges of panel elements, HM (*hot melt*) adhesives based on EVA (*ethylene vinyl acetate*) in the version with or without fillers, APAO (*alpha-polyolefins*), PA (*polyamide*), and PUR (*polyurethane*) are mainly used. They are characterized by many advantages in the ability to wet substrates with different polarity, good pre-adhesion, short open time, high setting speed, high resistance of glue lines to tearing, and beneficial features from the point of view of environmental protection, which predestines them for numerous applications in woodworking industry [22, 23].

Taking into account the consolidating trends, especially in kitchen and office furniture, manufacturers are increasingly introducing multicolored, with different thickness of edges, for example, based on ABS, PVC, PS polymers. Adhesives used to glue these edges are required, first of all, with very good adhesion and obtaining a transparent and thin adhesive glue line. In this context, it is increasingly common to

Property	Marking					
	S-1	S-2	S-3	S-4	S-5	S-6
Color	Transparent	Yellow	White	Green	Green	Transparent
Density [g/cm^3]	0.90	0.90	0.85	0.90	0.90	0.90
Dynamic viscosity [mPa·s]	140	300	35	50	60	30
Solid content [%]	14	16	13	12	12	12
Recommended amount of application [g/m^2]	5–10					
Destination	Foils and edges					

Table 1.
Properties of the solvent-borne adhesion promoters [13].

Property	Marking			
	W-1	W-2	W-3	W-4
Color	Green	Yellow	Yellow	Transparent
Density [g/cm^3]	1.0 ± 0.05			
Dynamic viscosity [mPa·s]	1000	1000	30 ± 10	600 ± 200
Solid content	27	28	30 ± 2	25 ± 2
pH value	7.5 ± 0.5			
Recommended amount of application [g/m^2]	5–10			
Destination	Foils and edges			

Table 2.
Properties of the waterborne adhesion promoters [13].

use HM EVA adhesives without filler and reactive PUR, ensuring obtaining glue lines with increased strength and thermal resistance [24–26].

2.3 Edges

The current range of offered types and varieties of foil and edging is very diverse, meeting the numerous expectations and requirements of designers, manufacturers, and users of individual final products.

Edges based on ABS, PS, and PVC were selected, also in the version without the adhesion promoters from the offer of products made in the technical conditions of PPUH SILPLAST/Poland Company/. Edges with a thickness of 3.0 mm and a width of 22 mm in the form of coils with a length of 100 m were purchased directly from their manufacturer. The properties of edges, based on the manufacturer's data, are presented in **Table 3**.

2.4 Application of adhesion promoters to edges

ABS, PS, and PVC edge tapes were selected for the research. The primers were applied in the laboratory (at 20 ± 2 °C and RH = 65 ± 5%). With the help of metal

Property	Polymer basis		
	ABS	PS	PVC
Hardness acc. to DIN 53505 standard (Shore methods) [N/mm^2]	73	75	81
Coefficient of thermal expandability [1/K × 10^{-6}]	85	95	80
Shrinkage (1 h in 90°C) [%]	< 0.3	< 0.7	< 2.0
Thermoresistance acc. to DIN 53460 standard (Vicat resistance) [°C]	96	90	78
Resistance to UV radiation acc. to the DIN 53388 standard	6.0	6.0	6.0–7.0
Resistance to cold liquid action acc. to the DIN 68861 standard (grade scale)	good	good	very good

Table 3.
Properties of edges used for experiments [13].

spreading strips (rakels), solvent-based and waterborne adhesion promoters were applied in the amount of 15 and 8 g/m^2, respectively. The solidification process was carried out under the following conditions:

- edging with temp. 20 ± 2°C, solidification under RT conditions
- edging with temp. 20 ± 2°C, forced air dryer solidification (60, 80 and 100°C, time 3 and 5 min)
- edging with temp. 60 ± 2°C, solidification in a forced air dryer (temp. 60, 80 and 100°C, time 3 min).

2.5 Preparation of samples for strength estimation and thermal resistance of glue lines

The process of edgebanding of particleboards with dimensions of 200 x 200 x 19 mm with ABS, PS, and PVC edges with applied primers was made using HM adhesives in the edgebanding prototype machine.

The tear strength tests were carried out in the Zwick 1445 test machine equipped with standard tooling in a set of rollers enabling tearing at an angle of 90°, at a loading speed of 1000 mm/min.

Visually, the degree of delamination occurring in the glued substrate under destructive loadings was carried out using the adopted scale (**Table 4**).

The determination of the thermal resistance of the glue lines contained in the narrow surfaces of the panel elements was made with a gradual increase in temperature. The samples were placed in a laboratory dryer with forced air circulation heated to 50 ± 2°C and heated. After 1 hour, the samples were subjected to a detailed visual assessment of the glued surfaces, checking whether they had not delaminated. If no delamination was found, the samples were placed in a dryer at a temperature of 60 ± 2°C and after 1 hour of soaking, another visual inspection was carried out. The determination was carried out until the first signs of deformation of the glue lines. If no delamination occurred, the tests were discontinued at 150°C.

2.6 Investigations of the rheological properties

The tests were carried out with the Rheotest-2 rotational rheoviscometer, conducting measurements at shear rates in the range of 2.7–1312 $^{s-1}$ as a function of temperature 15, 20, 25, and 30°C. Based on the experience of rheometric data, shearing stresses and apparent viscosity were determined.

Grades	Delamination degree [%]
1	100
2	≥90
3	≥80
4	≥60
5	<60

Table 4.
Adopted scale for the assessment of the results of the tests of the resistance of glue lines to tearing [13].

Subsequently, the experimental data were approximated to the appropriate rheological model and the values of its parameters were determined. Based on earlier research results, a rheological power model of Ostwald de Waele was used in the form of:

$$\tau = k^{\cdot} (\gamma)^{n}{}_{1} \tag{1}$$

in which:
τ—shear stresses
k—coefficient of consistence
γ—shear rate $[s^{-1}]$
n_1—exponent
In turn, the analysis of rheological models describing the relationship $\acute{\eta}' = f(\tau)$ for rheostable fluids allowed to conclude that in the studied area of γ experimental data can be correctly approximated using the three-parameter Ellis model, in the form of:

$$\eta' = \eta_0 / 1 + (\eta / \eta_{1/2})^{\alpha}{}_{1}^{-1} \tag{2}$$

The parameters of this model are
η_0 (Pa· s)—viscosity in the Ellis model
$\tau_{1/2}$ (Pa)—shear stresses in the Ellis model
α_1—rheological parameter
For the approximation of experimental data to the formula of the Ellis model, the random Brooks gradient method was used [13].

2.7 Wettability

The surface of the substrate subjected to gluing should be characterized by adequate wettability. Appropriate adhesion between the substrate (foil, edge) and the binder (primer, glue) is possible only if monolayers and molecular contact are formed between the wetting liquid and the material [13, 27].

On the basis of the assumptions of adsorbent adhesion theory and the Young-Dupre equation, it is possible to determine adhesive relations based on the value of the interactions of surface forces of contacting materials [28–30].

One of the most important adhesive parameters is surface-free energy together with dispersion and polar shares [31, 32].

It was assumed that good bonding is achieved when the surface-free energy of the substrate was higher than the surface tension of the wetting liquid.

Measurements of the angle of wetting with redistilled water were carried out with a PG-3 pocket goniometer, recording the results 15 s after applying a drop of redistilled water.

On the basis of the obtained results, surface-free energy was determined together with dispersion and polar shares [31, 33].

3. Results and discussion

3.1 Rheological properties of adhesion promoters

Table 5 shows the values of the rheological parameters of this model and the correlation coefficients. The values of r^2 obtained in the calculations indicate the

Amount of hardener [%]	Temperature [°C]	Model parameters		Correlation coefficient R^2
		k [Pa.s]	n_1 [−]	[−]
0	15	6.83	0.67	0.987
	20	6.08	0.67	0.987
	25	6.30	0.66	0.978
	30	3.74	0.73	0.985
2.5	15	7.87	0.65	0.988
	20	8.33	0.63	0.987
	25	6.96	0.65	0.992
	30	6.45	0.65	0.986
5.0	15	7.91	0.62	0.991
	20	6.80	0.66	0.982
	25	5.14	0.68	0.990
	30	2.54	0.77	0.994

Table 5.
Influence of the amount of catalyst added to the waterborne adhesion promoter on the formation of rheological parameters of the Ostwald de Waele model as a function of temperature [13].

accuracy of the selection of the approximated rheological model. For all the cases under consideration, the power exponent $n_1 < 1$, which, according to literature data, confirms that these systems decreases with increasing γ. The systems in question therefore represent the category of rheostable liquids, not showing a flow limit, diluted by shear. In Polish literature, these fluids are referred to as pseudoplastic, while in foreign-language literature, they are called liquids with apparent viscosity.

Analysis of the data in **Table 5** shows that the most sensitive rheological parameter in the Ostwald de Waele model, subject to noticeable changes in the range of factors under consideration, is the consistency coefficient k_1, whose values are in the range of 2.54–8.33. A general analysis of the obtained data indicates that as the share of the catalyst in the system increases, there is a tendency to increase the value of the k_1 factor. It can also be stated that a clear decrease in the value of this coefficient occurs with an increase in temperature. In turn, the power exponent n_1, which is a measure of the deviation of a given fluid from the Newtonian liquid, undergoes much smaller fluctuations at the level of 0.6–0.7. The more the values of n_1 differed from unity, the more pronounced the non-Newtonian properties of a given liquid became.

The values of the rheological parameters determined for each system in the Ellis model are given in **Table 6**. By assessing the course of changes in the values of rheological parameters in the Ellis model determined for individual systems, it is possible to determine certain regularities in the parameters of limit viscosity η_0 and shearing stress $\tau_{1/2}$ at different measurement temperatures. The values of parameter a were in the numerical range of 0.69–1.02 decreasing with increasing temperature and the share of the hardener in the W-1 adhesion promoter. According to [34], relations in terms of the formation of values η_0 and $\tau_{1/2}$ for the studied systems can be expressed by means of an indicator constituting the quotient of the value of these parameters, called the characteristic fluid time. **Table 6** summarizes the calculated values of this indicator.

Amount of hardener	Temperature	Model parameters			Characteristic time
[%]	[°C]	η_o [Pa.s]	$\tau^{1/2}$ [Pa]	α_1 [−]	$\eta_o/\tau^{1/2}$ [−]
0	15	0.17	0.21	1.02	0.81
	20	0.14	0.20	0.87	0.70
	25	0.12	0.20	0.83	0.60
	30	0.10	0.19	0.77	0.53
2.5	15	0.15	0.22	0.91	0.68
	20	0.14	0.21	0.87	0.67
	25	0.12	0.20	0.83	0.60
	30	0.11	0.20	0.80	0.55
5.0	15	0.14	0.22	0.87	0.64
	20	0.12	0.20	0.84	0.60
	25	0.10	0.19	0.77	0.53
	30	0.08	0.17	0.69	0.47

Table 6.
Influence of the amount of catalyst added to the waterborne adhesion promoter on the formation of rheological parameters in the Ellis model as a function of measurement temperature.

Analysis of the data contained in this table proves that the participation of the catalyst in the W-1 adhesion promoter causes an increase in the value of the parameter α_1.

3.2 Wettability

When presenting the results in the field of wettability, the citation and detailed analysis of the wetting angle values obtained in the measurements, which were used to carry out the relevant calculations, were abandoned, focusing mainly on discussing the relationship in the formation of surface-free energy for individual substrate-adhesion promoter-adhesive systems.

For substrates covered with adhesion promoters included in the work, the values of surface-free energy (γ_S) were determined on the basis of measurements of the angle of wetting with redistilled water, together with the dispersion ($\gamma_S{}^d$) and polar ($\gamma_S{}^P$) shares.

Figure 1 presents the relevant values for the surface-free energy with dispersion and polar shares for tested surface with and without adhesion promoters. A general analysis of these data indicates that both film and periphery tapes are characterized by very low values of γ_S contained depending on the base polymer in the range of 28.42–39.17 mJ/m^2. Covering the surface of these materials with adhesion promoters resulted in a clear increase in the value of γ_S, extremely beneficial from the point of view of the theoretical assumptions of adsorption theory of adhesion. These changes occurred primarily due to an increase in the polar component. For example, for PS-based edge tape, the value of this component after covering the surface with individual adhesives changed from 1.26 to over 13 mJ/m^2. In the comparative system, a slightly more effective solution for this group of substrates turned out to be a waterborne adhesion promoter in a catalyzed version.

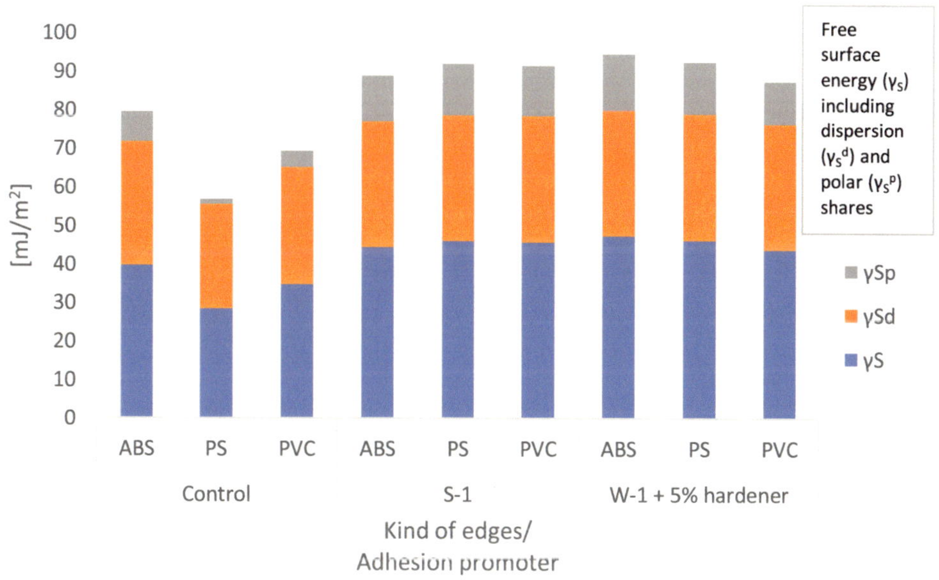

Figure 1.
Surface-free energy (γ_S) including dispersion (γ_S^d) and polar (γ_S^p) shares for edges covered with adhesion promoters.

3.3 Peel strength

A clear influence of the type of adhesive on the strength of glue lines in the edge-banded boards was also observed. In **Figure 2** results of the strength estimation are given.

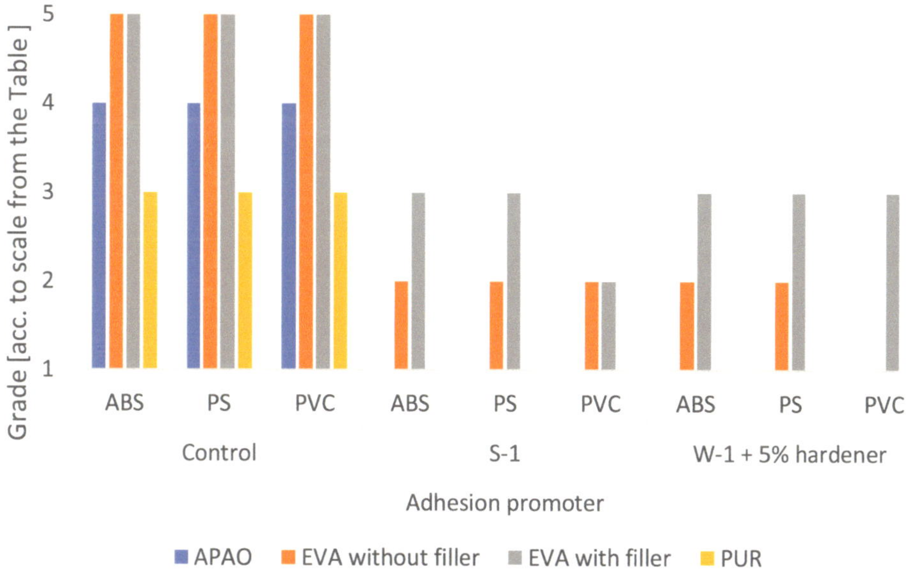

Figure 2.
Influence of adhesion promoter into peel strength.

A general analysis of the presented data proves that the type of adhesive significantly affects the quality of the joints. The non-stick coating of the surface of the edge tapes resulted in a clear improvement in the share of damage in the substrate during the delamination of the glue lines, respectively, from HM PUR glue from 80–85% (grade 3) to 100% (grade 1), in the case of HM APAO from 65% (grade 4) to 100% (grade 1), HM EVA without filler from 50% (grade 5) to 85–95% (grade 1–2 depending on the type of edging tape), and what should be emphasized for HM with filler from 20% (grade 5) up to 80% (Grade 3). Therefore, the tested HM adhesives can be ranked in terms of tear strength as follows (from the highest to the lowest):

PUR ≥ APAO > EVA without filler > EVA with filler

It can be concluded that the glue lines obtained as a result of the use of adhesion promoters for the preparation of the surface of foil and edging tapes for gluing constitute in terms of tearing strength, carried out, which should be exposed in conditions of shock forces at a load rise rate of 1000 mm / min, a coherent, high-quality system, the weakest link of which is the chipboard substrate, delamination at relatively low values of destructive loadings.

3.4 Thermoresistance of glue lines

In **Figure 3**, results of the thermoresistance are given. A very significant effect of the type of glue on the thermal resistance of glue lines was found. The use of adhesion promoters resulted in an increase in the thermal resistance of joints for individual edge tapes and HM adhesives respectively for: EVA without filler 43–57% (30–40°C), APAO by 44–63% (+40–50°C), PUR by 36–50% (+40–50°C), EVA with filler 33–40% (+20°C). In terms of thermal resistance of glue lines from narrow surfaces of plate elements with edges HM adhesives (from the highest to the lowest) can therefore be ranked as follows:

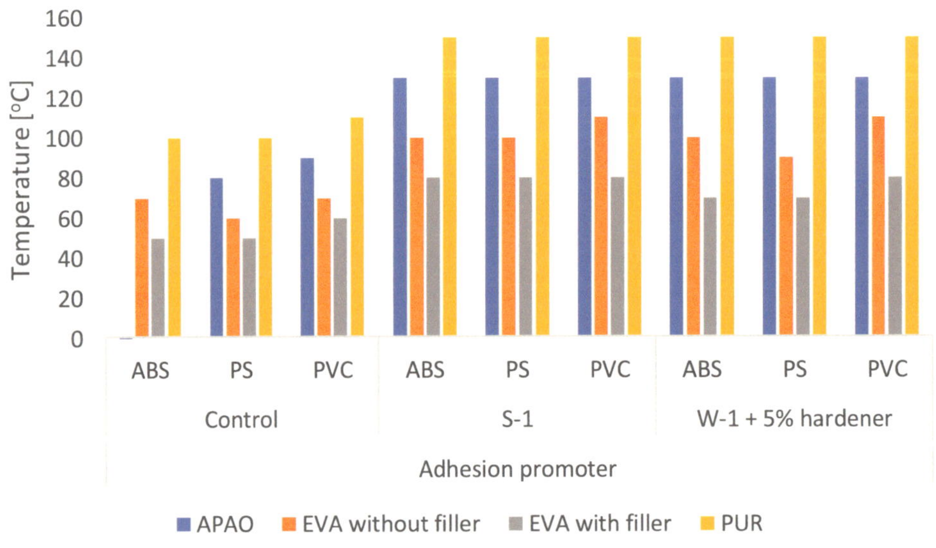

Figure 3.
Influence of adhesion promoter into thermoresistance of glue lines from HM adhesives.

PUR > APAO > EVA without filler > EVA with filler

however, taking into account the relative increase in thermal resistance:

APAO > EVA without filler > PUR > EVA with filler

Analyzing the type of edge material used for edgebanding, it can be concluded that the most advantageous product in terms of heat resistance in comparison with particleboard and adhesives included in the experiments is PVC edge, while ABS and PS turned out to be slightly inferior (the level of heat resistance lower by 10–20°C). It certainly results from the formation of mechanical and thermal properties of the base polymers of the tapes during heating. In the course of conducting, these studies, for example, changes in the thermal expansion of the tested tapes were observed during the experiments. In the case of ABS and PS edges, the maximum thermal expansion over the sample length of 2 mm was recorded at the time of delamination of the glue lines.

In the application works carried out in laboratory and industrial conditions, it was established that the solvent-borne adhesion promoter should be applied to individual substrates in the form of thin layers in the amount of at least 15 g/m^2 and solidified at an air temperature of 20 ± 2°C and RH = 65 ± 5% in about 5 minutes. On the other hand, a waterborne adhesion promoter with the participation of a 5% isocyanate catalyst in an amount of at least 8 g / m^2 and after drying at 60°C for 5 min.

4. Conclusions

1. Carried out research has indicated the opportunity of using solvent-borne and waterborne adhesion promoters for furniture production.

2. The waterborne adhesion promoters were classified as rheostable liquids diluted by shearing not showing a flow limit (pseudoplastic liquids). There was no effect of the hardener on the rheological characteristics of the adhesion promoter mixtures.

3. The greatest usefulness for approximating experimental data in terms of descriptions of flow curves was shown by the of Ostwald de Waele rheological model. The most sensitive parameter in this model was the consistency factor k_1. Along with the increase in the share of the catalyst, the value of this coefficient increased.

4. The Ellis model showed the greatest usefulness for the approximation of experimental data describing the relationship of the formation of apparent viscosity in the function of shearing stresses. The values of the rheological parameter characteristic in this model α_1 decreased with the increase in the temperature of the system and the amount of catalyst.

5. Covering the ABS, PS, PVC edge surfaces with adhesion promoters caused a clear increase in surface-free energy. These changes occurred primarily due to an increase in the polar share.

6. Adhesion promoters on the ABS, PS, PVC edge surfaces caused a clear improvement in the delaminations of glue lines in the substrate.

7. The use of adhesives resulted in an increase in the thermal resistance of joints from edges and HM adhesives.

Author details

Tomasz Krystofiak
Laboratory of Gluing and Finishing of Surface, Department of Wood Science and Thermal Techniques, Poznan University of Life Sciences, Poznan, Poland

*Address all correspondence to: tomasz.krystofiak@up.poznan.pl

IntechOpen

© 2022 The Author(s). Licensee IntechOpen. This chapter is distributed under the terms of the Creative Commons Attribution License (http://creativecommons.org/licenses/by/3.0), which permits unrestricted use, distribution, and reproduction in any medium, provided the original work is properly cited.

References

[1] Anonymous. Thermoplastische Kanten auch für Wohnmöbel. HK - Holz und Kunststoffverarbeitung. 1996;**7-8**:68-69

[2] Windmann H. Kantenbearbeit ungsmaschine für die Frontenfertigung. HK - Holz und Kunststoffverarbeitung. 1988;**5**:522-526

[3] Anonymous. Auftragsgeräte für PUR-Schmelzkleber. Adhäsion. 1989;**33**(10):44

[4] Heydt F. Hochwärmefeste und wasserdampfbeständige Kantenverleimung mit PU-Schmelzklebstoffen. HK - Holz und Kunststoffverarbeitung. 1989a;**5**:654-655

[5] Heydt F. Hochwärmfeste und wasserdampfbeständige Kantenverleimung mit PU-Schmelzklebstoffen. HOB – Die Holzverarbeitung. 1989b;**36**(5):102-104

[6] Becker H, Meyer zu Drewer J. Möbelkanten - alternative thermoplastische Werkstoffe. HK - Holz und Kunststoffverarbeitung. 1994;**10**:1062-1065

[7] Hackbarth W. Klebertechniken für thermoplastische Kantenwerkstoffe. HK - Holz und Kunststoffverarbeitung. 1994;**4**:443-445

[8] Kunkel D, Hippold T. Hochleistung für den Hochbau. Schmelzklebstoffe für Fenster, Türen, Boden. In: 6 Jowat Symposium Die Klebstofftechnologie auf dem Weg ins Jahr 2000. 1998. pp. 35-45

[9] Starck F. Ein fall für zwei. In: 7 Jowat Symposium Innovationen für die Welt des Klebens. 2000. pp. 38-41

[10] Zeppenfeld G. Kleben von Holz und Holzwerkstoffen - Bedingungen für die Herstellung fehlerfreier Klebverbindungen. Holztechnologie. 1990;**30**(6):291-295

[11] Pizzi A. A brief, non-mathematicalreview of adhesion theories as regards their applicability to wood. Holzforschung und Holverwertung. 1992;**1**:6-10

[12] Baghdachi JA. Fundamentals of adhesion. Journal of Coatings Technology. 1997;**69**(870):85:91

[13] Krystofiak T. Badania nad zastosowaniem środków proadhezyjnych do klejenia wybranych materiałów w przemyśle drzewnym (Investigations of the use of adhesion promoters for gluing selected materials in woodworking industry) [PhD thesis]. Poznan; 2002. pp. 1-181

[14] Anonymous. Neue Wege, Kunststoffe zu kleben. Adhäsion. 1993;**37**(7-8):21-23

[15] Kammer HW. Adhesion between polymers. Acta Polymerica. 1983;**34**(2):112-118

[16] Proszyk S, Krystofiak T, Baranowska A. Study of adhesion phenomenon of some glues to the surface lacquer coatings on the wood. XIV. In: Symposium Adhesives in Woodworking Industry. Vinné, Slovakia; 1999. pp. 193-196

[17] Wake WC. Theories of adhesion and uses of adhesives: A review. Polymer. 1978;**19**(3):291-308

[18] Żenkiewicz M. Adhezja i modyfikowanie warstwy wierzchniej tworzyw wielkocząsteczkowych. Wydawnictwa Naukowo-Techniczne/ Scientific and Technical Publisher/ Warszawa ss. 2000;**361**

[19] Zorll U. Chemische und mechanische Haftverbindungen bei Polymeren. Adhäsion. 1978a;**22**(11):356-364

[20] Cornyn J. Contact angles and adhesive bonding. International Journal of Adhesion and Adhesives. 1992;**12**(3):145-149

[21] Mantanis GI, Young RA. Wetting of wood. Wood Science and Technology. 1997;**31**(5):339-353

[22] Seeliger B. EVA-Polyamid-Polyolefine-Polyurethane. Aktuelle anwendungstechnische Informationen für die Schmalflächenbelegung und Profilummantelung. BM – Bau und Möbelschreiner. 1993;**3**:65-67

[23] Erb A. No Limits in den Kurven. Klebstoff - Technologien für's BAZ. In: 7 Jowat Symposium Die Innovationen für die Welt des Lebens. 2000. pp. 42-46

[24] Sonje Z. Untersuchungen über die Festigkeiten von Verklebungen mit reaktiven PUR-Schmelzklebstoffen. Holz als Roh und Werkstoff. 1992;**50**(10):401-406

[25] Proszyk S, Kotzian S, Krystofiak T. Studies of the properties of unfilled HM adhesives. In: XIV. Symposium Adhesives in Woodworking Industry. Vinné, Republika Słowacji; 1999. pp. 189-192

[26] Proszyk S, Hanyżak M, Krystofiak T. Studies on selected properties of reactive HM PUR adhesives. In: IIIrd. International Symposium. Wood Agglomeration. Zvolen; 2000. pp. 194-197

[27] Krystofiak T, Proszyk S. Investigations of the surface free energy and adhesion of the hot melt adhesive. In: Gliwickie Seminarium Polimerowe'97. 1997. pp. 275-278

[28] Zisman WA. Surface energetic of wetting, spreading and adhesion. Journal of Painting Technology. 1972;**44**(564):42-57

[29] Kloubek J. Calculation of surface free energy components of ice according to its wettability by water, chlorobenzene and carbon disulfide. Journal of Colloid and Interface Science. 1974;**49**(2):185-190

[30] Wu S. Polar und nonpolar interactions in adhesion. Journal of Adhesion. 1973;**5**(1):39-55

[31] Liptáková E. Studium fazoveho rozhrania dreva s filmotvrnymi materialami. In: Zbornik Vedeckych Prac, Drevarska Fakulta. Zvolen: VŠLD; 1980. pp. 55-67

[32] Liptáková E, Kúdela J. Analysis of the wood - wetting process. Holzforschung. 1994;**48**(2):139-144

[33] Potente H, Krüger R. Bedeutung polarer und disperser Oberflächenspannungsanteile von Plastomeren und Beschichtungsstoffen für die Haftfestigkeit von Verbundsystemen. Farbe und Lack. 1978;**84**(2):72-75

[34] Whorlow RW. Rheological Techniques. New York-Chichester-Brisbane-Toronto: Ellis Horwood Limited. John Wiley & Sons; 1980. p. 447

Chapter 8

Preparation, Properties, and Advanced Functional Applications of Nanocellulose

Kaimeng Xu, Yu Chen, Guanben Du and Siqun Wang

Abstract

Cellulose is the most abundant natural polymer on earth, which widely exists in various biomasses such as wood, bamboo, and other forestry and agricultural crops. Nanocelluloses isolated by various physical, chemical, and mechanical ways, as the second-generation cellulose products, facilitate the special microstructural formation such as rigid nano crystals and flexible nano fibrils, which display the high specific surface area, the excellent comprehensive mechanical strengths and thermal stability, as well as easy tailorability. Nanocellulose has been considered as a most important renewable, biodegradable, high-added-value bioresource for the development of novel functional bio-products in the future of wood industry and its industrial cross fields, including construction, polymer adhesives, composite fabrication and reinforcement, green energy storage and adsorption system. This chapter aims to introduce the important preparation and isolation methods, the basic and special properties, and several novel advanced functional applications of nanocellulose.

Keywords: nanocellulose, nanocellulose crystals, nanocellulose fibrils, preparation, properties, advanced functional materials

1. Introduction

A green renewable era for novel biomass materials application is approaching due to the continuous shortage of petroleum and environmental pollution caused by non-biodegradable synthetic polymers. Biomass with inherent advantages of renewability, biodegradation, low cost, and zero carbon dioxide emissions has attracted great interest in academic and industrial fields to effectively mitigate environmental pollution, global warming, and energy crisis. Cellulose (CE), extracted from various biomass sources including wood, bamboo, cotton, flax, hemp, crop straws, bagasse, leaf, fruit, and other microorganisms [1], is the most abundant and widely distributed natural biopolymer in the world with an estimated annual production of 7.5×10^{10} tons [2]. The chains of cellulose consist of the repeating β-(1–4)-linked-D-glucose units, which assemble into microfibrils via the interactions of hydrogen bonding and van der Waals forces [3]. Cellulose has been widely used in the paper, textile, and chemical industries for several centuries.

IntechOpen

The rapid development of nanotechnology and wood industry has ushered in a new global nano era in different fields. Nanocelluloses isolated by various physical, chemical, and mechanical methods as well as their combinations facilitate the formation of nanocrystals and nanofibrils. Compared with conventional celluloses, nanocelluloses with outstanding properties including high specific surface area, excellent tensile strength and Young's modulus, thermal stability, easy adaptability and processing, high barrier, and interesting optical properties [4], have drawn considerable attention in various cross fields of wood industry, such as construction, composite fabrication, wood adhesives, gas barrier materials, filtration systems, sensors systems, energy storage, and other environmental-friendly products. Nanocellulose has been considered as a critical renewable high-added-value bioresources for the development of novel functional bio-products in future wood industry. According to the Global Industry Analysts, the market for nanocellulose-based materials exceeded a billion dollars by 2020.

2. Preparation and properties of nanocellulose

2.1 Structure of cellulose

Cellulose $(C_6H_{10}O_5)_n$ is a long polymer chain with ringed glucose molecules and a ribbon-like conformation [5]. The unique properties of cellulose such as hydrophilicity, insolubility in aqueous solvents, infusibility, and ease of functionalization are attributed to the intramolecular and intermolecular hydrogen bond as well as polymer chain length [6], as shown in **Figure 1**.

Cellulose molecules are usually assembled into elementary nanofibrils (protofibrils). The protofibrils are further assembled via hydrogen bonding into microfibrils corresponding to dimensions varying from 2 to 20 nm [5]. These inter- and intra-hydrogen bonding networks enhance the durability and the axial rigidity of cellulose fibrils. There are two major domains of native cellulose corresponding to crystalline and amorphous regions. The crystallinity ranges from 40 to 70% depending on the biomass source and the extraction method with enhanced resistance to chemical, mechanical, and enzymatic effects [2]. Furthermore, cellulose can form different crystal types via molecular orientations, intramolecular and intermolecular

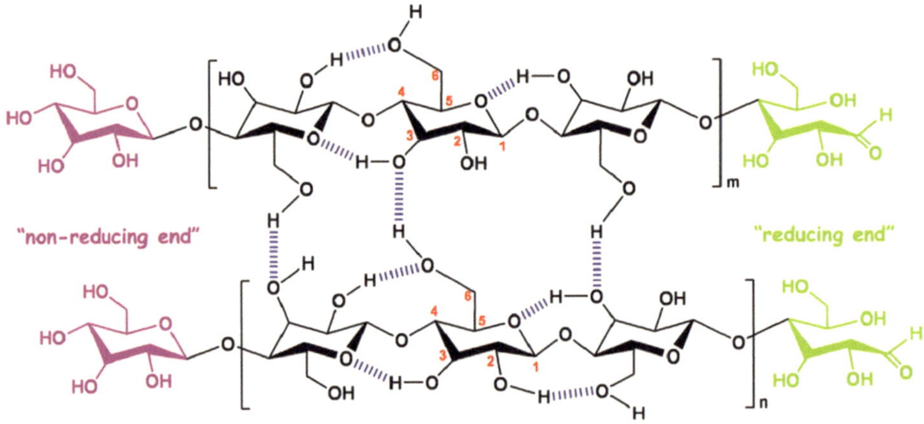

Figure 1.
Schematic representation of the chemical structure and intra-, intermolecular hydrogen bonds in cellulose [2, 6].

interactions, and van der Waals forces, and they can transform into each other by different forms of isolation and treatment [7, 8]. The amorphous region exhibits a lower density and easily reacts with other chemical groups [9].

2.2 Types of nanocellulose and their properties

The term "nano" originates from the Greek word "nanos" or Latin word "nanus," which generally means "dwarf." "Nano" represents a tiny scale of one in a billion. Generally, cellulose measuring nanometers in size in at least one dimension is considered nanocellulose. The basic properties of nanocellulose are similar to common cellulose including weak water solubility and ease of chemical modification despite various micro-morphologies under different physical, chemical, and biological treatments. However, they show outstanding mechanical properties, excellent thermal stability, large specific surface area, unique rheological and optical properties. The common nanocellulose can be categorized in two major types, cellulose nanocrystals (CNCs) and cellulose nanofibrils (CNFs) depending on their preparation methods, micro-morphology, and characteristics. The specific structures, properties, and yields of nanocellulose are closely related to the source of cellulose and isolation conditions [10].

The isolation of cellulose into nanocellulose generally entails two major stages: pretreatment of lignocellulosic feedstocks to obtain pure cellulose and transformation of cellulose to nanocellulose. Specifically, the hemicelluloses and lignin as well as extracts including fat, sugar, rosin, tannins, resin, terpenoids, terpene, flavonoids, waxes, and fatty acids in various biomass feedstocks are eliminated by different pretreatments [11]. The pure cellulose is then isolated by top-down methods such as physical, chemical, and mechanical techniques and their combinations. In addition, bacterial cellulose (BC) and cellulose nanofibers obtained by electrospinning (ECNF), which are generated by bottom-up methods, are also considered as nanocellulose. BC is self-assembled from low-molecular-weight sugars via bacterial metabolism, whereas ECNF are formed by electrospinning using different solvents of cellulose [12].

2.2.1 Cellulose nanocrystals

CNCs are also known as cellulose nanowhiskers or nanocrystalline celluloses. CNCs are rigid with a high modulus of elasticity (about 140 GPa) owing to their inherent crystallinity and orientation of hydrogen bonding, which is a rod-like or needle-like microstructure. The diameter and length of CNCs are less than 100 nm and around 100–400 nm, respectively. The degree of crystallinity usually changes from 54 to 84% [2]. Acid hydrolysis is a facile process used primarily. The crystallinity and size of CNCs are determined by the types of cellulose, the methods of isolation, and the corresponding parameters (hydrolysis time and temperature). The short rod-like CNCs with high degree of crystallinity originate mainly in the woody biomass and are obtained by acid hydrolysis. However, the CNCs with higher aspect ratios are typically obtained from bacteria and tunicates [13], as seen in **Figure 2**.

2.2.2 Cellulose nanofibrils

Cellulose nanofibrils (CNFs) with the same name, such as cellulose nanofibers, nanofibrillar cellulose, microfibrillated cellulose, and cellulose microfibrils, are long and flexible nanofibers, entangled into a mesh, which can be isolated mechanically (**Figure 3**). Their diameter and length range from 2 to 50 nm and 500 nm to several

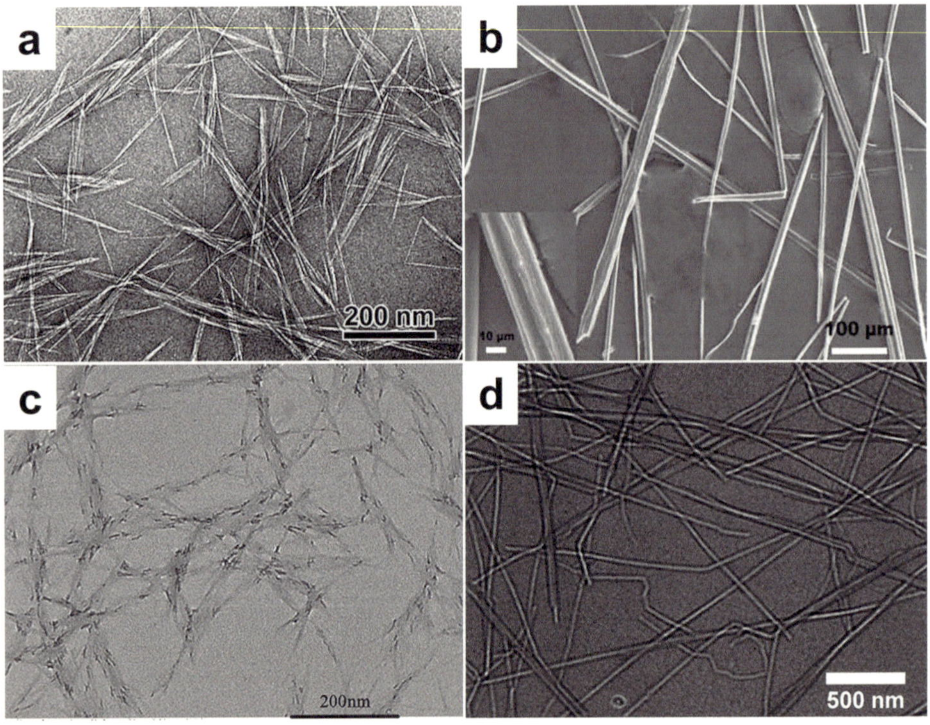

Figure 2.
Transmission electron microscope (TEM) images of cellulose nanocrystals derived from (a) wood, (b) bamboo, (c) straw, and (d) tunicate [14–17].

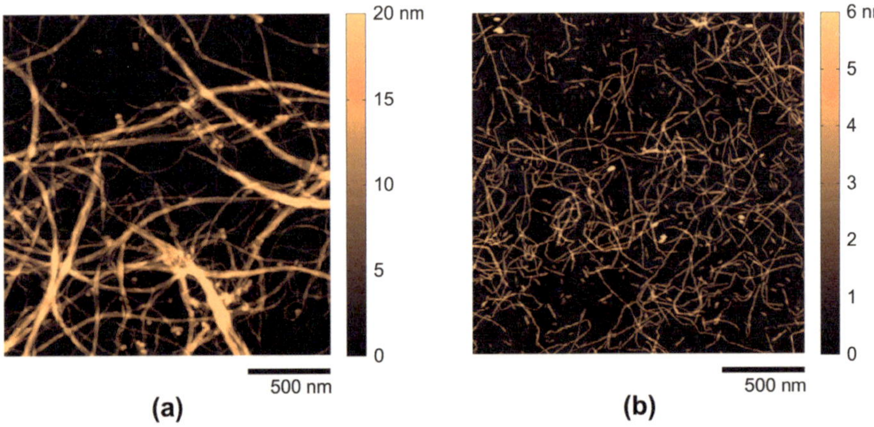

Figure 3.
Atomic force microscopy (AFM) images of cellulose nanofibrils from hardwood kraft pulp [12].

microns, respectively [10]. CNFs exhibit a stable configuration mainly due to their cellulosic molecular chains connected by hydrogen bonds. Typical mechanical ways including homogenization, refining, grinding, microfluidization, cryocrushing, and ultrasonication are used to defibrillate the cellulose, thus producing CNFs [12]. Some chemical pretreatments can be introduced to synergistically break the cellulose hydrogen bonds, resulting in enhanced accessibility of hydroxyl groups, which change the crystallinity and promote the reactivity of fibers. The inherent mechanical properties of CNFs are excellent corresponding to the ultimate strength of 2–6 GPa and an elastic modulus of 138 GPa in the crystalline region [18, 19]. The longer length with the higher aspect ratio and surface area as well as additional hydroxyl groups, which are easily modified on the surface of CNFs compared with CNCs. CNFs also exhibit outstanding thermal stability, optical transmittance, and gas barrier properties.

2.2.3 Electrospun cellulose nanofibers

Electrospinning is a novel, facile, and efficient way to fabricate continuous submicron or nanocellulose fiber. They have great potential for various applications due to their unique interwoven porous structure, low carbon footprint, and green synthesis. Electrospinning can be also used for the orientation and assembly of nanofibers to decrease the Gibbs free energy. During the electrospinning process, the cellulose solution is in a high voltage electric field. The droplets overcome the surface tension and then jet in a filament to the collection device through the air during solvent evaporation. The electrospinning process is influenced by the source of cellulose, concentration, viscosity, and surface tension of cellulose solution as well as electric field intensity, the receiving distance, and air temperature and humidity. In recent decades, the ECNFs and their derivatives have attracted great interest. The selection and development of the appropriate solvent system are the most important prerequisite and guarantee for the preparation of high-quality cellulose nanofibers by electrospinning.

2.2.4 Bacterial cellulose nanofibers

Bacterial cellulose (BC) is synthesized by specific microorganisms in the sugar source. Its chemical structure contains linear glucan molecules connected via hydrogen bonds, similar to the plant cellulose, and is free of lignin, hemicelluloses, and pectin. BC is assembled by twisting ribbons with cross-sectional area of 210–420 nm^2 and length of 1–9 μm. The degree of polymerization and crystallinity of BC are about 3000–9000 and 80–90%, respectively [20, 21]. Approximately 200,000 glucose molecules are formed via polymerization by a single *Acetobacter xylinum* cell per second. The cellulose synthase or terminal complexes existing in surface pores enter the media [22], which typically form ribbon-like bundles. Some pore-like sites are arranged in rows along the cell axis and juxtaposed with the cellulosic ribbon outside the cell [23]. A discrete lipopolysaccharide layer is formed as the extruding sites for precellulosic polymer in several chain groups assemble into subfibrils and microfibrils. A fibrillar ribbon with a width of 50–80 nm finally was formed by tightly aggregation [24].

2.3 Isolation methods of nanocellulose

See **Figure 4**.

2.3.1 Isolation methods of CNF

Mechanical isolation of CNF is usually performed after chemical pretreatment of cellulose. An appropriate pretreatment changes the crystallinity of cellulose and increases its reactivity. Cellulosic nanofibers are usually prepared under high-speed shear force and friction to dissociate the raw material into microfilament bundles with nanometer width and micron length. The main processing equipment utilizes

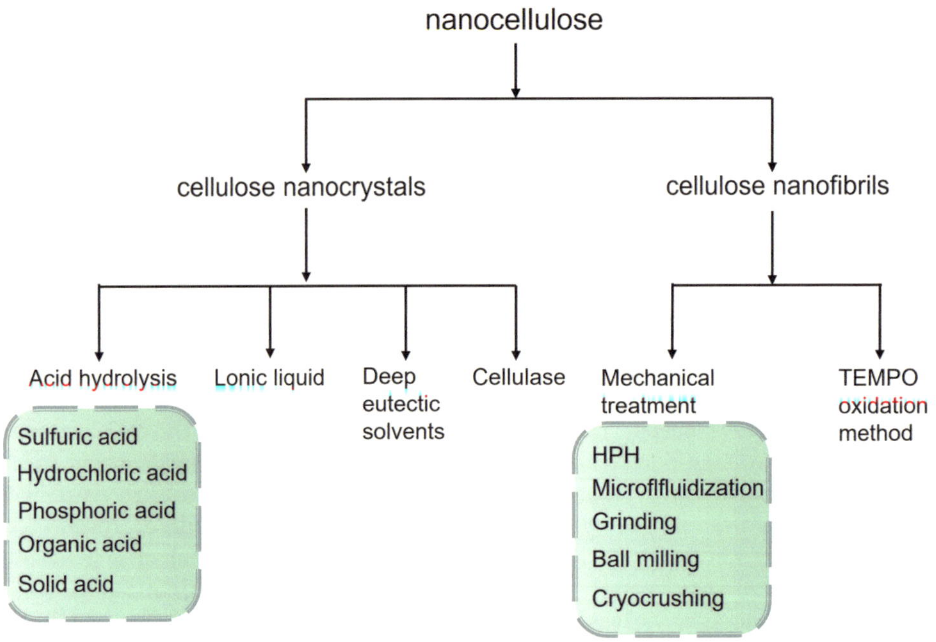

Figure 4.
Preparation method of nanocellulose.

high-pressure homogenization (HPH), microfluidization, grinding, ball milling, and cryocrushing. The first three techniques are the most common methods of mechanical isolation, as shown in **Figure 5**.

2.3.1.1 High-pressure homogenization

HPH is the most widely utilized method for preparing CNFs. It was first used to prepare CNFs from wood pulp in 1983 [26]. HPH is performed by sending the fiber slurry suspension into the container through a small nozzle, which generates high shear in the suspension under high speed, high pressure, and fluid impact, thereby reducing the fiber size to the nanometer scale [27]. HPH is a highly efficient isolation technique for refining cellulose fiber sheets owing to its simplicity and lack of organic solvents. Many researchers have attempted to use various feedstocks in HPH. Sugar beet was successfully isolated at 30 MPa for 10–15 cycles by Leitner et al. [28]. Habibi et al. [29] used bleached cellulose residues to extract about 2–5 nm wide CNFs through HPH of 15 times at 50 MPa. Clogging is one of the most significant limitations of HPH. Due to uneven particle distribution, small orifice size, and high homogenization pressure, homogenization often leads to pipe clogging and pump wear. In addition, the homogenization time is prolonged and the energy consumption is increased.
To overcome the disadvantages of clogging and wearing, the size is usually reduced prior to HPH. Therefore, a series of experiments were carried out using kenaf bast fibers to produce nanofibers [30]. Kenaf bast fibers were pretreated by refining and low-temperature crushing to obtain 10–90 nm wide nanofibers. CNFs with a width of 20–25 nm and 15–80 nm were obtained by pretreatment of kenaf core and stem by grinding. Zimmermann et al. [31] used milling pretreatment of wheat straw and wood fiber prior to homogenization of 150 MPa to obtain the nanofibrous cellulose.

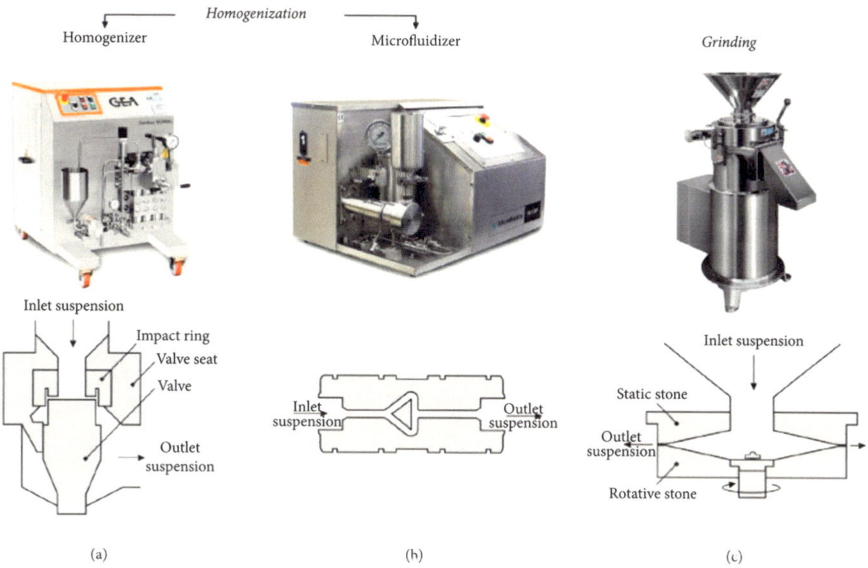

Figure 5.
The most common mechanical method for preparing CNF: (a) homogenization, (b) microfluidization, (c) grinding [25].

2.3.1.2 Microfluidization

Microfluidization is also a common method used to produce CNFs from pretreated cellulose based on a principle similar to HPH. Microfluidization is mainly conducted in a homogeneous cavity under a pressurizing mechanism, with usually "N" and "Y" types inside the homogeneous chamber. The microfluidizer combines the advantages of microfluidization and ultrahigh pressure (>300 MPa). Cellulose is passed through an N-shaped or Y-shaped channel at Mach speed in a pressurized chamber. It is simultaneously subjected to shear force, high-frequency oscillation, cavitation, and shocking, resulting in the breakdown of intermolecular hydrogen bonds of cellulose and the fibrillation [32].

2.3.1.3 Grinding

Grinding is a facile and low energy consumption method. It facilitates the possibility of industrial manufacture of CNFs. Generally, slurry is passed through static and rotating grinding stones in the instrument. The process of fibrillation in the shredder disrupts the hydrogen bonds and destroys the cell wall structures using shear forces to turn cellulose raw materials into nanoscale fibers [33]. Compared with HPH, traditional disc grinding has a lower efficiency due to the difficulty in tuning the gap of the two disks after gradually reducing the cellulose size. Meanwhile, the improper adjustment of the two grinding disks at a high speed of rotation results in collision and friction with the metal or inorganic fragments. In addition, the cellulose is easily embedded in the grooves of grinding discs during the grinding process, resulting in uneven scale. New grinding methods such as supermasscolloider and planetary ball milling have been shown to overcome the disadvantage of low efficiency. Furthermore, due to the presence of holes inside the chamber, it is easy to incorporate cellulose during the grinding process. The grinding procedure, however, is difficult to clog, and a large quantity of raw materials can be treated simultaneously. However, heat is easily generated by high-speed rotating disc grinding and cannot be dissipated rapidly (**Figure 6**).

2.3.1.4 Cryocrushing

The cryocrushing technique is used to obtain CNFs at low temperature via mechanical fibrillation. Cryocrushing of fibers is generally preceded after chemical pretreatment. The celluloses are rapidly frozen under liquid nitrogen, followed by treatment with high shear force, resulting in longitudinal decomposition and formation of CNFs [12]. The width of the CNFs extracted by cryocrushing is between 5 and 80 nm, and the length is several thousands of nanometers [35]. This technique is rarely used in commercial applications due to its limited ability to produce CNFs.

2.3.1.5 Oxidation

Oxidation via 2,2,6,6-tetramethylpiperidine-1-oxyl (TEMPO) is used for surface modification of native cellulose, which results in the oxidation of hydroxyl groups into carboxyl groups in mild aqueous systems. This method preserves the fibrous morphology of native cellulose, and the oxidation reaction only occurs on the cellulose surface. The surface negative charges lead to mutual repulsion between fibers, which facilitates the disintegration of fine fiber bundles and nanofibrillation. The most common oxidation method used is TEMPO/NaBr/NaClO in the aqueous system at pH = 9–11, TEMPO and NaBr play a catalytic role, and NaClO oxidizes the fiber surface [36]. Saito et al. used TEMPO for carboxylation of cellulose surface and successfully obtained fibers with a width of 3–4 nm and a length of several micrometers with a mechanical method involving pure nanofibrils [37]. To prevent side reactions,

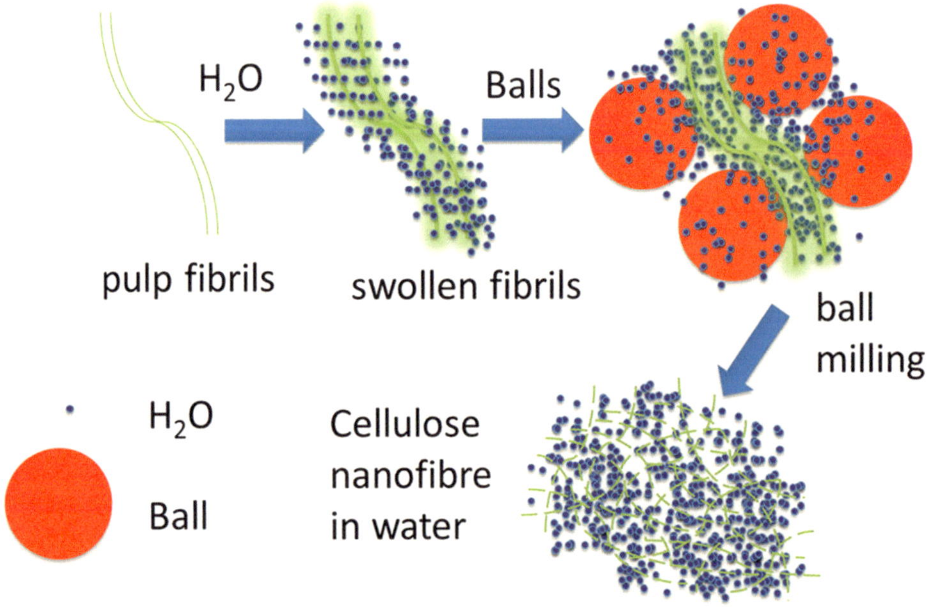

Figure 6.
Schematic diagram of the preparation of CNF by ball milling [34].

such as the degradation or discoloration of oxidized cellulose due to aldehyde groups, Hirota et al. utilized a TEMPO/NaClO/$NaClO_2$ oxidation system in neutral or slightly acidic conditions at pH 4.8–6.8 and a reaction temperature of 60°C, the carboxyl content can reach 1.87 mmol g^{-1} [38]. Further, the TEMPO/NaClO/$NaClO_2$ oxidation system can maintain the original polymerization of cellulose with uniform diameter and basically no aldehyde groups. Although the TEMPO oxidation method introduces a large number of carboxyl groups, which may reduce the degree of cellulose molecule polymerization, the crystal structure and crystallinity of cellulose are basically unchanged. The nanofibrils are uniformly dispersed in water, and the aspect ratio of the fibers is larger possibly due to many functional groups such as carboxyl groups on the surface.

2.3.2 Isolation methods of CNC

Acid hydrolysis is used as a facile process for the isolation of cellulose nanocrystals. This process involves acid-induced decomposition with the diffusion of acid molecules into cellulose microfibrils. The preparation of CNC via acid hydrolysis is mainly based on the difference in hydrolysis kinetics between the amorphous and the crystalline regions. It disrupts the glycosidic bonds in the cellulose molecular chain along the amorphous domains of the cellulose fibers, resulting in fracture of the hierarchical structure of cellulose bundles into CNCs. Acid hydrolysis decreases the degree of polymerization of CNCs. When the cellulose is partially hydrolyzed, a large amount of water is added for dilution, and the residual acid and impurities are removed by centrifugal dialysis.

2.3.2.1 Sulfuric acid hydrolysis

Historically, sulfonated cellulose nanocrystals (SCNCs) were successfully prepared for the first time in 1947 via sulfuric acid hydrolysis by Nickerson [39]. The concentration, temperature, and time of sulfuric acid hydrolysis play an important role in particle size, morphology, and physicochemical properties of CNCs [40]. Therefore, the reaction parameters and cellulose raw materials should be considered. Nagarajan et al. [41] reported incomplete hydrolysis when sulfuric acid concentration is less than 63 wt%. In this process, particles with low crystallinity are produced and small amounts of amorphous and aromatic polymers are dissolved. The productivity is enhanced when the sulfuric acid concentration ranges between 63% and 64% and the temperature is between 45°C and 60°C for 30–120 min [40, 42]. Similarly, when the concentration of sulfuric acid is greater than 65 wt%, there is a possibility of swelling of the crystalline region [43]. Sulfuric acid hydrolysis occurs between sulfuric acid and sodium hydroxyl groups on the surface of the crystal sulfate of electric charge. When the sulfate group is introduced into the surface of nano crystal, its dispersibility in water is improved, but its thermal stability is reduced.

2.3.2.2 Hydrochloric acid hydrolysis

Hydrochloric acid hydrolysis is another available method for preparing CNCs. The efficiency of hydrochloric acid hydrolysis of CNCs is enhanced at an acid concentration of 2.5–6.0 N and a temperature of 60–105°C for 2–4 h [44, 45]. Compared with sulfuric acid hydrolysis, CNCs hydrolyzed by hydrochloric acid carry no charged groups on the surface, so the dispersibility of the product in water is limited, resulting in easy aggregation and flocculation. The rheological properties of the two acid-hydrolyzed cellulose nanocrystals are different. The viscosity of nanocrystal suspensions obtained by hydrolysis of sulfuric acid is not correlated with time. However, the nanocrystal suspension hydrolyzed by hydrochloric acid exhibits thixotropy when the mass fraction is above 0.5 wt%, and anti-thixotropy when the mass fraction is below 0.3 wt% [45]. The nanocrystals obtained by blending sulfuric acid and hydrochloric acid have the same size as the nanocrystals hydrolyzed by sulfuric acid. However, the surface charge of the nanocrystals can be adjusted by changing the ratio of the two components.

2.3.2.3 Phosphoric acid hydrolysis

Phosphoric acid hydrolysis is a mild method. The CNCs prepared via phosphoric acid hydrolysis were thermally stable than those obtained by sulfuric acid [46]. Nevertheless, the colloidal stability of the suspension obtained after hydrolysis is not comparable to that of sulfuric acid hydrolysis. Acid concentration of 70–75 wt%, duration between 80 and 120 min, and temperatures from 100 to 120°C resulted in higher efficiency of phosphoric acid hydrolysis [47]. In addition, the phosphoric-acid-hydrolyzed CNCs exhibited better dispersibility in polar solvents than sulfuric-acid-hydrolyzed CNCs, and it can also be used as flame retardants and bio-bone scaffold materials [48].

2.3.2.4 Organic acid hydrolysis

Organic acids are recyclable, milder, and environmentally friendlier than other classical inorganic acids. Xie et al. [49] reported that 91 ± 2% of oxalic acid was recycled when sulfuric acid/oxalic acid mixture was used to prepare CNCs. Further, these organic acids are less corrosive to the processing equipment. Therefore, organic acid hydrolysis will be increasingly utilized in industrial manufacture of CNCs. Li et al. [50] reported a method of CNC synthesis from formic acid under mild conditions. Initially, the amorphous domains of cellulose are destroyed by formic acid (FA), releasing CNCs. Further oxidation using TEMPO increased the charge density on the CNC surface. The CNCs hydrolyzed by formic acid and modified by TEMPO exhibit higher crystallinity and surface charge density. The hydrolytic efficiency was further improved by Du et al. using $FeCl_3$ addition to the formic acid hydrolysis system [51]. The results indicated that the particle size of the synthesized CNCs was decreased with increasing ferric chloride dosage in the formic acid hydrolysis.

2.3.2.5 Solid acid hydrolysis

Although most reports of the preparation of nanocellulose crystals entail inorganic acid hydrolysis, the method has disadvantages such as easy corrosion of equipment, environmental pollution, difficult to control the degree of hydrolysis, and low yield. The strong acid cation exchange resin in the solid acid catalyst can be used to replace the homogeneous acid catalysts such as sulfuric acid and hydrochloric acid. The preparation of CNCs via solid acid hydrolysis is environmentally friendly and increases the recoverable yield. Tang et al. [52] used solid acid hydrolysis to prepare CNC from MCC by mixing the strong acid cation exchange resin with water in a ratio of 1:12 with continuous stirring. The crystallinity of the CNCs is higher than that of the CNCs prepared by sulfuric acid. However, the reaction time is long and the reaction efficiency is low due to the limited contact area between solid acid and cellulose. Therefore, it is still in the stage of laboratory research.

2.3.2.6 Enzymatic hydrolysis

Enzymatic hydrolysis of CNCs is a cheaper alternative to acid hydrolysis, which eliminates harsh chemicals and requires less energy consumption for fibrillation. Cellulose can be selectively degraded by the enzyme in the amorphous or crystalline regions. Cellulase is a multicomponent enzyme system with synergistic actions. It comprises endoglucanases (EGs), cellobiohydrolases (CBHs), and β-glucosidase (GBs) depending on the different catalytic reactions. EGs randomly cleave the amorphous regions within the cellulose polysaccharide chain, producing oligosaccharides of different lengths and new chain ends [53]. CBH acts on the ends of cellulosic polysaccharide chains to release glucose or cellobiose. GB hydrolyzes cellobiose to yield two molecules of glucose [12]. Under the action of cellulase, not only the amorphous region is cleaved by EG but also the crystalline region is destroyed by CBHs. Therefore, the degradation of CBHs to the cellulose crystal region should be avoided during enzymatic hydrolysis. The three components of cellulase are separated from each other by pretreatment. Amorphous regions of cellulose are maintained for EG hydrolysis, while additional crystalline regions are preserved during enzymatic hydrolysis.

3. Advanced functional applications of nanocellulose

3.1 Modifier of wood adhesives

Wood adhesive is the one of the most important components in the manufacture of wood-based composites such as medium-density fiberboards (MDF), particle boards (PB), and plywoods, which directly determines the comprehensive properties of panels. Urea-formaldehyde (UF), phenolic-formaldehyde (PF), and melamine-urea-formaldehyde (MUF) adhesives are widely used in the wood industry. Several studies reported chemical modification of wood adhesive but few described modifications of nanocellulose [54]. Surface morphology, chemistry, and adhesive properties affect the interfacial bonding and sufficient cross-linking reaction between wood and adhesives during the curing process. Nanocellulose with an inherent advantage of high stiffness and specific surface area at an appropriate amount improves the viscosity and stiffness of the wood adhesives. Nanocellulose can also fill the rough surface and hole in wood-unit surface, resulting in decreased porosity [55]. Nanocelluloses generated via various methods of isolation and modification exhibit differential effects on the bonding between wood and adhesive. The entangled microfibrillated cellulose (MFC) was prepared by a strong mechanical shearing resulted in high viscosity of adhesive [56]. TEMPO-CNF with long fibrillated morphology and negatively charged surface improves the CNF dispersion in the polar adhesive. Surface wettability of wood adhesive can be altered by various levels of energy dissipation with the addition of the modified nanocellulose. Aminopropyltriethoxysilane modification effectively reduced the surface energy of CNC, leading to a remarkable increase in the contact angle of CNC and urea formaldehyde resin [57].

Stress concentration at the bonding interface of wood and brittle adhesives (UF, PF, and MUF) is high corresponding to the density of cross-linked methylene and the degree of crystallinity. The reaction of hydroxyl groups and methylol groups in nanocellulose and UF promotes the ductility of adhesives. The crystalline regions improve the hydrolytic stability, resulting in reduced release of formaldehyde. The formaldehyde emission can be reduced by 13% by adding the modified CNCs at optimum levels (1 wt%) [57]. The major challenge for the adhesive modification by nanocellulose is the suspension of nanocellulose during the synthesis [58]. The higher the content of nanocellulose suspension incorporated, the higher the content of water in the adhesive, which reduces the solid content, resulting in slow curing process. The UF resin can be synthesized in various reaction conditions including weak acid, alkaline, and strong acids. Therefore, positively charged or uncharged nanocellulose under strong acid environment is essential due to the easy agglomeration of TEMPO-CNF at pKa = 3.50 via hydrogen bonding. The addition of nanocellulose or other cross-linkers such as poly(vinyl alcohol) effectively promotes the adhesive properties [59]. This provides a novel way to produce eco-friendly wood adhesives and reduce the use of petroleum-based polymers in wood adhesives in the future.

3.2 Novel energy storage application

Nanocellulose for novel energy storage application has received considerable attention due to its inherent structure and properties. Lithium-ion batteries (LIBs) with excellent properties including high energy density, non-memory effect, long-life cycles and low self-discharge rates, are key contributors to green energy storage [60]. Carbonaceous materials pyrolyzed by various precursors are the most utilized anodes industrially in lithium-ion batteries, resulting in low cost and various allotropic forms and morphologies [61]. Most anodes derived from natural cellulose are based on modified or synthetic porous carbon using chemical solvents or metals.

Nevertheless, directly pyrolyzed natural cellulose is an alternative candidate with acceptable electrochemical performance. The CNF carbon as anode in LIBs exhibited higher capacity but a weaker rate compared with CNC carbon. The disordered carbons used as LIB anodes were obtained by pyrolysis of microcrystalline cellulose in the temperature range of 950–1100°C [62]. Natural bacterial cellulose-based carbon treated by freeze-drying and carbonization showed good properties because of low charge transfer resistance and high specific surface area. To effectively promote the electronic conductivity of carbonaceous materials, nitrogen (N) doping in carbonaceous materials with similar atomic radii leads to desirable lattice mismatch, improves interfacial characteristics of the electrolyte and electrode, which facilitate electrical conductivity [63]. Unlike the traditional petroleum-based precursors from melamine or polyacrylonitrile for synthesizing N-doped carbons, novel chitosan (CS) contains 40% carbon and 8% nitrogen [64]. The N-doped porous carbon anodes derived from chitosan for the supercapacitance were successfully prepared by fine-tuning the hydrothermal carbonization parameters [65].

The natural nitrogen-doped porous carbon anode in LIBs was prepared by CS/CNC biocomposites using a facile procedure [60]. The N-doping content, the interfacial compatibility, and the pyrolysis temperature have a synergistic effect on the electrochemical performance of anodes. The outstanding cycling stability and coulombic efficiency of anodes are found at a pyrolyzed temperature of 1200°C. The addition of CNC has a positive effect on the rate retention and cycling performance. The CS/CNC anodes at the ratio of 10 wt% have high porosity, C/N ratio, and the multiscale pore distribution, resulting in an average specific capacity of 333 mAh g^{-1} at 100 mA g^{-1}, retention capacity of 251 mAh g^{-1} at 2000 mA g^{-1}, and almost constant capacity of 327 mAh g^{-1} after cycling. The CE/CS composite nanofibrous mats were obtained by single-nozzle and coaxial-nozzle electrospinning and then pyrolyzed at 900°C. The porous structure of carbon nanofibrous mats releases partial mechanical stress generated by the insertion and extraction of lithium ions. Their rough surface was conductive to the formation of solid electrolyte film, reducing the co-intercalation of solvent molecules and improving the cycling stability. The conventional carbon nanofibrous mats with a CE/CS ratio of 5:5 showed optimum electrochemical performance including a good rate performance (399 mAh g^{-1} at 30 mA g^{-1}), a high specific capacity (327 mAh g^{-1} at 100 mA g^{-1}), and an excellent cycling stability after 300 cycles. The carbon nanofibrous mats with the core-shell structure (CE as core and CS as shell) and the same ratio of CE/CS had higher pyridinic-N and pyrrolic-N content but a lower degree of graphitization and specific surface area in comparison with the common one. The N was more uniformly doped into the carbon nanofibrous mats via single-nozzle electrospinning compared with the coaxial technique, leading to a promotion for comprehensive electrochemical performance [66].

The separator of LIBs has two major functions: (1) preventing the direct contact of two electrodes; (2) enabling lithium-ion transportation by the electrolyte reservoir. It plays a significant role in LIB performance, such as cycle life, safety, and power density. The CNF film as a separator for LIBs exhibits high mechanical strength, thermal stability, and electrolytic property. Further, the CNF separator effectively promotes electrolyte wettability, ionic conductivity, and dimensional stability compared with commercialized separators fabricated from polypropylene/polyethylene/polypropylene. The CNF separators derived from *Cladophora* showed a small pore size but high Young's modulus and ionic conductivity, corresponding to 5.9 GPa and 0.4 mS cm^{-1}, respectively [67]. The CNF separators displayed high thermal stability under 150°C and were electrochemically inert in the potential range of 0–5 V compared with Li^+/Li. The $LiFePO_4$/Li cell with a CNF separator exhibited an excellent cycling performance (99.5%) and capacity retention [68].

3.3 Reinforcement of polymers

3.3.1 Reinforcement of thermoplastic resins

The role of nanocellulose in reinforcing polylactic acid (PLA)-based composites has been studied in recent decades. Most studies report that the mechanical strength and elastic modulus are improved after the incorporation of appropriate levels of nanocellulose. The poor interfacial compatibility between the nanocellulose with hydrophilic groups and the thermoplastic resins with hydrophobic groups limits the addition of nanocellulose in PLA. The ideal addition level of nanocellulose required to reinforce polymers is only 0.5–2 wt%. The surface properties of nanocellulose are generally modified by chemical or physical methods, which improved their dispersion and compatibility in PLA matrix. The CNC-graft-PLA/PLA nanocomposites modified by dicumyl peroxide were fabricated via reactive extrusion with a high grafting efficiency of 66% [69], which effectively promoted the interfacial bonding between CNCs and the PLA matrix, as well as the thermal stability of composites. The tensile strength of the composites increased by 40%, and its Young's modulus significantly rose by 490%.

Compared with the rigid CNCs, CNFs with flexible long chains exhibit possible entanglement with the resin matrix. A novel micro encapsulation-mixing and melt-compression technique to obtain CNF-reinforced PLA composites with uniform dispersion was reported by Wang and Drzal [70]. The PLA microparticles were obtained via solvent evaporation and mixed with CNFs generated by HPH. The dense PLA/CNFs composite sheets were prepared by membrane filtration and compression molding. This approach prompted the dispersion of the CNFs in the matrix even at high levels (32 wt%), which increased the modulus by 58% and the strength by 210%, respectively. The introduction of CNFs alters the crystallization of the PLA. Homogeneous and stable crystals can be obtained by increasing CNF loading, where CNFs act as the nucleating agents to accelerate crystallization of PLA particles and reduce the cold crystallization temperature [71]. An electrospinning technique incorporating CNCs with PLA improved the dispersion of CNCs in the composites [72]. A CNC loading of 2–3 wt% can effectively increase the elastic modulus by 17% and tensile strength by 14%, as well as contribute to stable ductility of the CNC/PLA composites.

3.3.2 Reinforcement of thermosetting resins

Phenol-formaldehyde (PF) resin is a typical and widely used thermosetting polymer. The mechanical properties of micro- and nanocellulose fibers as reinforcements for PF composites were compared [73]. The nanocomposite showed better mechanical properties than the micro-composites. The CNFs facilitate stress transfer in composites. The hydrophilicity of CNF enhanced the interfacial compatibility between CNF and PF. The CNFs immersed and dispersed in PF before polymerization, resulting in strong bonding in the outer layer of CNFs corresponding to strong fiber-matrix adhesion, which explains the higher strength of the CNF-reinforced PF composites compared with cellulose microfibril-reinforced PF composites. The commercial glass fibers with addition amount of 20 wt% promote the mechanical strengths of PF. However, the incorporation of natural CNF into the PF significantly elevated the tensile strength, flexural strength, and impact strength of CNF/PF composites by 142, 280, and 133%, respectively, at low CNF loading [73, 74]. The TEMPO-CNF/PF composites were prepared by a three-step procedure including mixing of CNFs and resin, ultrafiltration, and hot molding. The special processes of ultrafiltration and drying effectively adsorbed the moisture and then released the residual stress of the composite films. The obtained films were flexible with an average elongation at break of 13–17%. The neutral pH, the high polymerization of CNF, and the special composite method may contribute to the excellent mechanical strength of the TEMPO-CNF/PF composites. The TEMPO-CNF/PF composite flexible films were obtained via impregnation of TEMPO-CNF with aqueous PF resin, which yielded a tensile stress and toughness of 248 MPa and 26 MJ m^{-3}, respectively [75].

3.4 Adsorption treatment of wastes

The traditional activated carbon and zeolites are two most widely used adsorbents for the wasted water and air treatment. Nanocellulose, as a potential bio-adsorbent with the advantages of sustainability, nontoxicity, biodegradation, tiny size, large specific surface area, and the numerous choices to surface functionalization, has attracted tremendous interests in environmental remediation including metal ions, anionic and cationic dyes, and air pollutants.

The CNFs modified by carboxylate groups have been proved to be an effective adsorbent to several metal ions such as Pb^{2+}, Cd^{2+}, and Ni^{2+}, even the radioactive UO_2^{2+} [76], which is attributed to the attraction of negative charges [77]. The maximum adsorption capacity (167 mg g^{-1}) for UO_2^{2+} can be achieved with a three times higher than other popular adsorbents including montmorillonite, silica, and hydrogels. The CNFs modified by 3-aminopropyltriethoxysilane showed a positive effect on adsorbing Ni^{2+}, Cu^{2+}, and Cd^{2+} in solutions [78]. The adsorption performance depends on the pH range. The mercerized nanocellulose modified by succinic anhydride can quickly adsorb Zn^{2+}, Cd^{2+}, Cu^{2+}, Ni^{2+}, and Co^{2+} above 50% within 5 min. The maximum adsorption capacities correspond to 1.6, 2, 2, 0.8, and 1.3 mmol g^{-1} [79]. CNC is also proved to be available for adsorption of Cd^{2+}, Ni^{2+}, and Pb^{2+} but corresponding to a low adsorption capacity of 8.55, 9.42, and 9.7 mg g^{-1} in 25 mg L^{-1} aqueous solutions [80]. The adsorption capacities of Ag^{+}, Cu^{2+}, and Fe^{3+} by CNC are 56, 20, and 6.5 mg g^{-1}. The modification of CNC using phosphate groups effectively improved the adsorption capacity for several metal ions, corresponding to 136, 117, and 115 mg g^{-1}, respectively [81]. The modification effect of CNC by succinic anhydride on the adsorption of Pb^{2+} and Cd^{2+} was investigated. There was a about 10-fold adsorption capacity higher for modified CNC than the control one. The CNC adsorbent can regenerate using a saturated sodium chloride solution without any loss of adsorption capacity after two recycles [82].

CNF and CNC were also investigated in the adsorption of anionic and cationic dyes. CNF obtained from kenaf by a combination of acidified-chlorite pretreatment, which was proved to have a good adsorption capacity on methylene blue (MB). The parameters for maximum adsorption capacity (123 mg g^{-1}) are at 20°C and pH of 9 within 1 min. CNF can be regenerated by an acidic medium and has a six adsorption-desorption available cycles [83]. CNCs can also remove the MB from aqueous solutions. The maximum adsorption equilibrium capacity fitted by Langmuir and Freundlich isotherm models was 118 mg dye g^{-1} when the temperature and pH were set at 25°C and 9. The TEMPO-oxidized CNC corresponds to a higher adsorption capacity (769 mg dye g^{-1}) [84]. Sodium-periodate-oxidized CNC modified by ethylenediamine has an effective adsorption capacity for acid red, light yellow K-4G, and Congo red 4BS anionic dyes corresponding to the adsorption capacities of 135, 183, and 200 mg g^{-1}, respectively [85].

In addition, the toxic hydrogen sulfide (H_2S) adsorption performance was also studied by modified microfibrillated cellulose, such as aminopropyltriethoxysilane (APS) and hydroxycarbonated apatite (HAP) [86]. The H_2S adsorption capacity corresponding to 103.95 and 13.38 mg g^{-1} for APS/MFC and HAP/MFC can be achieved when the initial concentration was 80 mg L^{-1}. Compared with activated carbons, montmorillonites, silica-aluminas, and mixed zinc/cobalt hydroxides with the maximum adsorption capacities of 2–70, 0.5–12, 117–207, and 24–228 mg g^{-1} [79], APS/MFC is considered a promising bio-adsorbent.

4. Conclusions

Nanocellulose shows a great potential and brilliant prospect to be a novel functional bio-product with many inherent advantages including excellent mechanical properties and thermal stability, high specific surface area, available tailorability, and other special properties in the future of wood industry and its industrial cross fields, such as wood construction, wood adhesives, fabrication and reinforcement of composites, green energy storage and adsorption system. The nanocellulose-based composites with the functional polymers, inorganics, and metals are also a promising direction for the developing green novel bio-products with the low or even zero carbon footprint in the future. However, the most important issue on nanocelluloses is its manufacture on a large scale due to the limited transition technology from lab-scale products to industrial production. Future works should focus on optimizing the industrial process and continuously developing new or combining methods to produce nanocellulose with the low energy consumption and high efficiency. Also, the life cycle assessment, regulation, and standardization of nanocellulose for safety and environmental properties will be necessary for next commercialization.

Acknowledgements

This work is supported by the following grants and programs: 1. Yunnan Provincial Applied and Basic Research Grants (202201AT070058, 2019FB067); 2. National Natural Science Foundation of China (32060381); 3. the High Level Innovative One-Ten-Thousand Youth Talents of Yunnan Province (YNWR-QNBJ-2020-203); 4. 111 Project (D21027).

Conflict of interest

There is no conflict of interest in this field.

Author details

Kaimeng Xu[1*], Yu Chen[1], Guanben Du[1] and Siqun Wang[2]

1 International Joint Research Center for Biomass Materials, Southwest Forestry University, Kunming, China

2 The University of Tennessee, Knoxville, USA

*Address all correspondence to: xukm007@163.com; swang@utk.edu

IntechOpen

© 2022 The Author(s). Licensee IntechOpen. This chapter is distributed under the terms of the Creative Commons Attribution License (http://creativecommons.org/licenses/by/3.0), which permits unrestricted use, distribution, and reproduction in any medium, provided the original work is properly cited.

References

[1] Rajinipriya M, Nagalakshmaiah M, Robert M, Elkoun S. Importance of agricultural and industrial waste in the field of nanocellulose and recent industrial developments of wood based nanocellulose: A review. ACS Sustainable Chemistry & Engineering. 2018;**6**:2807-2828. DOI: 10.1021/acssuschemeng.7b03437

[2] Habibi Y, Lucia LA, Rojas OJ. Cellulose nanocrystals: Chemistry, self-assembly, and applications. Chemical Reviews. 2010;**110**:3479-3500. DOI: 10.1021/cr900339w

[3] Heise K, Kontturi E, Allahverdiyeva Y, Tammelin T, Linder MB, Ikkala O. Nanocellulose: Recent fundamental advances and emerging biological and biomimicking applications. Advanced Materials. 2021;**33**:2004349. DOI: 10.1002/adma.202004349

[4] Dufresne A. Nanocellulose processing properties and potential applications. Current Forestry Reports. 2019;**5**:76-89. DOI: 10.1007/s40725-019-00088-1

[5] Trache D, Hussin MH, Haafiz MM, Thakur VK. Recent progress in cellulose nanocrystals: Sources and production. Nanoscale. 2017;**9**:1763-1786. DOI: 10.1039/c6nr09494e

[6] Lin N, Dufresne A. Nanocellulose in biomedicine: Current status and future prospect. European Polymer Journal. 2014;**59**:302-325. DOI: 10.1016/j.eurpolymj.2014.07.025

[7] Thakur VK. Lignocellulosic Polymer Composites: Processing, Characterization, and Properties. Beverly, MA: John Wiley & Sons; 2014. p. 564. DOI: 10.1002/9781118773949

[8] Thakur VK. Nanocellulose Polymer Nanocomposites: Fundamentals and Applications. Beverly, MA: John Wiley & Sons; 2014. p. 516. DOI: 10.1002/9781118872246

[9] Kargarzadeh H, Ahmad I, Thomas S, Dufresne A. Handbook of Nanocellulose and Cellulose Nanocomposites. Weinheim: John Wiley & Sons; 2017. p. 920. DOI: 10.1002/9783527689972

[10] Alle M, Bandi R, Lee S, Kim J. Recent trends in isolation of cellulose nanocrystals and nanofibrils from various forest wood and nonwood products and their application. In Husen A, Jawaid M. Nanomaterials for Agriculture and Forestry Applications. Amsterdam: Elsevier; 2020. p. 41-80. DOI: 10.1016/B978-0-12-817852-2.00003-2

[11] Chen W, Yu H, Lee S, Wei T, Li J, Fan Z. Nanocellulose: A promising nanomaterial for advanced electrochemical energy storage. Chemical Society Reviews. 2018;**47**:2837-2872. DOI: 10.1039/c7cs00790f

[12] Nechyporchuk O, Belgacem MN, Bras J. Production of cellulose nanofibrils: A review of recent advances. Industrial Crops and Products. 2016;**93**:2-25. DOI: 10.1016/j.indcrop.2016.02.016

[13] Valentini L, Cardinali M, Fortunati E, Torre L, Kenny JM. A novel method to prepare conductive nanocrystalline cellulose/graphene oxide composite films. Materials Letters. 2013;**105**:4-7. DOI: 10.1016/j.matlet.2013.04.034

[14] Neto WPF, Putaux J, Mariano M, Ogawa Y, Otaguro H, Pasquini D, et al. Comprehensive morphological and structural investigation of cellulose

I and II nanocrystals prepared by sulphuric acid hydrolysis. RSC Advances. 2016;**6**:76017-76027. DOI: 10.1039/c6ra16295a

[15] Liu D, Zhong T, Chang PR, Li K, Wu Q. Starch composites reinforced by bamboo cellulosic crystals. Bioresource Technology. 2010;**101**:2529-2536. DOI: 10.1016/j.biortech.2009.11.058

[16] Xu K, Liu C, Kang K, Zheng Z, Wang S, Tang Z, et al. Isolation of nanocrystalline cellulose from rice straw and preparation of its biocomposites with chitosan: Physicochemical characterization and evaluation of interfacial compatibility. Composites Science and Technology. 2018;**154**:8-17. DOI: 10.1016/j.compscitech.2017.10.022

[17] Sacui IA, Nieuwendaal RC, Burnett DJ, Stranick SJ, Jorfi M, Weder C, et al. Comparison of the properties of cellulose nanocrystals and cellulose nanofibrils isolated from bacteria, tunicate, and wood processed using acid, enzymatic, mechanical, and oxidative methods. ACS Applied Materials & Interfaces. 2014;**6**:6127-6138. DOI: 10.1021/am500359f

[18] Saito T, Kuramae R, Wohlert J, Berglund LA, Isogai A. An ultrastrong nanofibrillar biomaterial: The strength of single cellulose nanofibrils revealed via sonication-induced fragmentation. Biomacromolecules. 2013;**14**:248-253. DOI: 10.1021/bm301674e

[19] Sakurada I, Nukushina Y, Ito T. Experimental determination of the elastic modulus of crystalline regions in oriented polymers. Journal of Polymer Science. 1962;**57**:651-660. DOI: 10.1002/pol.1962.1205716551

[20] Brown EE, Laborie MG. Bioengineering bacterial cellulose/poly (ethylene oxide) nanocomposites. Biomacromolecules. 2007;**8**:3074-3081. DOI: 10.1021/bm700448x

[21] Stevanic JS, Joly C, Mikkonen KS, Pirkkalainen K, Serimaa R, Rémond C, et al. Bacterial nanocellulose-reinforced arabinoxylan films. Journal of Applied Polymer Science. 2011;**122**:1030-1039. DOI: 10.1002/app.34217

[22] Hestrin S, Schramm M. Synthesis of cellulose by *Acetobacter xylinum*. 2. Preparation of freeze-dried cells capable of polymerizing glucose to cellulose. Biochemical Journal. 1954;**58**:345. DOI: 10.1042/bj0580345

[23] Brown RM, Willison JH, Richardson CL. Cellulose biosynthesis in *Acetobacter xylinum*: Visualization of the site of synthesis and direct measurement of the in vivo process. Proceedings of the National Academy of Sciences. 1976;**73**:4565-4569. DOI: 10.1073/pnas.73.12.4565

[24] Vitta S, Thiruvengadam V. Multifunctional bacterial cellulose and nanoparticle-embedded composites. Current Science. 2012;**102**:1398-1405

[25] Xie H, Du H, Yang X, Si C. Recent strategies in preparation of cellulose nanocrystals and cellulose nanofibrils derived from raw cellulose materials. International Journal of Polymer Science. 2018;**2018**:1-25. DOI: 10.1155/2018/7923068

[26] Henriksson M, Henriksson G, Berglund LA, Lindström T. An environmentally friendly method for enzyme-assisted preparation of microfibrillated cellulose (MFC) nanofibers. European Polymer Journal. 2007;**43**:3434-3441. DOI: 10.1016/j.eurpolymj.2007.05.038

[27] Nakagaito AN, Yano H. The effect of morphological changes from pulp

fiber towards nano-scale fibrillated cellulose on the mechanical properties of high-strength plant fiber based composites. Applied Physics A: Materials Science & Processing. 2004;**78**:547-552. DOI: 10.1007/s00339-003-2453-5

[28] Leitner J, Hinterstoisser B, Wastyn M, Keckes J, Gindl W. Sugar beet cellulose nanofibril-reinforced composites. Cellulose. 2007;**14**:419-425. DOI: 10.1007/s10570-007-9131-2

[29] Habibi Y, Mahrouz M, Vignon MR. Microfibrillated cellulose from the peel of prickly pear fruits. Food Chemistry. 2009;**115**:423-429. DOI: 10.1016/j.foodchem.2008.12.034

[30] Jonoobi M, Harun J, Tahir PM, Shakeri A, Saifulazry S, Makinejad MD. Physicochemical characterization of pulp and nanofibers from kenaf stem. Materials Letters. 2011;**65**:1098-1100. DOI:10.1016/j.matlet.2010.08.054

[31] Zimmermann T, Bordeanu N, Strub E. Properties of nanofibrillated cellulose from different raw materials and its reinforcement potential. Carbohydrate Polymers. 2010;**79**:1086-1093. DOI: 10.1016/j.carbpol.2009.10.045

[32] Li J, Wang Y, Wei X, Wang F, Han D, Wang Q, et al. Homogeneous isolation of nanocelluloses by controlling the shearing force and pressure in microenvironment. Carbohydrate Polymers. 2014;**113**:388-393. DOI: 10.1016/j.carbpol.2014.06.085

[33] Spence KL, Venditti RA, Habibi Y, Rojas OJ, Pawlak JJ. The effect of chemical composition on microfibrillar cellulose films from wood pulps: Mechanical processing and physical properties. Bioresource Technology. 2010;**101**:5961-5968. DOI: 10.1016/j.biortech.2010.02.104

[34] Zhang L, Tsuzuki T, Wang X. Preparation of cellulose nanofiber from softwood pulp by ball milling. Cellulose. 2015;**22**:1729-1741. DOI: 10.1007/s10570-015-0582-6

[35] Bhatnagar A, Sain M. Processing of cellulose nanofiber-reinforced composites. Journal of Reinforced Plastics and Composites. 2005;**24**:1259-1268. DOI: 10.1177/0731684405049864

[36] Siró I, Plackett D. Microfibrillated cellulose and new nanocomposite materials: A review. Cellulose. 2010;**17**:459-494. DOI: 10.1007/s10570-010-9405-y

[37] Saito T, Nishiyama Y, Putaux J, Vignon M, Isogai A. Homogeneous suspensions of individualized microfibrils from TEMPO-catalyzed oxidation of native cellulose. Biomacromolecules. 2006;7:1687-1691. DOI: 10.1021/bm060154s

[38] Hirota M, Tamura N, Saito T, Isogai A. Surface carboxylation of porous regenerated cellulose beads by 4-acetamide-TEMPO/NaClO/$NaClO_2$ system. Cellulose. 2009;**16**:841-851. DOI: 10.1007/s10570-009-9296-y

[39] Nickerson RF, Habrle JA. Cellulose intercrystalline structure. Industrial & Engineering Chemistry. 1947;**39**:1507-1512. DOI: 10.1021/ie50455a024

[40] Bondeson D, Mathew A, Oksman K. Optimization of the isolation of nanocrystals from microcrystalline cellulose by acid hydrolysis. Cellulose. 2006;**13**:171-180. DOI: 10.1007/s10570-006-9061-4

[41] Nagarajan KJ, Balaji AN, Thanga Kasi Rajan S, Sathick BK. Effect of sulfuric acid reaction time on the properties and behavior of cellulose nanocrystals from Cocos nucifera var-Aurantiaca peduncle's cellulose microfibers. Materials

Research Express. 2019;**6**:125333. DOI: 10.1088/2053-1591/ab5a9d

[42] Elazzouzi-Hafraoui S, Nishiyama Y, Putaux J, Heux L, Dubreuil F, Rochas C. The shape and size distribution of crystalline nanoparticles prepared by acid hydrolysis of native cellulose. Biomacromolecules. 2008;**9**:57-65. DOI: 10.1021/bm700769p

[43] Ioelovich M. Study of cellulose interaction with concentrated solutions of sulfuric acid. ISRN Chemical Engineering. 2012;**2012**:1-7. DOI: 10.5402/2012/428974

[44] Yu H, Qin Z, Liang B, Liu N, Zhou Z, Chen L. Facile extraction of thermally stable cellulose nanocrystals with a high yield of 93% through hydrochloric acid hydrolysis under hydrothermal conditions. Journal of Materials Chemistry A. 2013;**1**:3938-3944. DOI: 10.1039/c3ta01150j

[45] Araki J, Wada M, Kuga S, Okano T. Flow properties of microcrystalline cellulose suspension prepared by acid treatment of native cellulose. Colloids and Surfaces A: Physicochemical and Engineering Aspects. 1998;**142**:75-82. DOI: 10.1016/S0927-7757(98)00404-X

[46] Le Gars M, Douard L, Belgacem N, Bras J. Cellulose nanocrystals: From classical hydrolysis to the use of deep eutectic solvents. In: Shabatina T, Bochenkov V, editors. Smart Nanosystems for Biomedicine, Optoelectronics and Catalysis. London: IntechOpen; 2019. pp. 77-94. DOI: 10.5772/intechopen.89878

[47] Vanderfleet OM, Osorio DA, Cranston ED. Optimization of cellulose nanocrystal length and surface charge density through phosphoric acid hydrolysis. Philosophical Transactions of the Royal Society A: Mathematical, Physical and Engineering Sciences. 2017;**376**:20170041. DOI: 10.1098/rsta.2017.0041

[48] Gan I, Chow WS. Synthesis of phosphoric acid-treated sugarcane bagasse cellulose nanocrystal and its thermal properties enhancement for poly(lactic acid) nanocomposites. Journal of Thermoplastic Composite Materials. 2019;**32**:619-634. DOI: 10.1177/0892705718772866

[49] Xie H, Zou Z, Du H, Zhang X, Si C. Preparation of thermally stable and surface-functionalized cellulose nanocrystals via mixed H_2SO_4/oxalic acid hydrolysis. Carbohydrate Polymers. 2019;**223**:115116. DOI: 10.1016/j.carbpol.2019.115116

[50] Li B, Xu W, Kronlund D. Cellulose nanocrystals prepared via formic acid hydrolysis followed by TEMPO-mediated oxidation. Carbohydrate Polymers. 2015;**133**:605-612. DOI: 10.1016/j.carbpol.2015.07.033

[51] Du H, Liu C, Mu X, Gong W, Lv D, Hong Y, et al. Preparation and characterization of thermally stable cellulose nanocrystals via a sustainable approach of $FeCl_3$-catalyzed formic acid hydrolysis. Cellulose. 2016;**23**:2389-2407. DOI: 10.1007/s10570-016-0963-5

[52] Tang L, Huang B, Ou W, Chen X, Chen Y. Manufacture of cellulose nanocrystals by cation exchange resin-catalyzed hydrolysis of cellulose. Bioresource Technology. 2011;**102**:10973-10977. DOI: 10.1016/j.biortech.2011.09.070

[53] Lynd LR, Weimer PJ, Van Zyl WH, Pretorius IS. Microbial cellulose utilization: Fundamentals and biotechnology. Microbiology and Molecular Biology Reviews. 2002;**66**:506-577. DOI: 10.1128/MMBR.66.3.506-577.2002

[54] Trache D, Tarchoun AF, Derradji M, Hamidon TS, Masruchin N, Brosse N, et al. Nanocellulose: From fundamentals to advanced applications. Frontiers in Chemistry. 2020;**8**:392. DOI: 10.3389/fchem.2020.00392

[55] Ayrilmis N, Kwon J, Lee S, Han T, Park C. Microfibrillated-cellulose-modified urea-formaldehyde adhesives with different F/U molar ratios for wood-based composites. Journal of Adhesion Science and Technology. 2016;**30**:2032-2043. DOI: 10.1080/01694243.2016.1175246

[56] Veigel S, Rathke J, Weigl M, Gindl-Altmutter W. Particle board and oriented strand board prepared with nanocellulose-reinforced adhesive. Journal of Nanomaterials. 2012;**2012**:1-8. DOI: 10.1155/2012/158503

[57] Zhang H, She Y, Song S, Lang Q, Pu J. Particulate reinforcement and formaldehyde adsorption of modified nanocrystalline cellulose in urea-formaldehyde resin adhesive. Journal of Adhesion Science and Technology. 2013;**27**:1023-1031. DOI: 10.1080/01694243.2012.727173

[58] Gindl-Altmutter W, Veigel S. Nanocellulose-modified wood adhesives. In: Oksman K, Mathew AP, Bismarck A, Rojas O, Sain M, editors. Handbook of Green Materials: Processing Technologies, Properties and Applications. Singapore: World Scientific and Engineering Academy and Society; 2014. pp. 253-264. DOI: 10.1142/97898145664690031

[59] Vineeth SK, Gadhave RV, Gadekar PT. Chemical modification of nanocellulose in wood adhesive. Open Journal of Polymer Chemistry. 2019;**9**:86-99. DOI: 10.4236/ojpchem.2019.94008

[60] Xu K, Du G, Zhong T, Chen D, Lin X, Zheng Z, et al. Green sustainable, facile nitrogen self-doped porous carbon derived from chitosan/cellulose nanocrystal biocomposites as a potential anode material for lithium-ion batteries. Journal of the Taiwan Institute of Chemical Engineers. 2020;**109**:79-89. DOI: 10.1016/j.jtice.2020.02.005

[61] Hagberg J, Maples HA, Alvim KS, Xu J, Johannisson W, Bismarck A, et al. Lithium iron phosphate coated carbon fiber electrodes for structural lithium ion batteries. Composites Science and Technology. 2018;**162**:235-243. DOI: 10.1016/j.compscitech.2018.04.041

[62] Kierzek K, Piotrowska A, Machnikowski J. Cellulose-based carbon-A potential anode material for lithium-ion battery. Journal of Physics and Chemistry of Solids. 2015;**86**:215-222. DOI: 10.1016/j.jpcs.2015.07.015

[63] Niu Q, Gao K, Tang Q, Wang L, Han L, Fang H, et al. Large-size graphene-like porous carbon nanosheets with controllable N-doped surface derived from sugarcane bagasse pith/chitosan for high performance supercapacitors. Carbon. 2017;**123**:290-298. DOI: 10.1016/j.carbon.2017.07.078

[64] Advani JH, Noor-Ul HK, Bajaj HC, Biradar AV. Stabilization of palladium nanoparticles on chitosan derived N-doped carbon for hydrogenation of various functional groups. Applied Surface Science. 2019;**487**:1307-1315. DOI: 10.1016/j.apsusc.2019.05.057

[65] Tong X, Chen Z, Zhuo H, Hu Y, Jing S, Liu J, et al. Tailoring the physicochemical properties of chitosan-derived N-doped carbon by controlling hydrothermal carbonization time for high-performance supercapacitor application. Carbohydrate Polymers. 2019;**207**:764-774. DOI: 10.1016/j.carbpol.2018.12.048

[66] Wang Z, Kang K, Wu J, Hu Q, Harper DP, Du G, et al. Comparative effects of electrospinning ways for fabricating green, sustainable, flexible, porous, nanofibrous cellulose/chitosan carbon mats as anode materials for lithium-ion batteries. Journal of Materials Research and Technology. 2021;**11**:50-61. DOI: 10.1016/j.jmrt.2021.01.009

[67] Pan R, Cheung O, Wang Z, Tammela P, Huo J, Lindh J, et al. Mesoporous Cladophora cellulose separators for lithium-ion batteries. Journal of Power Sources. 2016;**321**:185-192. DOI: 10.1016/j.jpowsour.2016.04.115

[68] Kim JH, Kim JH, Choi ES, Yu HK, Wu Q, Chun SJ, et al. Colloidal silica nanoparticle-assisted structural control of cellulose nanofiber paper separators for lithium-ion batteries. Journal of Power Sources. 2013;**242**:533-540. DOI: 10.1016/j.jpowsour.2013.05.142

[69] Dhar P, Tarafder D, Kumar A, Katiyar V. Thermally recyclable polylactic acid/cellulose nanocrystal films through reactive extrusion process. Polymer. 2016;**87**:268-282. DOI: 10.1016/j.polymer.2016.02.004

[70] Wang T, Drzal LT. Cellulose-nanofiber-reinforced poly (lactic acid) composites prepared by a water-based approach. ACS Applied Materials & Interfaces. 2012;**4**:5079-5085. DOI: 10.1021/am301438g

[71] Song Y, Tashiro K, Xu D, Liu J, Bin Y. Crystallization behavior of poly (lactic acid)/microfibrillated cellulose composite. Polymer. 2013;**54**:3417-3425. DOI: 10.1016/j.polymer.2013.04.054

[72] Martinez-Sanz M, Lopez-Rubio A, Lagaron JM. Optimization of the dispersion of unmodified bacterial cellulose nanowhiskers into polylactide via melt compounding to significantly enhance barrier and mechanical properties. Biomacromolecules. 2012;**13**:3887-3899. DOI: 10.1021/bm301430j

[73] Neelamana IK, Thomas S, Parameswaranpillai J. Characteristics of banana fibers and banana fiber reinforced phenol formaldehyde composites-macroscale to nanoscale. Journal of Applied Polymer Science. 2013;**130**:1239-1246. DOI: 10.1002/app.39220

[74] Joseph S, Sreekala MS, Oommen Z, Koshy P, Thomas S. A comparison of the mechanical properties of phenol formaldehyde composites reinforced with banana fibres and glass fibres. Composites Science and Technology. 2002;**62**:1857-1868. DOI: 10.1016/S0266-3538(02)00098-2

[75] Qing Y, Sabo R, Cai Z, Wu Y. Resin impregnation of cellulose nanofibril films facilitated by water swelling. Cellulose. 2013;**20**:303-313. DOI: 10.1007/s10570-012-9815-0

[76] Sehaqui H, de Larraya UP, Liu P, Pfenninger N, Mathew AP, Zimmermann T, et al. Enhancing adsorption of heavy metal ions onto biobased nanofibers from waste pulp residues for application in wastewater treatment. Cellulose. 2014;**21**:2831-2844. DOI: 10.1007/s10570-014-0310-7

[77] Ma H, Hsiao BS, Chu B. Ultrafine cellulose nanofibers as efficient adsorbents for removal of UO_2^{2+} in water. ACS Macro Letters. 2012;**1**:213-216. DOI: 10.1021/mz200047q

[78] Hokkanen S, Repo E, Suopajärvi T, Liimatainen H, Niinimaa J, Sillanpää M. Adsorption of Ni (II), Cu (II) and Cd (II) from aqueous solutions by amino modified nanostructured

microfibrillated cellulose. Cellulose. 2014;**21**:1471-1487. DOI: 10.1007/s10570-014-0240-4

[79] Mahfoudhi N, Boufi S. Nanocellulose as a novel nanostructured adsorbent for environmental remediation: A review. Cellulose. 2017;**24**:1171-1197. DOI: 10.1007/s10570-017-1194-0

[80] Kardam A, Raj KR, Srivastava S, Srivastava MM. Nanocellulose fibers for biosorption of cadmium, nickel, and lead ions from aqueous solution. Clean Technologies and Environmental Policy. 2014;**16**:385-393. DOI: 10.1007/s10098-013-0634-2

[81] Liu P, Borrell PF, Božič M, Kokol V, Oksman K, Mathew AP. Nanocelluloses and their phosphorylated derivatives for selective adsorption of Ag^{+}, Cu^{2+} and Fe^{3+} from industrial effluents. Journal of Hazardous Materials. 2015;**294**:177-185. DOI: 10.1016/j.jhazmat.2015.04.001

[82] Yu X, Tong S, Ge M, Wu L, Zuo J, Cao C, et al. Adsorption of heavy metal ions from aqueous solution by carboxylated cellulose nanocrystals. Journal of Environmental Sciences. 2013;**25**:933-943. DOI: 10.1016/S1001-0742(12)60145-4

[83] Chen S, Zou Y, Yan Z, Shen W, Shi S, Zhang X, et al. Carboxymethylated-bacterial cellulose for copper and lead ion removal. Journal of Hazardous Materials. 2009;**161**:1355-1359. DOI: 10.1016/j.jhazmat.2008.04.098

[84] Batmaz R, Mohammed N, Zaman M, Minhas G, Berry RM, Tam KC. Cellulose nanocrystals as promising adsorbents for the removal of cationic dyes. Cellulose. 2014;**21**:1655-1665. DOI: 10.1007/s10570-014-0168-8

[85] Jin L, Li W, Xu Q, Sun Q. Amino-functionalized nanocrystalline cellulose as an adsorbent for anionic dyes. Cellulose. 2015;**22**:2443-2456. DOI: 10.1007/s10570-015-0649-4

[86] Hokkanen S, Repo E, Bhatnagar A, Tang WZ, Sillanpää M. Adsorption of hydrogen sulphide from aqueous solutions using modified nano/micro fibrillated cellulose. Environmental Technology. 2014;**35**:2334-2346. DOI: 10.1080/09593330.2014.903300